THE

CATHOLIC DOGMA:

"Extra Ecclesiam Nullus omnino Salvatur."—

(*"Out of the Church there is positively no Salvation."*—FOURTH LAT. COUNC., IN 1215.)

"Error, cui non resistitur, approbatur; et Veritas, cum minime defensatur, opprimitur."—

"Not to oppose erroneous Doctrine is to approve of it, and not to defend at all true Doctrine is to suppress it.—INNOCENT III.

—— BY ——

MICHAEL MÜLLER, C.SS.R.

Permissu Superiorum.

COPYRIGHT, 1888, BY ELIAS FREDERICK SCHAUER.

Copyright 2007 Catholic Authors Press

ISBN: 978-0-9782985-1-7

Catholic Authors Press

Hartford, Connecticut

www.CatholicAuthors.org

PREFACE.

Necessary to be Read.

St. Paul, in his epistle to St. Timothy, exclaims: " O Timothy, keep that which is committed to thy trust, avoiding the profane novelties of words, and oppositions of knowledge falsely so called." (I. Tim. vi. 20.) " Who is at present this Timothy?" asks Vincent of Lerins, and he answers: It is the Body of the Pastors of the Church, and therefore every Pastor must apply these words of St. Paul to himself: O Timothy, O Pastor, O Doctor, O Priest, " Keep that which is committed to thy trust," pure and undefiled, " earnestly contend for the faith once delivered to the saints;" (Jude, v. 3); never depart from the *sacred words* of God, "once put into thy mouth." (Isai. lix. 21.) " You, therefore," says Bishop Hay, "must never know what it is to temporize in religion, in order to please men, nor to adulterate even one iota of the Gospel of Christ to humor them. You must declare the sacred truths revealed by Jesus Christ in their original simplicity, without seeking to adorn them with the persuasive words of human wisdom, much less disguise them in a garb not their own. Truth, plain and unadorned, is the only weapon you must employ against your adversaries, regardless of their censure or their approbation. 'This is the truth,' you must say, 'revealed by God; this you must embrace, or you can have no part with him.' If the world looks upon what you say as foolishness, you must not be surprised, for you know that 'the sensual man perceiveth not the things that are of the spirit of God; for it is foolishness to him, and he cannot understand' (I. Cor. ii. 14.); ' but that the foolishness of

God is wiser than men;' and pitying this blindness you must earnestly pray to God to enlighten them, 'with modesty admonishing them . . . if, peradventure, God may give them repentance to know the truth.' (II. Tim. ii. 25.)

"If there ever was a time when it was especially necessary for every Pastor of the Church to watch over the purity of faith and morals which the Church has entrusted to him, it is the present age and country, in which so many condescensions and compliances are admitted and received at the expense of the purity of Catholic faith and morals, and the narrow way that leads to life is converted, in the opinion of men, to the broad road that leads to destruction.

"This remark applies especially to that latitudinarian principle so common now-a-days, that *a man may be saved in any religion, provided he lives a good moral life, according to the light he has;* for, by this, the faith of Christ is evacuated, and the Gospel rendered of no avail; a Jew, a Turk, a Heathen, are all comprehended in this scheme, and if they live a good moral life have as good a right to salvation as a Christian!

"To be a member of the Church of Christ is no longer necessary, since, if we lead a good moral life, we are in the state of salvation, whether we belong to her or not! What a wide field does this give to the passions of men! What liberty to all the whims of the human mind! It is therefore of the utmost consequence to state and to show plainly the revealed Catholic truth that '*there is no salvation out of the Catholic Church.*'"

It must be remembered that every Catholic dogma is a revealed truth that has always been held by the Fathers of the Church from the beginning and must, therefore, be interpreted, not according to modern opinions and latitudinarian principles, but according to the faith of the Fathers and Doctors of the Church; and therefore Vincent of Lerins says: " A true Catholic is he who loves the truth revealed by God, who loves the Church, the Body of Christ, who esteems religion, the Catholic faith, higher than any human authority, talents, eloquence, and philosophy; all this he holds in contempt, and remains firm and unshaken in the faith which, he knows, has always from the beginning been held by the Catholic Church; and if he notices that any one, no matter who he may be, interprets a dogma in a manner different from that of the Fathers of the Church, he understands that God permits such an interpretation to be made, not for the good of religion, but as a temptation, according to the words of St. Paul: 'For there must be also heresies; that they also, who are reproved, may be made manifest among you.' (I. Cor. xi. 19.) 'And indeed, no sooner are novel opinions proclaimed, than it becomes manifest what kind of a Catholic a man is.' (Commonit.) Hence, as St. Augustine says, 'a theologian who is humble, will never teach anything as true Catholic doctrine, unless he is perfectly certain of the truth which he asserts, and proves it from Holy Scripture and the Tradition of the Church.' 'Those who have learned theology well,' says St. Basil, 'will not allow one iota of Catholic dogmas to be betrayed. They will, if necessary, willingly undergo any kind of death in their defence.'

" They will propose each dogma, especially the all-important dogma, " *out of the Church there is No salvation,*" in the words of the Church and explain it as she understands it; they are most careful not to weaken in the least the meaning of this great dogma, by the way of proposing or explaining it. Why does not St. Paul say: if any one preach to you a Gospel *contrary* to that instead of *beside* that which we have preached to you? 'It is,' says St. John Chrysostom, ' to show us that one is *accursed* who *even indirectly* weakens the least truth of the Gospel.' (Cornelius a Lapide in Epist. ad Gal. I. 8.) "

" As there is," says Pius IX., " but one God the Father, one Christ his Son, one Holy Ghost, so there is also only one divinely revealed truth, only one divine faith—the beginning of man's salvation and the foundation of all justification, by which (faith) the just man lives, and without which it is impossible to please God and to be admitted to the Communion of his children; and there is but one true, holy, Catholic, Roman Church and divine teaching Authority, (cathedra) founded upon Peter by the living voice of the Lord, *out of which (Church) there is neither the* TRUE FAITH *nor* ETERNAL SALVATION, since no one can have God for his Father, who has not the Church for his Mother." (Encycl. Letter, March 17, 1856.)

"The Holy Ghost," says St. Augustine, "is to the Body of Christ, which is the Church, what the human soul is to the human body. It is by the soul that each member of the body lives and acts. In like manner, it is by the Holy Ghost that the just man lives and acts. As the soul does not follow a member which is cut off from the body, so, in like manner, does the Holy Ghost not follow a member which has been justly cut off from the Body of Christ. He, therefore, who wishes to obtain life everlasting, must remain vivified by the Holy Ghost; and in order to remain vivified by the Holy Ghost we must keep charity, love the truth, and desire unity." (Serm. 267.) "Therefore no one can find life everlasting except in the Catholic Church." (Serm. ad Cæsareenses) "Where unity is wanting, there can be no divine charity. Hence it is that divine charity can be kept only in the Catholic Church." (Contr. lit. Petil., lib. ii., cap 77.) Now, as no one can obtain salvation without having the spirit of Christ, or divine charity, and as this spirit or divine virtue, which is called the soul of the Church, is kept only in the unity of the Church, it is evident that out of the Church there is positively no salvation.

It must be remembered that every dogma is exclusive, and admits of no interpretation contrary to that which it has received from the beginning. To every dogma, therefore, may be added what Pius IX. added to the definition of the Immaculate Conception of the Ever Blessed Virgin Mary, namely: "Wherefore, if any persons—which God forbid—shall presume to think in their hearts otherwise than we have defined, let them know that they are condemned by their own judgment, that they have suffered shipwreck in faith, and have fallen away from the unity of the Church."

Preface.

"Let those, therefore," says Vincent of Lerins, "who have not learned theology well, learn it better; let them try to understand of each dogma as much as they are able, and let them believe what they are not able to understand; let them remember the words of St. Paul: 'If any one shall teach you anything besides that which you have received, let him be anathema.' (Ephes. i. 9.) Dediscant bene quod didicerant non bene; et ex toto Ecclesiæ dogmate quod intellectu capi potest capiant, quod non potest credant. O Timothee, depositum custodi, devitans prophanas vocum novitates. Si quis vobis annuntiaverit præterquam quod accepistis, anathema sit. (Commonit.)" It is according to this Catholic and apostolic spirit that we have endeavored to explain our religion, and especially the great dogma "Out of the Catholic Church there is positively no salvation." But our explanation, it seems, is too Catholic for some individuals, because we have not admitted into it any modern opinions and latitudinarian principles. Believing, therefore, that "they would do a service to God" and to their fellow-men, especially to their separated brethren, they have, through the Buffalo *Catholic Union and Times*, made known that we have misrepresented Catholic belief concerning the dogma "Out of the Church there is no salvation."

The Right Reverend George Hay, Bishop of Edinburgh, Scotland, who, when yet a Protestant, took the vow to do all he could to extirpate Popery, wrote a treatise entitled "*An Inquiry whether Salvation can be had without true faith and out of the Communion of the Church of Christ.*" In this treatise, the pious and very learned Prelate of the Church proves most clearly that "out of the true Church no one can be saved," and adds "that it is *only of late* that that loose way of thinking and speaking about the necessity of true faith, and of being in communion with the Church of Christ, has appeared among the members of the Church, and that this is one of the strongest grounds of its condemnation. It is a novelty, it is a new doctrine; it was unheard of from the beginning; nay, it is directly opposed to the uniform doctrine of all the great lights of the Church in all former ages. It is, therefore, a matter of surprise that anybody should call this point in question; that indeed this can only be accounted for from the general spirit of dissipation and disregard for all religion, which so universally prevails now-a-days; for the first authors of the so-called reformation, and some of their most candid followers, seeing the strong proofs from Scripture for this point, and not finding the smallest foundation in the Sacred Writings to support the contrary, have solemnly acknowledged it, however much it made against themselves; for the Protestant Church of Scotland, in her Confession of Faith, agreed upon by the divines of Westminister, approved by the General Assembly in the year 1646, and ratified by Act of Parliament in 1649, in the chapter on the Church speaks thus: "The visible Church, which is also Catholic or universal under the gospel (not confined to one nation, as before, under the law), consists of all those throughout the world that profess the true religion, and of their children, and is the kingdom of the Lord Jesus Christ, the house and family of God, out of which there is no ordinary possibility of salvation." (Confession of Faith, chap. xxv.)

"But their predecessors in the preceding century, when the Presbyterian religion first began in Scotland, speak no less clearly on the same subject; for in their Confession of Faith, authorized by Parliament in the year 1560, 'as a doctrine grounded upon the infallible word of God,' they speak thus, Article xvi.: 'As we believe in one God, Father, Son, and Holy Ghost, so we do most constantly believe, that from the beginning there hath been, and now is, and to the end of the world shall be one Kirk—that is to say, one company and multitude of men, chosen by God, who rightly worship and embrace him by true faith in Jesus Christ; . . . which Kirk is Catholic—that is, universal; because it containeth the elect of all ages, etc.; out of which Kirk there is neither life nor eternal felicity: and therefore we utterly abhor the blasphemy of them that affirm that men who live according to equity and justice shall be saved, what religion so-ever they have professed.' This confession of the original Kirk of Scotland was reprinted and published in Glasgow in the year 1771, from which this passage is taken. Calvin himself confesses the same truth, in these words, speaking of the visible Church: 'Out of its bosom,' says he, 'no remission of sins, no salvation is to be hoped for, according to Isaiah, Joel, and Ezekiel ; . . . so that it is always highly pernicious to depart from the Church;' and this he affirms in his Institutions themselves, B. iv., c. 1, § 4.

"We shall add one testimony more, which is particularly strong; it is of Dr. Pearson, a bishop of the Church of England, in his exposition of the Creed, edit. 1669, where he says, 'The necessity of believing the Catholic Church appeared, *first*, in this, that Christ hath appointed it as the only way to eternal life. We read at the first, Acts ii. 47, "That the Lord added to the Church daily such as should be saved;" and what was then daily done hath been done since continually. Christ never appointed two ways to heaven; nor did he build a Church to save some, and make another institution for other men's salvation (Acts iv. 12): "There is no other name under heaven given among men, whereby we must be saved, but the name of Jesus;" and that name is not otherwise given under heaven than in the Church. As none were saved from the deluge but such as were within the ark of Noe, framed for their reception by the command of God; as none of the first-born of Egypt lived but such as were within those habitations whose doorposts were sprinkled with blood, by the appointment of God, for their preservation; as none of the inhabitants of Jericho could escape the fire or sword, but such as were within the house of Rahab, for whose protection a covenant was made;—so NONE shall ever escape the eternal wrath of God who belong not to the Church of God.' Behold how far the force of truth prevailed among the most eminent members of the Reformation before latitudinarian principles had crept in among them!

"It is true, indeed, that, though the founders of these

Churches, convinced by the repeated and evident testimonies of the Word of God, professed this truth, and inserted it in the public standards of their religion, yet their posterity now disclaim it, and accuse the Catholic Church of being uncharitable for holding it; but this only shows their inconsistency, and proves that they are devoid of all certainty in what they believe; for if it was a divine truth, when these religions were founded, that *out of the true Church, and without the Catholic faith, there is no salvation,* it must be so still; and if their first founders were mistaken on this point, what security can their followers now have for any other thing they taught? But the Catholic Church, always consistent and uniform in her doctrine, always preserving the *words once put in her mouth* by her Divine Master, at all times and in all ages has believed and taught the same doctrine as a truth revealed by God, that 'out of the true Church of Christ, and without his true faith, there is no possibility of salvation;' and the most authentic public testimony of her enemies proves that this is the doctrine of Jesus, and of his holy Gospel, whatever private persons, from selfish and interested motives, may say to the contrary. 'What a reproach must this be before the judgment-seat of God to those members of the Church of Christ who call in question or seek to invalidate this great and *fundamental truth,* the *very fence* and *barrier* of the true religion; which is so repeatedly declared by God in his Holy Scriptures, professed by the Church of Christ in all ages, attested in the strongest terms by the most eminent lights of Christianity, and candidly acknowledged by the most celebrated writers and divines of the Reformation! Will not every attempt to weaken the importance of this divine truth be considered by the great God as betraying his cause and the interests of his holy faith? and will those who do so be able to plead even their favorite *invincible ignorance* in their own defence before him?' (From *Sincere Christian,* American Edition.)

But let us hear a greater Authority speaking on this all-important subject.

In his Encyclical Letters, dated Dec. 8, 1849; Dec. 8, 1864; and Aug. 10, 1863, and in his Allocution on Dec. 9, 1854, Pope Pius IX. says:—

"It is not without sorrow that we have learned another not less pernicious error, which has been spread in several parts of Catholic countries, and has been imbibed by many Catholics, *who are of opinion that all those who are not at all members of the true Church of Christ, can be saved.* Hence they often discuss the question concerning the future fate and condition of those who die without having professed the Catholic faith, and give the most frivolous reasons in support of their wicked opinion . . . . .

"It is indeed of faith that no one can be saved outside of the Apostolic, Roman Church; that this Church is the one ark of salvation; that he who has not entered it, will perish in the deluge. . . .

"We must mention and condemn again that most pernicious error, which has been imbibed by certain Catholics, who are of the opinion that those people who live in error and have not the true faith, and are separated from Catholic unity, may obtain life everlasting. Now this opinion is most contrary to Catholic faith, as is evident from the plain words of our Lord, (Matt. xviii. 17; Mark xvi. 16; Luke x. 16; John iii. 18) as also from the words of St. Paul, (II. Tit. iii. 11) and of St. Peter (II. Peter. ii. 1). To entertain opinions contrary to this Catholic faith is to be an impious wretch.

"We therefore again reprobate, proscribe, and condemn all and every one of these perverse opinions and doctrines, and it is our absolute will and command that all sons of the Catholic Church shall hold them as reprobated, proscribed, and condemned. It belongs to our Apostolic office to rouse your Episcopal zeal and watchfulness to do all in your power to banish from the minds of the people such impious and pernicious opinions, which lead to indifference of religion, which we behold spreading more and more, to the ruin of souls. Oppose all your energy and zeal to these errors and employ zealous priests to impugn and annihilate them, and to impress very deeply upon the minds and hearts of the faithful the great dogma of our most holy religion, *that salvation can be had only in the Catholic faith.* Often exhort the clergy and the faithful to give thanks to God for the great gift of the Catholic faith."

Now is it not something very shocking to see such condemned errors and perverse opinions proclaimed as Catholic doctrine in a Catholic newspaper, and in books written and recently published by Catholics?

We have, therefore, deemed it our duty to make a strong, vigorous, and uncompromising presentation of the great and fundamental truth, the very fence and barrier of the true religion,—"OUT OF THE CHURCH THERE IS POSITIVELY NO SALVATION," against those soft, weak, timid, liberalizing Catholics, who labor to explain away all the points of Catholic faith offensive to non-Catholics, and to make it appear that there is no question of life and death, of heaven and hell, involved in the differences between us and Protestants.

Not to free your neighbor from religious errors, says Pope Leo, when it is in your power to do so, is to show to be in error yourself, and "therefore," says Pope Gregory, "he whose duty it is to correct his neighbor when he is in fault, and yet omits to make the correction, makes himself guilty of the faults of his neighbor." "Indeed," says Pope Innocent III. of those whose duty it is to keep the deposit of faith pure and undefiled, "not to oppose erroneous doctrine is to approve of it, and not to defend at all true doctrine is to suppress it."

CONTENTS.

                                                                    Page

PREFACE iii

CHAPTER I Introductory 5
    II. The infallible and only true guide to heaven........... 12
    III. The great revolt against Christ 27
    IV. Dishonesty of His Impudence Bishop Coxe 45
    V. Refutation of the false assertions of Rev'ds Sir Oracle, Cronin and Young, divided into two parts.......... 67

PART I.

There is no salvation out of the Church.

§ 1. S. O. begins to comment on some answers, contained in our little work, "Familiar Explanation of Christian Doctrine," (first edition) 74

§ 2 S. O. continues to speak ex cathedra 75

§ 3. S O. examines and explains the question and answer, "Have Protestants any faith in Christ? A. They never had"......... 79

§ 4 What Catholic faith is 80

§ 5. What Protestants' belief in Christ is....................... 87

§ 6 More false oracles of Sir Oracle 98

§ 7. S O declares truth to be rant and abuse 101

§ 8 S. O continues to declare false what is true 108

§ 9 S O declares wholly untrue what he cannot understand ... 115

§ 10 S O avows that our conclusion is correct, but tells more d—d lies 122

§ 11 S O declares that the final sentence of the Eternal Judge, "I know you not—Depart from me, etc." will fall, not on Protestants, but only on bad Catholics; but from his own words it is proved that Protestants, too, are included in that sentence 124

§ 12. S O declares the honest life of Protestants a standing reproach to bad Catholics 128

§ 13. S O's. pharisaical language 130

PART II.

Those who live in heresy without being guilty of the sin of heresy.

§ 1. Natural Law... 136
§ 2. The written Law... 136
§ 3. The New Law or the Law of Grace............................ 140
§ 4 Conscience in general.. 144
§ 5 Kinds of conscience:
    1. The right or true conscience........................... 146
    2. The certain conscience................................. 148
    3. The timorous or tender conscience...................... 150
    4. The doubtful conscience................................ 150
    5. The lax conscience..................................... 156
    6. The perplexed conscience............................... 156
    7. The scrupulous conscience.............................. 157
    8 The erroneous or false conscience 157
§ 6. What heretics are not guilty of the sin of heresy—Refutation of Rev. A. Young's erroneous doctrine on the divine faith of material heretics.. 166
§ 7. Invincible or inculpable ignorance neither saves nor damns a person.. 211
§ 8. How Almighty God leads to salvation those who are inculpably ignorant of the truths of salvation............................. 218
§ 9. Those who sincerely seek the true religion................. 236
§ 10. S O on Confession... 250
§ 11. S. O points out the road to heaven for heathens and Protestants of every denomination... 253
§ 12. S O gives us credit for our correct doctrine in a way very dishonorable to himself... 262
§ 13. S O. as Catechist... 264
§ 14. Liberalism condemned by the Church....................... 267

CHAPTER I.

INTRODUCTORY.

In 1874 we wrote a little volume, entitled *Familar Explanation of Christian Doctrine*. Our Mother, the holy Catholic Church, has wisely decreed that no book treating of faith and morals shall be printed without the approbation of the Bishop of the diocese, and that no Bishop shall give his approbation before the Manuscript has been submitted to the criticism of a learned and pious theologian, in order that the reader of the book may know that it contains nothing contrary to faith and morals. (See Third Plenary Council of Baltimore. p. 120, No. 220.) The Rule of the Redemptorist Fathers, however, requires that a book written by one of them must be examined by two learned theologians, before it appears in print. We submitted our little volume to the criticism of the late very learned Rev. A. Konings, C. SS. R., Professor of Moral Theology and Canon Law at the Redemptorist College, Ilchester, Md., to the late Rev. Doctor Francis J. Freel, then the beloved Pastor of the Church of St. Charles Borromeo, Brooklyn, L. I., to the late Rev. Father M. Sheehan, a learned priest of Ireland, and to James A. Mc. Master, the late learned Editor of the New York Freeman's Journal. As the little book was very favorably criticised, it received the *Imprimatur* of the Most Rev. J. Roosevelt Bailey, Archbishop of Baltimore, and of the Very Rev. Jos. Helmpraecht, the Provincial of the Redemptorist Society in the U. S., and was published in 1875. The little volume had a wide circulation for these fifteen years. Last year we published, by Benziger Brothers, a new edition of this little volume, considerably improved and enlarged.

In the little volume (first edition) we have shown, from page 12 to page 86, that only the Roman Catholic Church is the true Church of Christ on earth, established for the salvation of mankind, that she is the only infallible interpreter of the Written and Unwritten Word of God, and that consequently all those who wish to be saved must die united to this Church.

From page 87 to page 124, we have given several popular reasons why salvation out of the Roman Catholic Church is impossible for those who live up to the principles and spirit of Protestantism. In the second part of this short treatise we speak of those Protestants who are not guilty of the spirit of Protestantism or the sin of heresy. *The Catholic Union and Times* of Buffalo, issued on January 26, 1888, contained an anonymous article, headed "A Queer Explanation of Christian Doctrine." The writer of the article endeavors to prove from a few questions and answers contained in our Familiar Explanation that we have misrepresented the Catholic Doctrine, "*There is no salvation out of the Roman Catholic Church.*" From the manner in which the article is written, it is evident that it is not written by an Irish priest, who was educated in Ireland; for if the whole article were put in the form of questions any Irishman or Irishwoman would confound the writer of that article by the way of answering those questions. The writer is probably a convert from the so-called Episcopalian Church, who was received into the Church without having the gift of divine faith, and consequently understood neither the spirit of the Catholic faith nor that of Protestantism. If he is not such a convert, then rest assured that he is a liberal-minded priest. He gives no other proof for the truth of his assertions than his own authority, and how great this is appears clearly from the fact that he did not sign the article, and therefore it deserves no more credit than a dream-book. The fact that the Rev. Editor of the *Buffalo Catholic Union and Times* calls the writer of the article "*the most prominent priest of the United States*" shows his want of prudence, for no sensible man would have called him so; he might have said, a prominent priest of the U. S.

Here is the editorial : "*The most prominent priest in the United States* has honored our columns this week with an article upon a most important matter. The recognized ability of the writer and the recent publicity given to the points he discusses deserve the editorial space given to the masterly communication. We hope our readers—and especially our esteemed Protestant readers—will give this article careful perusal. *We endorse his every statement* and heartily thank the writer for his able and timely criticism."

Strange, to call a priest THE *most prominent* priest in the United States without giving the public his name. The Cardinal Archbishop, and all other Archbishops and Bishops, and all the priests, and even every Catholic of the United States would have thanked him for letting them know who, in his opinion, is not only a prominent, but even THE MOST prominent priest in the United States. For brevity's sake we shall call him "Sir Oracle."

The Rev. Editor and his brother-priest, the writer of "Queer article," are peremptory and self-sufficient in proclaiming their erroneous opinions, as if they had nothing better to learn from the Church and her holy doctors. To them may be applied what St. Francis Xavier wrote one day to one of the Jesuit Fathers, namely: "You, like so many others who resemble you, are greatly mistaken, when you fancy you can follow your opinions and judgment, merely for the reason that you are Members of the Society." (*Life of St. Fr. Xav.*)

"Did you read in the *Buffalo Union and Times*, the article 'Queer Explanation?'" I asked a priest. "I did," he answered. "What did you think of it?"—"I thought, the writer of it is an illustration of what Cardinal Manning says in his work *The Vatican Council* namely: 'A school of errors partly sprung up in Germany by contact with Protestantism, and partly in England, by the agency of those who, being born in Protestantism, have entered the Catholic Church, but have never been liberated from certain erroneous habits of thought.'"

"What does your Reverence advise me to do in the matter? Will it be well for me to return to "Sir Oracle" the compliments which he has made to the author of 'Familiar Explanation of Christian Doctrine?'"—"Indeed, it is not only well, but even a duty for you to do so, on account of the readers of the B. U. and T., some of whom may have received false impressions, especially liberal Catholics, who never learned well the reasons of the faith that is in them. Hence, if you were silent, and omit to give strong proofs for the Catholic doctrine in question, Catholics and even Protestants who read the article "Queer Explanation" would, in fact, begin to doubt your doctrine, and that writer would triumphantly assert that you had been silenced by the anonymous assertions brought forward by him, and published by the Rev. Editor of the *B. U. and T.*, who has made that article all his own by cheerfully endorsing every statement of it. Expose, therefore, to the Public his counterfeit theology by contrasting it with sound theology, so clearly explained, that even the most ignorant can understand it."

"Should these compliments be returned through the *B. U. and T.?*" "*The B. U. and T.* would indeed be bound to communicate them to all its readers; but as the instructions conveyed through a newspaper are easily forgotten, and often thrown into the waste basket, I advise you to have them printed and published in pamphlet form through the energetic Publishers, Benziger Brothers. If you write these compliments, like all your other works, and have them published at a cheap price, they will have a wide circulation, and thousands of *Catholics and non-Catholics* will devour them and be benefited by them. If certain priests are so very ignorant in matters of great importance, how ignorant must not be those who never had an opportunity to learn sound Catholic theology concerning certain dogmatical truths.

"That there are such also among the German Clergy, is

evident from the fact that, in 1886, the Rev. A. Klug published, in Germany, a new catechism, in which he asserts that 'Protestants are saved in those truths which they hold with us in common.' Cardinal Manning also says in his work, *The Vatican Council*, 'that many of the clergy were brought up in dangerous *traditional* errors during two hundred years, up to the time of the Vatican Council; that their errors were owing to the fact that they never conceived a clear and precise idea of the Church, because they never had a clear and precise knowledge of the supreme power of her Head; that, unless this be distinctly understood, the doctrine of the Church will always be proportionally obscure; the doctrine of the Church does not determine the doctrine of the Primacy; but the doctrine of the Primacy does precisely determine the doctrine of the Church.'

"Many are still affected by those errors and entertain erroneous views of certain Catholic doctrines; you know, it is not an easy task to get rid of the errors of the intellect, and of lying spirits. If you, then, clearly show the errors of these men, you will earn the thanks of the greater part of the American clergy and laity, and even of many honest Protestants, who are eager to know the true religion."

These remarks of a pious priest are very correct.

The present age is completely absorbed in speculations of every kind—political, commercial, literary, scientific, and even religious; so that the source whence the rising generation ought to derive more knowledge of their moral and religious duties is contaminated by invincible pride, immoderate luxury, ridiculous fashion, self-interest, and general ignorance of the doctrine of salvation. Hence the predominant tendency of the present generation is to enjoy material life, indulge the passions, gratify the sensitive and appetitive powers, and neglect the religious cultivation of the intellect, heart, and soul. It is, therefore, the indispensable duty of priests, parents, and of all those who have the spiritual direction of children and Christian families, to communicate to all *sound Catholic doctrine* as the great means to oppose and to cure the moral leprosy of the age. This is the only object we had in view in publishing our catechisms and other larger works for every class of society. Quack doctors in all sciences, speculating pedants in literature, monopolists of every kind, and hypocrits in religion and politics, are contemptible in every age and nation and deserve universal animadversion. This language may tickle and fret some individuals. The exposition of Catholic doctrine in our smaller as well as in our larger works is too Catholic for the consciences of certain men, who, on this account, will not fail to heap upon us their rancorous and vindictive criticisms in pharisaical language. One day St. Alphonsus said that he thought he could bear in silence every insult offered to him except one : that of being called a heretic. We, too, are ready to bear in silence personal insults, except one—that of having misrepresented Catholic doctrine in any of our works. Even from our childhood the study of our religion has been our greatest pleasure ; we have always loved it too much to misrepresent any truth whatsoever. We have taken unspeakable pains to make it plain and attractive to all classes of society, even to the little ònes. We have never published a line that was not read by excellent theologians before it went into the hands of the printer. Hence we have felt it our duty to vindicate, in strong language, the insult which has publicly been offered to us in the *B. U. and T.* We have now one foot in the grave, and the other shall soon follow it. We, therefore, have no reason to be a coward in publishing the truths of the Catholic religion and in opposing erroneous principles. It would, indeed, be a great shame for us to keep silence in a matter of the greatest importance. If there are priests who are bold enough to make false and fallacious assertions concerning our holy religion, without any due respect to learned and pious Prelates and priests and the Catholic Press in general, who have bestowed high praises upon our works, for their orthodox and solid teaching, we must not be less bold in showing to the Public the ignorance of those priests in matters in which the salvation of souls is at stake.

Since we wrote the above we have received a copy of the *Buffalo Catholic Union and Times*, issued March 22, 1888, in which an article is published, headed "*Have Protestants Divine Faith?*" The writer of it is the Rev. Alfred Young, a Paulist Father of New York. The article is written to corroborate at least part of that written by the "Most Prominent Priest of the U. S." He praises the Rev. Father Cronin for having published that article "Queer Explanation." We are very sorry for the grave errors which these priests have taught the Public, not of course, intentionally, but because they knew not what they were doing.

In showing their erroneous doctrine on Catholic and Protestant belief in Christ, ect., we will chiefly follow the doctrine of St. Thomas Aquinas, and other doctors and eminent theologians of the Church.

"That method of teaching," says Pope Leo XIII., " which rests on the authority and judgment of individual professors, has a changeable basis, and hence arise different and conflicting opinions which cannot present the mind of the holy Doctor (Thomas Aquinas) and foster dissensions and controversies which have agitated Catholic schools for a long time and *not without great detriment to Christian Science.*" (Brief, June 19. 1886). "St. Thomas, indeed, is a most wise doctor, who walks within the confines of truth; who not only never disputes with God, the Head and Fount of all truth, but is always strictly in full accord with Him, and is always docile to Him when disclosing his secrets in any manner whatever; who no less piously listens to the Roman Pontiff when speaking, reveres in him the divine authority, and fully holds that *submission to the Roman Pontiff is necessary to salvation.* (Opusc. contra errores Græcorum). In following St. Thomas Aquinas as our author and master, we safely teach without any danger of passing over the boundaries of truth. But to gather and scatter opinions according to our own will and pleasure is to be reputed the vilest license, lying, and false science, a disgrace and slavery of the mind." (Encyc., Dec. 21., 1887.)

CHAPTER II.

The Infallible and Only True Guide to Heaven.

Many years ago a celebrated architect built a magnificent palace. When he had completed the costly edifice he gave it to some friends for their dwelling. But these soon behaved badly, and became a scandal to the whole neighborhood. People often said: "Why was so splendid a palace erected for such wicked wretches?" At last the king arrived and took possession of the palace. He pardoned the servants and tried to make them good again. Then the people said: "Now we understand why this magnificent palace was built; it was for the king."

The architect in this parable is God the Father. He built a magnificent palace—the world. He put into it his friends—Adam and Eve. They soon behaved badly; and the angels asked, "Why was so splendid a palace—the world—created for these wicked people?"

At last the King, Jesus Christ, arrived. He pardoned the servants and tried to make them good again, and the angels exclaimed: "Now we understand why this great palace—the world—was made; it was for Jesus Christ, the King of the world."

God decreed from all eternity to create the world as a dwelling-place for men, where, by a holy life, they should gain an eternal reward. He foresaw from all eternity that men would not live up to the end of their creation. God would then have been frustrated in his design, had he not decreed from all eternity the Incarnation for the redemption of the human race. It was, therefore, principally for the sake of the God-Man that the world was created. He was to come for the justification and glorification of man.

The Infallible and Only True Guide to Heaven. 13

Hence St. Thomas Aquinas says: *Ordo naturæ creatus est et institutus propter ordinem gratiæ.*

The principal end of the creation of the universe is, first, Jesus Christ, and, secondly, that the elect may receive here below the grace of God through Christ. Although it is true that the world existed before the Son of God became man, nevertheless, in the plan of creation and redemption, Jesus Christ is prior to the world. On this account St. Paul calls Jesus Christ the beginning, the *first-born from the dead*, that, in all things, he may hold the primacy: because in him it hath pleased the Father that all fulness should dwell, and through him to reconcile all things unto himself, making peace through the blood of the cross, both as to the things on earth, and the things that are in heaven. (Coloss. i. 18-20.)

There is, therefore, a certain intimate union between the creation of the world and the nativity of Christ. God did not wish that Christ should be born except in this world; and again, he did not wish that this world should exist without Jesus Christ. Nay, it was chiefly for his sake, as we have said, that God created the world and for his sake has preserved it and shall continue to preserve it to the end of time.

God had decreed to institute through him the order of grace, that is, the order of the justification and glorification of the elect.

As the artist produces his work according to his conception and knowledge, so, also, God created man to his own image, which is his Son, his eternal Wisdom, the prototype of all things. Now, when a work of art is deteriorated by time or accident, it is restored by the skilful hand of the artist to its original state; so, in like manner, the image of God in man being disfigured in Adam, its source, the Son of God became man to repair his image. "As the children are partakers of flesh and blood, so Jesus also made himself partaker of the same: wherefore it behooves him in all things to be made like unto his brethren, that he might become a merciful and faithful High Priest before God, and be a propitiation for the sins of the people." (Heb. ii. 14, 17.) Thus we receive our sonship or adoption of children of God from him who is the Son of God by his nature. "And if sons, heirs also of God, and joint-heirs with Christ." (Rom. viii. 17.)

Hence it has always been, from the beginning, absolutely necessary for salvation to know, by divine faith, God as the Creator of heaven and earth and the eternal Rewarder of the good and the wicked, and the Incarnation of the Son of God, and consequently the mystery of the Most Holy Trinity; "For he that cometh to God," says St. Paul, "must believe that he is, and is a rewarder of those who seek him." (Heb. xi. 6.) Upon these words of the great Apostle, Cornelius a Lapide comments as follows:

"The knowledge of God acquired from the contemplation of the world teaches only that God is the Author of the world and of all natural blessings, and that only these natural goods can be obtained and asked of him. But God wishes to be honored and loved by men, not only as the Author of natural goods, but also as the Author of the supernatural and everlasting goods in the world to come; and no one can in any other way come to him and to his friendship, please him, and be acceptable to him. Hence true, divine faith is necessary, because it is only by the light of divine faith that we know God, not only as the Author of nature, but also as the Author of grace and eternal glory; and therefore the Apostle says that to know that there is a God, who rewards the good and punishes the wicked, is to know him as such, not only from natural knowledge, and belief, but also from supernatural knowledge and divine faith.

"But if St. Paul speaks here only of these two great truths, it does by no means follow, that he wishes to teach that the supernatural knowledge of these two truths only and divine faith in them are sufficient to obtain justification, that is, to obtain the grace to become the children of God; but they are necessary in order to be greatly animated with hope in undergoing hard labors and struggles for the sake of virtue. However, to obtain the grace of justification, we must also believe other supernatual truths, especially the mystery of the Incarnation of Christ and that of the Most Holy Trinity." (Comm. in Ep. ad Heb., ix. 6.)

"Some theologians," says St. Alphonsus, "hold that the belief of the two other articles—the Incarnation of the Son of God, and the Trinity of Persons—is strictly commanded, but not necessary, as a means without which salvation is impossible; so that a person inculpably ignorant of them may be saved. But according to the more common and truer opinion, the explicit belief of these articles is necessary as a means without which no adult can be saved." (First Command. No. 8.) According to St. Augustine (De Praedest. Sanctorum C. 15.) and other Theologians, the predestination, election, and Incarnation of Christ alone were owing, not to the foreseen merit of any one, not even to that of Christ himself, but only to the good pleasure of God However, the predestination of all men in general, or the election of some in preference to others, is all owing to the merit of Christ, on account of which God has called all men to life everlasting and gives them sufficient grace to obtain it, if they make a proper use of his grace, especially that of prayer.

"That faith," says the same great Doctor of the Church, "is sound, by which we believe that neither any adult nor infant could be delivered from sin and the death of the soul, except by Jesus Christ, the only Mediator between God and man." (Ep. 190, olim 157, parum a principio.) Hence St Thomas says: Almighty God decreed from all eternity the mystery of the Incarnation, in order that men might obtain salvation through Christ. It was therefore necessary at all times, that this mystery of the Incarnation should, in some manner, be explicitly believed. Undoubtedly, that means is necessarily a truth of faith, by which man obtains salvation. Now men obtain salvation by the mystery of the Incarnation and Passion of Christ; for it is said in the Holy Scripture: "There is no other name

under heaven given to men whereby we must be saved."
(Acts, iv. 12.) Hence it was necessary at all times that the
mystery of the Incarnation of Christ should be believed by
all men in some manner (aliqualiter, either implicitly or
explicitly), however, in a different way, according to the
circumstances of times and persons.

Before the fall, man believed explicitly the Incarnation
of Christ. Ante statum peccati homo habuit explicitam
fidem de Christi incarnatione, secundum quod ordinabatur ad
consummationem gloriæ, non autem secundum quod ordinabatur ad liberationem a peccato per passionem et resurrectionem, quia homo non fuit præscius peccati futuri. But
that he had the knowledge of Christ's Incarnation seems
to follow from his words: " Wherefore a man shall leave
father and mother, and shall cleave to his wife." (Gen.
ii. 24.) And St. Paul calls this *a great sacrament in Christ
and in the Church*; (Eph. v. 32.) and therefore it cannot
be believed that the first man was ignorant of this sacrament.

After the fall of man, the mystery of the Incarnation
of Christ was explicitly believed, that is, not only the
Incarnation itself, but also the Passion and Resurrection of
Christ, by which mankind is delivered from sin and death;
for otherwise they could not have prefigured Christ's
Passion by certain sacrifices offered as well before as also
after the Written Law, the meaning of which sacrifices was
well known to *those whose* duty it was to teach the religion
of God; but as to the rest of the people, who believed that
those sacrifices were ordained by God to foreshadow Christ
to come, they had thus implicit faith in Christ.

As the mystery of the Incarnation was believed from
the beginning, so, also, was it necessary to believe the
mystery of the Most Holy Trinity ; for the mystery of the
Incarnation cannot be explicitly believed without faith in
the Most Holy Trinity, because the mystery of the Incarnation teaches that the Son of God took to himself a human
body and soul by the power of the Holy Ghost. Hence, as
the mystery of the Incarnation was explicitly believed by

the teachers of religion, and implicitly by the rest of the people, so, also, was the mystery of the Most Holy Trinity explicitly believed by the teachers of religion and implicitly by the rest of the people. But in the New Law it must be explicitly believed by all." (De Fide, Q ii., art. vii. et viii.)

God revealed these great truths of salvation to our first parents immediately after the fall. He preserved the knowledge of them through the holy patriarchs and prophets who, in clear language, foretold that the Redeemer would come, and " be a priest upon his throne " (Zach. vi. 13.), " a priest according to the order of Melchisedech," (Ps. cix. 4.), and that he himself would be the victim offered up for the sins of mankind.

From these great, fundamental truths of religion we easily understand why St. Paul wrote to the Hebrews: " Jesus Christ yesterday, and to-day, and the same forever" (Heb. xiii. 8.), " through whom it hath well pleased the Father to reconcile all things unto himself, making peace through the blood of the cross, both as to the things on earth and the things that are in heaven." (Coloss. i. 20.)

The great apostle means to say: O Hebrews, Jesus Christ, the God-Man and High Priests, was *yesterday*, that is, he was in the time before you from the beginning. Jesus was the victim and priest before the Law, not in person, but in figure. He was the victim in figure in the lamb and other animals which priests and patriarchs offered in sacrifices. The faithful worshippers saw Christ in those sacrifices 'either explicitly or implicitly; and they believed in him. They believed that he would come and redeem the world. By this spiritual knowledge they guided their lives. Thus their sins were forgiven both as to their guilt and their punishment. The sacrifice of Abel was acceptable to God, because in the lamb which he sacrificed he saw not merely the lamb, but also a better victim—that is, the Saviour, and he believed in him, and therefore God had regard to Abel and his offering; and " God the Father," says St. Augustine, " reconciles to himself, through Christ, the things on earth, and the things in heaven, by offering pardon to all men, on account of Christ, and by giving those who make themselves worthy of it the seats of glory which the fallen angels have lost." (See Cornel. a Lap., Epist. ad Ephes., c. i., from v. 1–10.)

We also learn from Christ and his Church, that the explicit faith in the mysteries of the Holy Trinity and of the Incarnation of the Son of God is also required as a necessary means of salvation.

"This is life everlasting," says our Saviour, "that they may know thee, the only true God, and Jesus Christ whom thou hast sent;" (John, xvii. 3.), for, says he, "I am the way, and the truth, and the life," that lead man to the Father. Hence "no man cometh to the Father but by me." (John, xiv. 6.)

But if a man act according to the dictates of his conscience, and follow exactly the light of reason which God has implanted in him for his guide, is that not sufficient to bring him to salvation?

"This is, indeed," says Bishop Hay, "a specious proposition; but a fallacy lurks under it. When man was created, his reason was then an enlightened reason. Illuminated by the grae of original righteousness, with which his soul was adorned, reason and conscience were safe guides to conduct him in the way of salvation. But by sin this light was miserably darkened, and his reason clouded by ignorance and error. It was not, indeed, entirely extinguished; it still clearly teaches him many great truths, but it is at present so influenced by pride, passion, prejudice, and other such corrupt motives, that in many instances it serves only to confirm him in error, by giving an appearance of reason to the suggestions of self-love and passion. This is too commonly the case, even in natural things; but in the supernatural, in things relating to God and eternity, our reason, if left to itself, is miserably blind. To remedy this, God has given us the light of faith as a sure and safe guide to conduct us to salvation, appointing his holy Church the guardian and depository of this heavenly light; consequently, though a man may pretend to act according to reason and conscience, and even flatter himself that he does so, yet reason and conscience, if not enlightened and guided by true faith, can never bring him to salvation.

"Nothing can be more striking than the words of Holy Scripture on this subject. 'There is a way,' says the wise man, 'that seemeth right to a man, but the ends thereof lead to death.' (Prov. xiv. 12.) What can be more plain than this, to show that a man may act according to what he thinks the light of reason and conscience, persuaded he is doing right, and yet, in fact, he is only running on in the way to perdition! And do not all those who are seduced by false prophets, and false teachers, think they are in the right way? Is it not under the pretext of acting according to conscience that they are seduced? and yet the mouth of truth itself has declared, that 'if the blind lead the blind, both shall fall into the pit.' (Mat. xv. 14.) In order to show us to what excess of wickedness man may go under the pretence of following his conscience, the same Eternal Truth says to his apostles, 'The hour cometh, that whosoever killeth you will think that he doth God a service;' (John xvi. 2.) but observe what he adds,—' And these things will they do, because they have not known the Father nor me.' (Ib. 3.) Which shows that, if one has not the true knowledge of God and of Jesus Christ, which can be obtained only through true faith in the Church, there is no enormity of which he is not capable while thinking he is acting according to reason and conscience. Had we only the light of reason to direct us, we would be justified in following it; but as God has given us an external guide in his holy Church, to assist and correct our blinded reason by the light of faith, our reason alone, unassisted by this guide, can never be sufficient for salvation.

"Nothing will set this in a clearer light than a few examples. Conscience tells a heathen that it is not only lawful, but a duty, to worship and offer sacrifice to idols, the work of men's hands. Will his doing so, according to his conscience, save him? or will these acts of idolatry be innocent or agreeable in the sight of God, because they are performed according to conscience? 'The idol that is made by hands is cursed, as well as he that made it; ... for that which is made, together with him that made it, shall suffer torments.' (Wis. xiv. 8, 10.) Also, 'He that sacrificeth to gods shall be put to death, save only to the Lord.' (Exod. xxii. 20.) In like manner, a Jew's conscience tells him that he may lawfully and meritoriously blaspheme Jesus Christ, and approve the conduct of his forefathers in putting him to death upon a tree. Will such blasphemy save him, because it is according to the dictates of his conscience? The Holy Ghost, by the mouth of St. Paul, says, 'If any man love not our Lord Jesus Christ, let him be anathema,' that is, 'accursed.' (I. Cor. xvi. 22.) A Mahometan is taught by his conscience that it would be a crime to believe in Jesus Christ, and not believe in Mahomet; will this impious conscience save him? The Scripture assures us that 'there is no other name given to men under heaven by which we can be saved,' but the name of Jesus only; and 'he that believeth not the Son shall not see life, but the wrath of God remaineth on him.' All the various sects which have been separated from the true Church, in every age, have uniformly calumniated and slandered her, speaking evil of the truth professed by her, believing in their conscience that this was not only lawful, but highly meritorious. Will calumnies and slanders against the Church of Jesus Christ save them because of their approving conscience? The Word of God declares, 'That the nation and the kingdom that will not serve her shall perish;' and 'there shall be lying teachers who shall bring in damnable heresies, bringing upon themselves swift destruction, ... through whom the way of truth shall be evil spoken of.' (II. Pet. ii. 1.) In all these, and similar cases, their conscience is their greatest crime, and shows to what a height of impiety conscience and reason can lead us, when under the influence of pride, passion, prejudice, and self-love. Conscience and reason, therefore, can never be safe guides to salvation, unless directed by the sacred light of revealed truth."

The Infallible and Only True Guide to Heaven. 21

"An effect," says St. Thomas, "is never greater than its cause, nor any act more efficacious than the active power which produces it, wherefore the enjoyment of eternal beatitude is not within the power of our natural faculties. So, man, left to his own powers, can only produce acts conformable to his nature and existence, such as to acquire art and science, to labor in any employment, and to enjoy private and social happiness, but he can never come to God and possess him without supernatural assistance. It is useless to adjust the strings of a harp or lyre; they remain silent until they are put in motion by the hand of a musician. A vessel is rigged out with its masts, cables, and sails, and ready for sailing, but wants a fair breeze to launch it into the deep. In like manner, people, to be saved, want the powerful hand of God to direct their course to another world, to assist and to enlighten them in their pilgrimage. Hence it is evident that the first step towards God and salvation is supernatural knowledge of God and divine faith in the four great truths of salvation as a necessary preparatory means to obtain the grace of justification; that neither invincible ignorance of the necessary truths of salvation, nor the mere knowledge of these truths can be means to convey sanctifying grace to the soul. To the knowledge of those truths must be joined supernatural divine faith in them, confident hope in the Redeemer, and perfect charity, which includes perfect sorrow for sin and the implicit desire to comply with God's will in all that he requires of the soul, to be saved.

These dispositions of the soul are the effects of the grace of God, and not of anything else whatsoever; and the infusion of sanctifying grace into the soul that is thus prepared is the gratuitous gift granted by the infinite mercy of God on account of the merits of the Redeemer.

St. Thomas asks the qestion: Did Jesus Christ, when he descended into Limbo, deliver the souls of children who died in original sin? To understand this, we must remember a certain principle and doctrine, namely: *There is no salvation possible for any one without being united to Jesus*

Christ crucified. Hence the great Apostle St. Paul says: "It is Jesus Christ whom God hath proposed to be a propitiation through faith in his blood." (Rom. iii. 25.) Now, those children were not united to Christ by their own faith, because they had not the use of reason, which is the foundation of faith; nor were they united to Christ by the faith of their parents, because the faith of their parents was not sufficient for the salvation of their children; nor were those children united to Christ by means of a sacrament, because there was no sacrament under the Old Law which had of itself the virtue of conferring either grace or justification.

Besides, life eternal is granted only to those who are in the state of sanctifying grace. "The grace of God is life everlasting in Jesus Christ our Lord." (Rom. vi. 23.) All those, therefore, who died at any age without perfect charity and faith in the Redeemer to come, as well as those who die without the sacrament of spiritual generation after the Passion and Death of Jesus Christ, are not purified from the mortal stain of original sin, and are, consequently, excluded from the kingdom of eternal glory. (De Incarn., Q. lii., art. vii.)

All this is also certain from what the Council of Trent has defined (Sess. 6. can. 3.) namely, that, without supernatural knowledge and faith, it is impossible to fulfil the Law of God, to be justified and become acceptable to him. (See Cornel. a Lap., Comment. in Ep. ad Rom., c. ii.)

Hence the foot-note, found on page 230 in *Catholic Belief* is not correct, namely: "A believer in one God who, without any fault on his part, does not know and believe that in God there are three divine Persons, is, notwithstanding, *in a state of salvation*, according to the opinion of most Catholic theologians.

No good theologian ever made such an assertion. All good theologians attribute justification neither to inculpable ignorance of, nor even to the knowledge of, the necessary truths of salvation; they attribute it to the infinite mercy of God, who unites himself with the soul only when it is prepared by the supernatural acts of divine faith, hope, and charity.

Therefore, only a theologian like "Sir Oracle" might easily endorse the above assertion.

"The three theological virtues," says St. Thomas, "incline and prepare man for supernatural happiness. Reason receives supernatural lights by faith, which gives us a foresight of eternal glory; the will tends by hope towards it as possible and attainable; and charity unites us to God, the eternal source of all joy and happiness."

"It is impossible" says O. A. Brownson, "to make Catholics and non-Catholics understand this great truth and conceive a correct idea of the spirit and essence of religion, unless it is clearly shown that our religion is based on divine revelation, and placed in the guardianship of a body of men divinely commissioned to teach the world, authoritatively and infallibly, all its sacred and immutable truths,—truths which all men are consequently bound in conscience to receive without hesitation. This is the fixed standard of Catholic belief; it is the basis upon which all dogmas rest. If this all-important truth be well understood by Catholics, the snares to entrap them may be very cunningly laid, yet they will not be easily caught in the meshes."

Nor can a discussion of doctrinal points be of any great use to one who is not thoroughly convinced of the divine authority of the Church. This being once accepted, everything else follows logically, as a matter of course. Hence, no one should be admitted to the one fold of Christ who does not firmly hold and declare that the Roman Catholic Church, ruled by the successors of St. Peter, is God's whole and sole appointed teacher of the Gospel on earth. However familiar persons may be with our doctrines, or however much they may believe our dogmas, without holding this, the fundamental truth of Catholic faith, they should not be allowed to join the Church. The moment it is well understood, and firmly believed, there need be but little delay about the abjuration.

The Church herself teaches us this lesson in her *Profession of Faith for Converts* and in her *Ritual*.

In the profession of faith which the Church requires converts to make before they are received into the Church, *the very first article of faith* reads as follows: "I, N. N., having before my eyes the holy Gospels which I touch with my hand, and *knowing that no one can be saved without that faith which the holy, Catholic, Apostolic, Roman Church holds, believes, and teaches*, against which I grieve that I have greatly erred," etc.

When a child is taken to church for baptism, the first question addressed to the child is: "What dost thou ask of *the Church of God?*" and the answer is: "Faith." What we must believe, etc., is learned from the Catholic Church alone. Hence it is that a Catholic, well instructed, when asked, "Why do you believe this?" answers: "Because the Church, our Mother, believes and teaches this." And "from whom did your Mother learn this?" "From God."

The Church, therefore, is not one religious body among many; it is *the only religious body*, inherent in the divine order of creation and representing it, as we said above.

What is here especially insisted upon is that, in treating of the Church, the reasons why salvation outside of her is impossible should be plainly stated, especially in our age, in which secret societies are doing all they can to undermine the divine teaching authority of the Church. The lesson, therefore, on the Church must be plain, and solid, and deeply impressed upon all who wish to be saved; all must learn and understand that *only* the Catholic Church is the Teacher from God, and the *reasons* why salvation out of her is impossible.

This doctrine is clearly expressed in the following words of the Athanasian Creed: "He, therefore, who wishes to be saved, must thus think of the Trinity," that is, he must believe the doctrine of the Holy Trinity as explained in this Creed. "Furthermore it is necessary to everlasting salvation that he also believe rightly the Incarnation of our Lord Jesus Christ. Hence St. Peter says: "Be it known to you, that there is no salvation in any other name than that of Jesus Christ; for there is no other name under heaven given to men whereby we must be saved." (Acts, iv. 10, 12). "Thus," says St. Alphonsus, "there is no hope of salvation except in the merits of Jesus Christ. Hence St. Thomas and all theologians conclude that, since the promulgation of the Gospel, it is necessary, not only as a matter of precept, but also as a means of salvation (necessitate medii, without which no adult can be saved), to believe explicitly that we can be saved only through our Redeemer." (Reflections on the Passion of Jesus Christ, Chapt. I., No. 19). The explicit belief in the mysteries of the Holy Trinity and of the Incarnation of the Son of God is therefore of the greatest importance. This belief teaches the origin of the world, its creation by God the Father; it teaches us the supernatural end of man, his fall, and the redemption of mankind by God the Son; it teaches the sanctification of souls by the gifts of the Holy Ghost.

The work which the Redeemer began in his Incarnation and completed in his Passion was not yet firmly established and secured; his Kingdom was not to come all at once, nor his dominion to be immediately established on the ruins of the empire of evil. The number of the elect must be gathered from all nations and generations of men. The merits of his Passion must be applied to the souls he has redeemed through all succeeding ages. This great mission is carried on through his Church, which, at Pentecost, came forth in the power of the Holy Spirit. Through her our Lord continues to act in the accomplishment of his designs.

"The Church, therefore," as Dr. O. A. Brownson, says, "is inherent in the divine order of creation and grace. God decreed her establishment and indestructibility when he decreed the order of creation and grace. Whatever is incompatible with her teaching, is incompatible with her divine order, aye, with the Divine Being Himself. As without God there is nothing, so without the Church, or outside of her, there is no religion, no spiritual life. All the pretended religions outside of her are shams, at best háve no basis, stand on nothing and are nothing, and can give no life or support to the soul, but leave it out of the divine order to drop it into hell.

"Catholics need to know this, and to be armed with principles and arguments that enable them to prove it against all gainsayers, or, at least, to enable them to defend themselves, and to be always on their guard against Protestant contamination and sophistry."

CHAPTER III.

The Great Revolt against Christ.

From the beginning of the world there have been two elements—the good and the bad—combating each other. "There must be scandals," says our Lord; St. Michael and Lucifer combat each other in heaven; Cain and Abel in the family of Adam; Isaac and Ismael in the family of Abraham; Jacob and Esau in the family of Isaac; Joseph and his brethren in the family of Jacob; Solomon and Absolom in the family of David; St. Peter and Judas in the company of Our Lord Jesus Christ; the Apostles and the Roman emperors in the Church of Christ; St. Francis of Assisi and Brother Elias, in the Franciscan Order; St. Bernard and his uncle Andrew, in the Cistercian Order; St. Alphonsus and Father Leggio in the Congregation of the Most Holy Redeemer; orthodox faith and heresy and infidelity, in the Kingdom of God on earth; the just and the wicked, in all places; in fact, where is the country, the city, the village, the religious community, or the family, howsoever small it may be, in which these two elements are not found in opposition. The parable of the sower and the cockle is everywhere verified; even should you be quite alone, grace and nature will combat each other. "And a man's enemies shall be they of his own household." (Matth. x. 36.) Strange to say, not only the good and the wicked are found in perpetual conflict; but God, for wise ends, permits that even the holiest and best of men are sometimes diametrically opposed to one another, and even incite persecution, one against the other, though each one may be led by the purest and holiest of motives.

There must be scandals,—a fatal, though divine warning!

There must be storms in nature to purify the air from dangerous elements. In like manner, God permits storms—heresies to arise in his Church on earth, in order that the erroneous and impious doctrines of heretics may, by way of contrast, set forth in clearer light the true and holy doctrines of the Church. As light is in the midst of darkness, gold contrasted with lead, the sun among the planets, the wise among the foolish,—so is the Roman Catholic Church among non-Catholics. "If two things of different natures," says the Wise Man, "be brought into opposition, the eye perceives their difference at once." "Good is set against evil, and life against death: so also is the sinner against the just man. And so look upon all the works of the Most High. Two and two, and one against another." (Eccl. xxxiii. 15.)

Christ, then, permits the storms of heresies to burst upon his Church, in order to bring forth into clearer light his divine doctrine, and to remove dangerous elements from his Mystic Body—the Roman Catholic Church.

At the beginning of the sixteenth century, with the exception of the Greek schismatics, a few Lollards in England, some Waldenses in Piedmont, scattered Albigenses or Manicheans, and a few followers of Huss and Zisca among the Bohemians, all Europe was Roman Catholic. England, Scotland, Ireland, Spain, Portugal, France, Italy, Germany, Switzerland, Hungary, Poland, Holland, Denmark, Norway, and Sweden,—every civilized nation was in the unity of the Catholic faith. Many of these nations were at the height of their power and prosperity. Portugal was pushing her discoveries beyond the Cape of Good Hope, and forming Catholic settlements in the East Indies. Christopher Columbus, a Roman Catholic, had discovered America, under the patronage of the Catholic Isabella of Spain. England was in a state of great prosperity. Her two Catholic Universities of Oxford and Cambridge contained, at one time, more than fifty thousand students. The country was covered with noble churches, abbeys, and monasteries, and with hospitals, where the poor were fed, clothed, and instructed.

However, the progress of civilization tended to foster a spirit of pride, and encourage the lust of novelties. The prosperity of the Church led to luxury, and in many cases to a relaxation of discipline. There were, as there always have been, in every period of the Church, the days of the apostles not excepted, bad men in the Church. The wheat and tares grow together until the harvest. The net of the Church encloses good and bad. The writings of Wickliffe, Huss, and their followers, had unsettled the minds of many. Princes were restive under the check held by the Church upon their rapacity and lusts. Henry VIII., for example, wanted to divorce a wife to whom he had been married twenty years, that he might marry a young and pretty one. He could not do this, so long as he acknowledged the spiritual supremacy of the Pope. Philip, Landgrave of Hesse, wanted two wives. No Pope would give him a dispensation to marry and live with two women at once. Then there were multitudes of wicked and avaricious nobles, who wanted but an excuse to plunder the churches, abbeys, and monasteries, whose property was held in trust for the education of the people and the care of the poor, aged, and sick, all over Europe. Then there were priests and monks eager to embrace a relaxed discipline, and many people who, incited by the cry of liberty, were ready to rush into license, and make war upon every principle of religion and social order, as soon as circumstances would favor the outbreak of this rebel spirit in individuals and masses. Now, when God, says St. Gregory, sees in the Church many revelling in their vices, and, as St. Paul observes, believing in God, confessing the truth of his mysteries, but belying their faith by their works, he punishes them by permitting that, after having lost grace, they also lose the holy knowledge which they had of his mysteries, and that, without any other persecution than that of their vices, they deny the faith. It is of these David speaks, when he says: "Destroy Jerusalem to its foundations;" (Ps. cxxxvi. 7.) leave not a stone upon stone. When the wicked spirits have ruined in a soul the edifice of virtue, they sap its foundation, which is faith. St. Cyprian, therefore, said: "Let no one think that virtuous men and good Christians ever leave the bosom of the Church; it is not the wheat that the wind lifts, but the chaff; trees deeply rooted are not blown down by the breeze, but those which have no roots. It is rotten fruits that fall off the trees, not sound ones; bad Catholics become heretics, as sickness is engendered by bad humors. At first, faith languishes in them, because of their vices; then it becomes sick; next it dies, because, since sin is essentially a blindness of spirit, the more a man sins, the more he is blinded; his faith grows weaker and weaker; the light of this divine torch decreases, and soon the least wind of temptation or doubt suffices to extinguish it." Witness the great defection from faith in the sixteenth century, when God permitted heresies to arise, in order to exercise his justice against those who were ready to abandon the truth, and his mercy toward those who remained attached to it; to prove, by trials, those who were firm in the faith, and to separate them from those who loved error; to exercise the patience and charity of the Church, and to sanctify the elect; to give occasion for the illustration of religious truth and the holy Scripture; to make pastors more vigilant, and value more the sacred deposit of faith; in fine, to render the authority of tradition more clear and incontestable. Heresy arose in all its strength; Martin Luther was its ringleader and its spokesman.

Martin Luther, an Augustinian friar, a bold man and a vehement declaimer, having imbibed erroneous sentiments from the heretical writings of John Huss of Bohemia, took occasion, from the publication of indulgences promulgated by Pope Leo X., to break with the Catholic Church, and to propagate his new errors, in 1517, at Wittenberg, in Saxony. He first inveighed against the abuse of indulgences; then he called in question their efficacy; and at last totally rejected them. He declaimed against the supremacy of the See of Rome, and condemned the whole

Church, pretending that Christ had abandoned it, and that it wanted reforming, as well in faith as discipline. Thus this new evangelist commenced that fatal defection from the ancient faith, which was styled "Reformation." The new doctrines, being calculated to gratify the vicious inclinations of the human heart, spread with the rapidity of an inundation. Frederick, Elector of Saxony, John Frederick, his successor, and Philip, Landgrave of Hesse, became Luther's disciples. Gustavus Ericus, King of Sweden, and Christian III., King of Denmark, also declared in favor of Lutheranism. It secured a footing in Hungary. Poland, after tasting a great variety of doctrines, left to every individual the liberty of choosing for himself. Munzer, a disciple of Luther, set up for doctor himself, and, with Nicholas Stark, gave birth to the sect of Anabaptists, which was propagated in Suabia, and other provinces in Germany, in the Low Countries. Calvin, a man of bold, obstinate spirit, and indefatigable in his labors, in imitation of Luther, turned reformer also. He contrived to have his new tenets received at Geneva, in 1541. After his death, Beza preached the same doctrine. It insinuated itself into some parts of Germany, Hungary, Bohemia, and became the religion of Holland. It was imported by John Knox, an apostate priest, into Scotland, where, under the name of Presbyterianism, it took deep root, and spread over the kingdom. But among the deluded nations, none drank more deeply of the cup of error than England. For many centuries this country had been conspicuous in the Christian world for the orthodoxy of its belief, as also for the number of its saints. But by a misfortune never to be sufficiently lamented, and by an an unfathomable judgment from above, its Church shared a fate which seemed the least to threaten it. The lust and avarice of one despotic sovereign threw down•the fair edifice, and tore it off the rock on which it had hitherto stood. Henry VIII., at first a valiant asserter of the Catholic faith against Luther, giving way to the violent passions which he had not sufficient courage to curb, renounced the supreme jurisdiction which the Pope had always held in the Church, presumed to arrogate to himself that power in his own dominions, and thus gave a deadly blow to religion. He then forced his subjects into the same fatal defection. Once introduced, it soon overspread the land. Being, from its nature, limited by no fixed principle, it has since taken a hundred different shapes, under different names, such as: the Calvinists, Arminians, Antinomians, Independents, Kilhamites, Glassites, Haldanites, Bereans, Swedenborgians, New-Jerusalemites, Orthodox Quakers, Hicksites, Shakers, Panters, Seekers, Jumpers, Reformed Methodists, German Methodists, Albright Methodists, Episcopal Methodists, Wesleyan Methodists, Methodists North, Methodists South, Protestant Methodists, Episcopalians, High Church Episcopalians, Low Church Episcopalians, Ritualists, Puseyites, Dutch Reformed, Dutch non-Reformed, Christian Israelites, Baptists, Particular Baptists, Seventh-day Baptists, Hardshell Baptists, Softshell Baptists, Forty Gallon Baptists, Sixty Gallon Baptists, African Baptists, Free-will Baptists, Church of God Baptists, Regular Baptists, Anti-mission Baptists, Six Principle Baptists, River Brethren, Winebremarians, Mennonites, Second Adventists, Millerites, Christian Baptists, Universalists, Orthodox Congregationalists, Campbellites, Presbyterians, Old School Presbyterians and New School Presbyterians, Cumberland Presbyterians, United Presbyterians, The Only True Church of Christ, 573 Bowery, N. Y., up stairs, 5th story, Latter-day Saints, Restorationists, Schwenfelders, Spiritualists, Mormons, Christian Perfectionists, etc., etc., etc. All these sects are called Protestants because they all unite in protesting against their mother, the Roman Catholic Church.

Some time after, when the reforming spirit had reached its full growth, Dudithius, a learned Protestant divine, in his epistle to Beza, wrote: "What sort of people are our Protestants, straggling to and fro, and carried about by every wind of doctrine, sometimes to this side, sometimes to that? You may, perhaps, know what their sentiments in matters of religion are to-day, but you can never tell precisely what they will be to-morrow. In what article of religion do these churches agree which have cast off the Bishop of Rome? Examine all from top to bottom, and you will scarce find one thing affirmed by one which was not immediately condemned by another for wicked doctrine." The same confusion of opinions was described by an English Protestant, the learned Dr. Walton, about the middle of the last century, in his preface to his Polyglot, where he says: "Aristarchus heretofore could scarce find seven wise men in Greece; but with us, scarce are to be found so many idiots. For all are doctors, all are divinely learned: there is not so much as the meanest fanatic who does not give you his own dreams for the word of God. The bottomless pit seems to have been opened, from whence a smoke has arisen which has darkened the heavens and the stars, and locusts have come out with stings, a numerous race of sectaries and heretics, who have renewed all the ancient heresies, and invented many monstrous opinions of their own. These have filled our cities, villages, camps, houses, nay, our pulpits, too, and lead the poor deluded people with them to the pit of perdition." "Yes," writes another author, "every ten years, or nearly so, the Protestant theological literature undergoes a complete revolution. What was admired during the one decennial period is rejected in the next, and the image which they adored is burnt, to make way for new divinities; the dogmas which were held in honor, fall into discredit; the classical treatise of morality is banished among the old books out of date; criticism overturns criticism; the commentary of yesterday ridicules that of the previous day, and what was clearly proved in 1840, is not less clearly disproved in 1850. The theological systems of Protestantism are as numerous as the political constitutions of France—one revolution only awaits another." (Le Semeur, June, 1840.) It is indeed utterly impossible to keep the various members of one single sect from perpetual disputes, even about the essential truths of revealed religion. And those religious differences exist not only in the same sect, not only in the same country and town, but even in the same family. Nay, the self-same individual, at different periods of his life, is often in flagrant contradiction with himself. To-day he avows opinions which yesterday he abhorred, and to-morrow he will exchange these again for new ones. At last, after belonging, successively, to various new-fangled sects, he generally ends by professing unmitigated contempt for them all. By their continual disputes and bickerings, and dividing and subdividing, the various Protestant sects have made themselves the scorn of honest minds, the laughing-stock of the pagan and the infidel.

These human sects, the "works of the flesh," as St. Paul calls them, alter their shape, like clouds, but "feel no blow, says Mr. Marshall, because they have no substance. They fight a good deal with one another, but nobody minds it, not even themselves, nor cares what becomes of them. If one human sect perishes, it is always easy to make another, or half a dozen. They have the life of worms, and propagate by corruption. Their life is so like death that, except by the putridity which they exhale in both stages, it is impossible to tell which is which, and when they are buried, nobody can find their graves. They have simply disappeared.

The spirit of Protestantism, or the spirit of revolt against God and his Church, sprung up from the Reformers' spirit of incontinency, obstinacy, and covetousness. Luther, in despite of the vow he had solemnly made to God of keeping continency, married a nun, equally bound as himself to that sacred religious promise; but, as St. Jerome says, "it is rare to find a heretic that loves chastity."

Luther's example had indeed been anticipated by Carlostadtius, a priest and ringleader of the Sacramentarians, who had married a little before; and it was soon followed by most of the heads of the Reformation.

Zwinglius, a priest and chief of the sect that bore his name, took a wife.

Bucer, a nember of the order of St. Dominic, became a Lutheran, left his cloister, and married a nun.

Œcolampadius, a Brigitin monk, became a Zwinglian, and also married.

Cranmer, Archbishop of Canterbury, had also his wife.

Peter Martyr, a canon-regular, embraced the doctrine of Calvin, but followed the example of Luther, and married a nun.

Ochin, General of the Capuchins, became a Lutheran, and also married.

Thus the principal leaders in the Reformation went forth preaching the new gospel, with two marks upon them : apostasy from faith, and open violation of the most sacred vows.

The passion of lust, as has been already said, hurried also Henry VIII. of England into a separation from the Catholic Church, and ranked him among the Reformers.

Those wicked men could not be expected to teach a holy doctrine; they preached up a hitherto unheard-of " evangelical liberty," as they styled it. They told. their fellow-men that they were no longer obliged to subject their understanding to the mysteries of faith, and to regulate their actions according to the laws of Christian morality ; they told that every one was free to model his belief and practice as it suited his inclinations. In pursuance of this accommodating doctrine, they dissected the Catholic faith till they reduced it to a mere skeleton ; they lopped off the reality of the body and blood of Christ in the Holy Eucharist, the divine Christian sacrifice offered in the Mass, confession of sins, most of the sacraments, penitential exercises, several of the canonical books of Scripture, the invocation of saints, celibacy, most of the General Councils of the Church, and all present Church authority ; they perverted the nature of justification, asserting that faith alone suffices to justify man ; they made God the author of sin, and maintained the observance of the commandments to be impossible.

As a few specimens of Luther's doctrine, take the following: "God's commandments are all equally impossible." (De Lib. Christ., t. ii., fol. 4.) "No sins can damn a man, but only unbelief." (De Captiv. Bab., t. ii., fol. 171.) "God is just, though by his own will he lays us under the necessity of being damned, and though he damns those who have not deserved it." (Tom. ii., foll. 434, 436.) "God works in us both good and evil." (Tom. ii., fol. 444.) "Christ's body is in every place, no less than the divinity itself." (Tom. iv., fol. 37.) Then, for his darling principle of justification by faith, in his eleventh article against Pope Leo, he says: "Believe strongly that you are absolved, and absolved you will be, whether you have contrition or no."

Again, in his sixth article: "The contrition which is acquired by examining, recollecting, and detesting one's sins, whereby a man calls to mind his life past, in the bitterness of his soul, reflecting on the heinousness and multitude of his offences, the loss of eternal bliss, and condemnation to eternal woe,—this contrition, I say, makes a man a hypocrite, nay, even a greater sinner than he was before."

Thus, after the most immoral life, a man has a compendious method of saving himself, by simply believing that his sins are remitted through the merits of Christ.

As Luther foresaw the scandal that would arise from his own and such like sacrilegious marriages, he prepared the world for it, by writing against the celibacy of the clergy and all religious vows; and all the way up, since his time, he has had imitators. He proclaimed that all such vows " were contrary to faith, to the commandments of God, and to evangelical liberty." (De Votis Monast.) He said again: "God disapproves of such a vow of living in continency, equally as if I should vow to become the mother of God, or to create a new world." (Epist. ad Wolfgang Reisemb.) And again: "To attempt to live unmarried, is plainly to fight against God."

Now, when men give a loose rein to the depravity of nature, what wonder if the most scandalous practices ensue? Accordingly, a striking instance of this kind appeared in the license granted, in 1539, to Philip, Landgrave of Hesse, to have two wives at once, which license was signed by Luther, Melanchthon, Bucer, and five other Protestant preachers.

On the other hand, a wide door was laid open to another species of scandal: the doctrine of the Reformation admitted divorces in the marriage state in certain cases, contrary to the doctrine of the Gospel, and even allowed the parties thus separated to marry other wives and other husbands.

To enumerate the errors of all the Reformers would exceed the limits of this treatise. I shall therefore only add the principal heads of the doctrine of Calvin and the Calvinists: 1. that baptism is not necessary for salvation; 2. good works are not necessary; 3. man has no free-will; 4. Adam could not avoid his fall; 5. a great part of mankind are created to be damned, independently of their demerits; 6. man is justified by faith alone, and that justification, once obtained, cannot be lost, even by the most atrocious crimes; 7. the true faithful are also infallibly certain of their salvation; 8. the Eucharist is no more than a figure of the body and blood of Christ. Thus was the whole system of faith and morality overturned. Tradition they totally abolished; and though they could not reject the whole of the Scripture, as being universally acknowledged to be the word of God, they had, however, the presumption to expunge some books of it that did not coincide with their own opinions, and the rest they assumed a right to explain as they saw fit.

To pious souls, they promised a return to the fervor of primitive Christianity; to the proud, the liberty of private judgment; to the enemies of the clergy, they promised the division of their spoils; to priests and monks who were tired of the yoke of continence, the abolition of a law which, they said, was contrary to nature; to libertines of all classes, the suppression of fasting, abstinence, and confession. They said to kings who wished to place themselves at the head of the Church as well as of the State, that they would be freed from the spiritual authority of the Church; to nobles, that they would see a rival order humbled and impoverished; to the middle classes and the vassals of the Church, that they would be emancipated from all dues and and forced services.

Several princes of Germany and of the Swiss cantons supported by arms the preachers of the new doctrines. Henry VIII. imposed his doctrine on his subjects. The King of Sweden drew his people into apostasy. The Court of Navarre welcomed the Calvinists; the Court of France secretly favored them.

At length Pope Paul III. convoked a General Council, at Trent, in 1545, to which the heresiarchs had appealed. Not only all the Catholic bishops, but also all Christian princes, even Protestants, were invited to come.

But now the spirit of pride and obstinacy became most apparent. Henry VIII. replied to the Pope that he would never intrust the work of reforming religion in his kingdom to any one except to himself. The apostate princes of Germany told the papal legate that they recognized only the emperor as their sovereign; the Viceroy of Naples allowed but four bishops to go to the council; the king of France sent only three prelates, whom he soon after recalled. Charles V. created difficulties, and put obstacles in the way. Gustavus Vasa allowed no one to go to the council. The heresiarchs also refused to appear. The council, however, was held in spite of these difficulties. It lasted over eighteen years, because it was often interrupted by the plague, by war, and by the deaths of those who had to preside over it. The doctrines of the innovators were examined and condemned by the council, at the last session of which there were more than three hundred bishops present; among whom were nine cardinals, three patriarchs, thirty-three archbishops, not to mention sixteen abbots or generals of religious orders, and one hundred and forty-eight theologians. All the decrees published from the commencement were read over, and were again approved and subscribed by the Fathers. Accordingly, Pius IV., in a consistory held on the 26th of January, in 1564, approved and confirmed the council in a book which was signed by all the cardinals. He drew up, the same year, a profession of faith conformable in all respects with the definitions of the council, in which it is declared that its authority is accepted; and since that time, not only all bishops of the Catholic Church, but all priests who are called to teach the way of salvation, even to children, nay, all non-Catholics, on abjuring their errors, and returning to the bosom of the Church, have sworn that they had no other faith than that of the holy Council.

The new heresiarchs, however, continued to obscure and disfigure the face of religion. As to Luther's sentiments in regard to the Pope, bishops, councils, etc., he says in the preface to his book, *De Abroganda Missa Privata:* "With how many powerful remedies and most evident Scriptures have I scarce been able to fortify my conscience so as to dare alone to contradict the Pope, and to believe him to be Antichrist, the bishops his apostles, and the universities his brothel-houses;" and in his book, *De Judicio Ecclesiæ de Gravi Doctrina,* he says: "Christ takes from the bishops, doctors, and councils both the right and power of judging controversies, and gives them to all Christians in general."

His censure on the Council of Constance, and those that composed it, is as follows: "All John Huss' articles were condemned at Constance by Antichrist and his apostles," (meaning the Pope and bishops), "in that synod of Satan, made up of most wicked sophisters; and you, most holy Vicar of Christ, I tell you plainly to your face, that all John Huss' condemned doctrines are evangelical and Christian, but all yours are impious and diabolical. I now declare," says he, speaking to the bishops, "that for the future I will not vouchsafe you so much honor as to submit myself or doctrine to your judgment, or to that of an angel from heaven." (Preface to his book *Adversus falso nominatum ordinem Episcoporum.*) Such was his spirit of pride that he made open profession of contempt for the authority of the Church, councils, and Fathers, saying : "All those who will venture their lives, their estates, their honor, and their blood, in so Christian a work as to root out all bishoprics and bishops, who are the ministers of Satan, and to pluck by the roots all their authority and jurisdiction in the world,—these persons are the true children of God and obey his commandments." (*Contra Statum Ecclesiæ et falso nominatum ordinem Episcoporum.*)

This spirit of pride and obstinacy is also most apparent from the fact that Protestantism has never been ashamed to make use of any arguments, though ever so frivolous, inconsistent, or absurd, to defend its errors, and to slander and misrepresent the Catholic religion in every way possible. It shows itself again in the wars which Protestantism waged to introduce and maintain itself. The apostate princes of Germany entered into a league, offensive and defensive, against the Emperor Charles V., and rose up in arms to establish Protestantism.

Luther had preached licentiousness, and reviled the emperor, the princes, and the bishops. The peasants lost no time in freeing themselves from their masters. They overran the country in lawless bands, burned down castles and monasteries, and committed the most barbarous cruelties among the nobility and clergy. Germany became at last the scene of desolation and most cruel atrocities during the Thirty Years' War (1618-1648). More than one hundred thousand men fell in battle ; seven cities were dismantled ; one thousand religious houses were razed to the ground ; three hundred churches and immense treasures of statuary, paintings, books, etc., were destroyed.

But what is more apparent and better known than the spirit of covetousness of Protestantism ? Wherever Protestantism secured a footing, it pillaged churches, seized Church property, destroyed monasteries, and appropriated to itself their revenues.

In France, the Calvinists destroyed twenty thousand Catholic churches ; they murdered, in Dauphiné alone, two hundred and twenty-five priests, one hundred and twelve monks, and burned nine hundred towns and villages. In England, Henry VIII. confiscated to the crown, or distributed among his favorites, the property of six hundred and forty-five monasteries and ninety colleges, one hundred and ten hospitals, and two thousand three-hundred and seventy-four free-chapels and chantries.

They even dared to profane, with sacrilegious hands, the remains of the martyrs and confessors of God. In many places they forcibly took up the saints' bodies from the repositories where they were kept, burned them, and scattered their ashes abroad. What more atrocious indignity can be conceived? Are parricides or the most flagitious men ever worse treated? Among other instances, in 1562, the Calvinists broke open the shrine of St. Francis of Paula, at Plessis-Lestours; and finding his body uncorrupted fifty-five years after his death, they dragged it about the streets, and burned it in a fire which they had made with the *wood of a large crucifix*, as Billet and other historians relate.

Thus at Lyons, in the same year, the Calvinists seized upon the shrine of St. Bonaventure, stripped it of its riches, burned the Saint's relics in the market-place, and threw his ashes into the river Saône, as is related by the learned Possevinus, who was in Lyons at the time.

The bodies also of St. Irenæus, St. Hilary, and St. Martin, as Surius asserts, were treated in the same ignominious manner. Such, also, was the treatment offered to the remains of St. Thomas, Archbishop of Canterbury, whose rich shrine, according to the words of Stowe, in his annals, " was taken to the king's use, and the bones of St. Thomas, by the command of Lord Cromwell, were burnt to ashes in September, 1538.

The Catholic religion has covered the world with its superb monuments. Protestantism has now lasted three hundred years; it was powerful in England, in Germany, in America. What has it raised? It will show us the ruins which it has made, amidst which it has planted some gardens, or established some factories. The Catholic religion is essentially a creative power, built up, not to destroy, because it is under the immediate influence of that Holy Spirit which the Church invokes as the Creative Spirit, "Creator Spiritus." The Protestant, or modern philosophical spirit, is a principle of destruction, of perpetual decomposition and disunion. Under the dominion of English Protestant power, for four hundred years, Ireland was rapidly becoming as naked and void of ancient memorials as the wilds of Africa.

The Reformers themselves were so ashamed of the progress of immorality among their proselytes, that they could not help complaining against it. Thus spoke Luther: "Men are now more revengeful, covetous, and licentious, than they were ever in the Papacy." (Postil. super Evang. Dom. i., Advent.) Then again: "Heretofore, when we were seduced by the Pope, every man willingly performed good works, but now no man says or knows anything else than how to get all to himself by exactions, pillage, theft, lying, usury." (Postil. super Evang. Dom. xxvi., p. Trinit.)

Calvin wrote in the same strain: "Of so many thousands," said he, "who, renouncing Popery, seemed eagerly to embrace the Gospel, how few have amended their lives! Nay, what else did the greater part pretend to, than, by shaking off the yoke of superstition, to give themselves more liberty to follow all kinds of licentiousness?" (*Liber de scandalis.*) Dr. Heylin, in his History of the Reformation, complains also of "the great increase of viciousness" in England, in the reforming reign of Edward VI.

Erasmus says: "Take a view of this evangelical people, the Protestants. Perhaps 'tis my misfortune, but I never yet met with one who does not appear changed for the worse." (Epist. ad Vultur. Neoc.) And again: "Some persons," says he, "whom I knew formerly innocent, harmless, and without deceit, no sooner have I seen them joined to that sect (the Protestants), than they began to talk of wenches, to play at dice, to leave off prayers, being

grown extremely worldly, most impatient, revengeful, vain, like vipers, tearing one another. I speak by experience."
(*Ep. ad Fratres Infer. Germaniœ.*)

M. Scherer, the principal of a Protestant school in France, wrote, in 1844, that he beholds in his Reformed Church "the ruin of all truth, the weakness of infinite division, the scattering of flocks, ecclesiastical anarchy, Socinianism ashamed of itself, Rationalism coated like a pill, without doctrine, without consistency. This Church, deprived alike of its corporate and its dogmatic character, of its form and of its doctrine, deprived of all that constituted it a Christian Church, has in truth ceased to exist in the ranks of religious communities. Its name continues, but it represents only a corpse, a phantom, or, if you will, a memory or a hope. For want of dogmatic authority, unbelief has made its way into three-fourths of our pupils."
(*L' Etat Actual de l' Eglise Reformée en France*, 1844.)

Such has been Protestantism from the beginning. It is written in blood and fire upon the pages of history. Whether it takes the form of Lutheranism in Germany, Denmark, and Sweden; Anglicanism in Great Britain, or Calvinism and Presbyterianism in Switzerland, France, Holland, Scotland, and America,—it has been everywhere the same. It has risen by tumult and violence; propagated itself by force and persecution; enriched itself by plunder, and has never ceased, by open force, persecuting laws, or slander, its attempt to exterminate the Catholic faith, and destroy the Church of Christ, which the fathers of Protestantism left from the spirit of lust, pride, and covetousness,—a spirit which induced so many of their countrymen to follow their wicked example; a spirit on account of which they would have been lost at all events, even if they had not left their mother, the One, Holy, Roman Catholic and Apostolic Church.

The main spirit of Protestantism, then, has always been to declare every man independent of the divine authority of the Roman Catholic Church, and to substitute for this divine authority a human authority. Pope Pius IX. spoke of Protestantism, in all its forms, as a "revolt against God, it being an attempt to substitute a *human* for a *divine* authority, and a declaration of the creature's independence of the Creator." "A true Protestant, therefore," says Mr. Marshall, "does not acknowledge that God has a right to teach him; or, if he acknowledges this right, he does not feel himself bound to believe all that God teaches him through those whom God has appointed to teach mankind. He says to God: If thou teachest me, I reserve to myself the right to examine thy words, to explain them as I choose, and admit only what appears to me true, consistent, and useful." Hence St. Augustine says: "You, who believe what you please, and reject what you please, believe yourselves or your own fancy rather than the Gospel." The faith of the Protestant, then, is based upon his private judgment alone; it is human. "As his judgment is alterable," says Mr. Marshall, "he naturally holds that his faith and doctrine is alterable at will, and is therefore continually changing it. Evidently, then, he does not hold it to be the truth; for truth never changes; nor does he hold it to be the law of God, which he is bound to obey; for if the law of God be alterable at will, it can only be altered by God himself, never by man, any body of men, or any creature of God."

CHAPTER IV.

BISHOP COXE'S DISHONESTY.

The story is told of a Western-bound train, flying along with lightning speed; the time was shortly after sunset. Suddenly a crash was heard: the train stopped. "What is the matter?" the passengers asked one another. A huge owl, dazzled by the glare, had struck against the reflector in front of the engine, shivered the glass, and tried to extinguish the light, and a great bull had set its head against the engine, to stop the train. The lamp was rekindled, the engine sped on, but the stupid owl and the obstinate bull were cast aside, dead, and left to rot and be devoured by wild beasts. An Irishman, on seeing them, exclaimed: "I admire your courage, but condemn your judgment."

This train may be likened to the holy Catholic Church, speeding on, on her heaven-sent mission, to lead men to heaven by the light of her holy doctrine. The foolish owl, the enemy of light and the friend of darkness, represents Lucifer, who, as the foe of God and of the light of God's holy religion, has always been endeavoring to extinguish the light of the true religion. The bull represents the kings and emperors, the heretics and members of secret societies, whom Lucifer uses to stop, if possible, the progress of the Catholic Church, the bearer of the light of faith. Although it is hard, in a certain sense, not to admire the courage of Lucifer's agents, yet we cannot but condemn their judgment, their folly, and wickedness, in opposing the work of God, and bringing down upon themselves the everlasting curse of the Almighty.

Our Divine Saviour, Jesus Christ, came to break the power of the devil over mankind; he came to banish idolatry, the worship of the devil, from among men, and lead them back to the worship and service of his heavenly Father by his holy example and divine doctrine. But no sooner had he begun to teach men his saving doctrine, than Satan opposed him. Satan is called, in Holy Scripture, the father of lies. From the beginning of the world he has tried to misrepresent every religious truth. He practised this black art in paradise; and so unhappily successful was he in it, that ever since he has practised it, in order to propagate error and vice among men. When our Saviour began to preach his holy religion, Satan practised his black art, even in the presence of Christ himself. By malicious men, the ministers of Satan, Christ was contradicted and misrepresented in his doctrine; for, instead of being believed, he was held up to the people as a blasphemer, for teaching that he was the Son of God, as the impious Caiphas declared him to be, saying, "He hath blasphemed, he is guilty of death." (Matt. xxvi. 65.) He was misrepresented in his reputation, for he was noble, of royal lineage, and yet was despised: "Is not this the carpenter's son?" (Matt. xiii. 55.) He is wisdom itself, and was represented as an ignorant man: "How doth this man know letters, having never learned?" (John vii. 17.) He was represented as a false prophet: "And they blindfolded him, and smote his face . . . saying: Prophesy who is this that struck thee?" (Luke, xxii. 64.) He was represented as a madman: "He is mad, why hear you him?" (John, x. 20.) He was represented as a winebibber, a glutton, and a friend of sinners: "Behold a man that is a glutton and a drinker of wine, a friend of publicans and sinners." (Luke, vii. 34.) He was represented as a sorcerer: "By the prince of the devils he casteth out devils." (Matt ix. 34.) He was represented as a heretic and possessed person: "Do we not say well of thee, that thou art a Samaritan, and hast a devil?" (John, viii. 48.) In a word, Jesus was represented to the people as so bad and notorious a man, that no trial was deemed necessary to condemn him, as the Jews said to Pilate : "If he were not a malefactor, we would not have delivered him up to thee." (John, xviii. 30.) If ever infamous calumny was carried to excess, it was undoubtedly in the case of our Saviour, "who knew not sin," who had never uttered a deceitful word, who "did all things well," and who "passed his life in doing good, and healing all kinds of infirmities." Christ's holy doctrine and his holy Church, the teacher of his divine doctrines, are still misrepresented by Lucifer's agents, now that he is on his throne, gloriously reigning in heaven.

Our divine Saviour and his holy Apostles spoke of these agents and warned the Christians to be on their guard against them. That the Protestant Bishop Coxe is one of them is a well-known fact. In several passages of Holy Scripture he is spoken of. We give some of them for his benefit:—

1. Our blesssd Saviour, foretelling the coming of false teachers, says, "Beware of false prophets, who come to you in sheep's clothing, but inwardly they are ravenous wolves; by their fruits ye shall know them;" and then he tells us, going on with the similitude of a tree, what shall be the portion of such false prophets. "Every tree that bringeth not forth good fruit shall be cut down and cast into the fire." (Matt. vii. 15, 19.) Such is the fate of false teachers, according to Jesus Christ. St. Paul describes them in the same light, and exhorts the pastors of the Church to watch against them, that they may prevent the seduction of the flock . "I know that after my departure ravening wolves shall enter in among you, not sparing the flock: and of your own selves shall arise men speaking perverse things, to draw away disciples after them; therefore watch." (Acts, xx. 29.) Such is the idea the word of God gives of all who depart from the doctrine of the Church of Christ and teach falsehood; they are *ravenous wolves, seducers of the people,* who *speak perverse things,* and whose end is *hellfire.*

2. St. Paul, concluding his Epistle to the Romans, warns them against such teachers in these words: "Now, I beseech you, brethren, to mark them who cause dissensions and offences contrary to the doctrine which ye have learned, and to avoid them: for they that are such serve not Christ our Lord, but their own belly, and by pleasing speeches and good words seduce the hearts of the innocent." (Rom. xvi. 17.) Can such as these, who cause dissensions contrary to the ancient doctrine, and seduce the souls redeemed by the blood of Jesus, who are not servants of Christ, but his enemies, and are slaves to their own belly—can these, I say, be in the way of salvation? Alas! the same holy Apostle describes their fate in another text, saying, "That they are enemies of the cross of Christ, whose end is destruction, whose god is their belly, and whose glory is in their shame." (Philip. iii. 18.)

3. In St. Paul's absence some false teachers had come in among the Galatians, and persuaded them that it was *necessary* for salvation to join circumcision with the gospel; on this account the apostle writes his epistle to correct this error; and though it was but an error on one point, and apparently not of great importance, yet, because it was false doctrine, the holy Apostle condemns it: "I wonder how you are so soon removed from him that called you to the grace of Christ, unto another gospel: which is not another; only there are some that trouble you, and would pervert the gospel of Christ. But though we, or an angel from heaven, preach a gospel to you besides that which we have preached to you, let him be accursed. As we said before, I say now again, if any one preach to you a gospel besides that which ye have received, let him be accursed." (Gal. i. 6.) This shows, indeed, the crime and fate of false teachers, though their doctrine was false only on a single point.

4. St. Peter describes these unhappy men in the most dreadful colors. "There shall be among you lying teachers, who shall bring sects of perdition" (or, as the Protestant translation has it, *damnable heresies*) " and deny the

Lord who bought them, bringing on themselves swift destruction." (II. Pet. ii. 1.) and going on to describe them, he says: "Their judgment of a long time lingereth not, and their destruction slumbereth not." (ver. 3.) "The Lord knoweth how . . . to reserve the unjust unto the day of judgment to be tormented; and especially them who . . . despise governments, audacious, pleasing themselves, they fear not to bring in sects blaspheming," (ver. 9.) "leaving the right way, they have gone astray." (ver. 15.) "These are wells without water, and clouds tossed with whirlwinds, to whom the mist of darkness is reserved." (ver. 17.) Good God! what a dreadful state to be in!

5. St. Paul, speaking of such as are led away by what St. Peter calls *damnable heresies*, says: "A man that is a heretic, after the first and second admonition, avoid; knowing that he that is such an one is subverted and sinneth, being condemned by his own judgment." (Tit. iii. 10.) Other offenders are judged and cast out of the Church by the sentence of the pastors; but heretics, more unhappy, leave the Church of their own accord, and by so doing give judgment and sentence against their own souls. (*Sincere Christian* by BISHOP HAY.)

Whilst writing this, we remember something remarkable that happened in France, in 1556. It may be well for Mr. Coxe to know it.

It is a well-known fact that the Catholic Church has received power from Jesus Christ to cast out devils and restrain them from injuring any of God's creatures. The Church often makes use of this power. She has instituted certain rites and prayers to be used by bishops and priests in casting out devils from possessed persons. In our little work, *Triumph of the Blessed Sacrament*, we have related how Almighty God permitted evil spirits to possess a certain person, called Nicola Aubry, of the town of Vervins, in France. The possession took place 1565, and lasted for several months. The Bishop of Laon, by Christ in the Blessed Sacrament, expelled the evil spirits forever, on February 8th, 1566.

When the strange circumstances of Nicola's possession became known everywhere, several Calvinist preachers came with their followers to "expose this popish cheat," as they said. On their entrance, the devil saluted them mockingly, called them by name, and told them that they had come in *obedience to him*. One of the preachers took his Protestant prayer-book, and began to read it with a very solemn face. The devil laughed at him, and, putting on a most comical face, he said: "Ho! ho! my good friend, do you intend to expel *me* with your prayers and hymns? Do you think that they will cause me pain? Don't you know that they are mine? I help to compose them?"

"I will expel thee in the name of God," said the preacher solemnly.

"You!" said the devil mockingly. "You will *not* expel me, either in the name of *God*, or in the name of the *devil*. Did you ever hear, then, of one devil driving out another?"

"I am not a devil," said the preacher angrily, "I am a servant of Christ."

"A servant of Christ, indeed!" said Satan with a sneer. "What! I tell you, you are worse than *I* am. *I* believe, and *you* do not want to believe. Do you suppose that *you* can expel me from the body of this miserable wretch! Ha! go first and expel all the devils that are in your own heart!"

The preacher took his leave, somewhat discomfited. On going away, he said, turning up the whites of his eyes: "Oh Lord, I pray thee, assist this poor creature!"

"And I pray Lucifer," cried the spirit, "that he may never leave you, but may always keep you firmly in his power, as he does now. Go about your business now. You are *all mine*, and I am your master." So they went away. They had seen and heard more than they wanted.

Bishop Coxe is well known as a famous exorcist. He does all in his power to prevent the devil (that is what he takes the Roman Catholic faith for) from taking possession of Protestants. He knows that, if this possession should really take place, he would have no power to expel the devil of idolatry. An ounce of preventive is, in his opinion, better than a pound of cure. In this, he imitates his ancestors.

St. Augustine tells us that the Manichees and the Donatists did all in their power to raise prejudices in the minds of the people against the Roman Catholic Church. They told men that the teaching of the Church was unsound and profane doctrine, that it was full of wicked principles and human inventions, instead of divine faith; and all these calumnies were spread abroad among the people, in order that they might not think of going to the Church to learn the truth, or even suspect her to be the Church of Christ. "The chief reason," says St. Augustine, "why I continued to live so long in the errors of the Manichees, and impugned the Catholic Church with so much violence, was, because I thought that all I heard against the Church was true. But when I found out that it was all false, I made known this falsehood to the world, in order to undeceive others who were caught in the same snare. I mingled joys and blushes, and was ashamed that I had now for so many years been barking and railing, not against the Catholic Faith, but only against the fictions of my carnal conceits. For so rash and impious was I; that those things which I might first have learned from Catholics by inquiry, I charged upon them by accusation. I was readier to impose falsehood than to be informed of the truth." This he did, deluded and deceived by the Manichees. Alas! this has not been the case of St. Augustine alone, but of almost as many as have given ear to the deserters of this Church; nay, it is at this very day the case of infinite numbers of Protestants and infidels, who, following St. Augustine in his errors, do not inquire how this thing is believed or understood by the Church, but insultingly oppose all, as if understood as they imagine. They make no difference between *that which the Catholic* Church teaches, and *what they think* she teaches. Thus they believe her guilty of as many absurdities, follies, and impieties, as the heathens did of old.

There is a Protestant. He considers the antiquity of the

Roman Catholic Church; her unity in faith; the purity and holiness of her doctrine; her establishment by poor fishermen all over the world, in spite of all kinds of opposition; her invariable duration from the time of the apostles; the miracles which are wrought in her; the holiness of all those who live according to her laws; the deep science of her doctors; the almost infinite number of her martyrs; the peace of mind and happiness of soul experienced by those who have entered her bosom; the fact that all Protestants admit that a faithful Catholic will be saved in his religion; the frightful punishment inflicted by God upon all the persecutors of the Catholic Church; the melancholy death of the authors of heresies; the constant fulfilment of the words of our Lord, that his Church would always be persecuted. He seriously considers all this; he is enlightened by God's grace to see that the Roman Catholic Church alone is the true Church of Jesus Christ; he is convinced that her authority is from God, and that to hear and obey her authority is to hear and obey God himself: and so he accepts and believes all that she teaches, because it comes to him on the authority of God, and therefore *must* be true; not because he himself sees *how* or *why* it is true. This is true divine faith—this is the right way to become a Catholic. Such faith is absolutely necessary. It is necessary by necessity of precept. Our blessed Lord says: "He that believeth and is baptized shall be saved. He that believeth not shall be condemned." This precept is affirmative, in as far as it obliges us to believe all that God has revealed; it is negative, in as far as it forbids us to hold any opinions contrary to the revealed truth.

Such faith is necessary by necessity of medium, for, "without faith, it is impossible to please God." (Heb. xi. 6.) "If you believe not, you shall die in your sins." (John, v. 38; viii. 27.)

Now, this Protestant is about to join the Catholic Church. Coxe hears of it. So he goes and lectures on the idolatry and errors of the Roman Catholic Church, to prevent him from falling, as he calls it, into bad hands.

Lord Stafford was a good Catholic, but his wife a strict Protestant. He had been living several years in Abbeville, France. He begged the Bishop of Amiens, Monseigneur de la Motte, to convert his wife. "God only can convert the soul," answered the Bishop; "you can do her more good by praying for her than I by talking to her."

Now Lady Stafford had a great esteem for St. Francis de Sales. "If I could meet a bishop like him," she said, "I might become a Catholic." She had an interview with the Bishop of Amiens. At first, he avoided the subject of religion, and sought to gain her confidence. One day he asked her if her conscience was entirely at rest, if she had no doubts about her religion, living thus separated from the Church. "With the Bible in my hand," she answered, "I fear no one. I am quite satisfied." The words of the bishop, however, made a deep impression on her. She began to doubt seriously of the truth of her sect. She consulted the bishop. She heard one of his sermons, and conceived a great desire to be able to profess the same religious belief as this saintly prelate. She had yet some doubts about holy Mass and purgatory. She consulted the bishop once more. Instead of settling her doubts immediately, the bishop said: "Madame, you are acquainted with the Protestant Bishop of London. You have evidently great confidence in him. Go, then, and lay before him what I now tell you: The Bishop of Amiens declares that he will become a Protestant, if you can disprove the fact that St. Augustine, whom you regard as one of the greatest lights of the Church, offered up the holy Mass, and offered it up for the dead, viz., for his own deceased mother." The proposition was accepted. Lady Stafford begged her husband to go to London, and there, *incognito*, place the written message in the hands of the Protestant bishop, and bring back his written answer. The Protestant bishop read the message, and, on being requested to write an answer, he said: "This lady has fallen into bad hands; she will be perverted. Whatever I might say will not hinder the evil. A letter from me would only give rise to misunderstandings and unpleasant recriminations." As we may imagine, Lady Stafford was greatly surprised at this answer. She was sincere. It was evident that the bishop did not wish to answer, because he could not.

These two thoughts especially moved her to take the final step: "1. No Catholic *ever* became a Protestant in order to do penance for his sins, and to return to God, while many Protestants have become Catholics for this very reason.

"2. The Protestants honor as saints many doctors and fathers of the Church who taught a doctrine just the reverse of Protestantism; and, consequently, Protestants must admit that one can become a saint by imitating these holy doctors, and by living and dying in their belief. Lady Stafford made the spiritual exercises for a few days in a convent, and finally became a good, fervent Catholic." (Herbert.)

Like the London Protestant bishop, Bishop Coxe, too, knows that many non-Catholics have fallen into bad hands and became very edifying Catholics. He knows that good Catholic books, that clearly explain the Catholic religion, are also bad hands by which many non-Catholics have been converted to the Catholic Church. He knows that *Familiar Explanation of Christian Doctrine* is also one of those bad hands. To prevent non-Catholics from reading this little book, which proves so clearly that *only* the Roman Catholic Church is the true Church of Christ, and that no salvation is possible out of her, he takes from it a few questions and answers, *dishonestly* detached from the context, and twists them, as he does Holy Scripture, to his own destruction and to that of his neighbor.

We have not learned what Bishop Coxe has said on these questions and answers; but, to judge from the anonymous article *Queer Explanation*, we understand that he used them as arguments to denounce the idolatry *and error of the Catholic religion.*

It is not from conviction that Mr. Coxe declares the Catholic religion idolatrous and full of errors, for he knows too well that idolatry was abolished by the Catholic Church, and that, if it were not for her, he himself would be an idolater. If Coxe slanders the Spouse of Christ in a most impious manner, it is from devilish hatred to her. And why is it that he and many other Protestants entertain a devilish hatred to the Catholic Church?

"The so-called Reformers," says Dr. O. A. Brownson, "supposed at first that they could maintain dogmatic religion by means of the Bible, without any divinely authorized interpreter or teacher, for they were not aware at first how much their interpretation of Scripture depended on the tradition of the Church in which they had all been educated. When shown this by Catholics, and shown still further that the Bible, interpreted by tradition, supported the claims of the papacy and the Catholic Church, from which they had separated, they were forced, in order to be consistent with themselves, either to return to the Catholic Church or to reject the traditional interpretation of the written word, and to rely henceforth solely, in their interpretation of the sacred text, on grammar and lexicon. But, interpreted solely by grammar and lexicon, it was soon discovered that no uniform and consistent dogmatic system could with any tolerable degree of certainty be educed from the Holy Scriptures. There is no denying the fact. The variations of Protestantism, even during the lives of the reformers, the multiplication of Protestant sects, all appealing alike to the sacred text, and the experience of three hundred and more years, render it indubitable. Hard pressed by their Catholic opponents, Protestants were driven to the sad alternative of either condemning their separation from the Church and returning to her communion, or of giving up dogmatic religion as unessential and falling back on interior feeling or sentiment.

"The reformers imagined that they had opposed a truth to the authority of the Church when they asserted the authority of the Bible; but in doing this they only changed the form of their denial. Their assertion of the authority of the Bible was purely negative, simply the denial of the authority of the Church to interpret it or declare and apply its sense. It meant neither more nor less; for the Church asserted and always had asserted the authority of the Bible, interpreted and applied by the divinely instituted court in the case. The Bible, Protestant experience has proved, without the Church as that court, is as unauthoritative as are the statutes of a kingdom or republic, left to the private judgment of the citizen or subject, without the civil court to interpret and apply them to the case in hand. They, then, did not oppose to the Church as the principle of their denial any truth or authority. Nothing but pure denial, historically as well as logically, Protestantism, in spite of every refuge or subterfuge, has reached its inevitable termination—the negation of all authority, external or internal, spiritual or secular, and therefore of all faith, of all objective truth, and of all religion; for the very nature of religion is to bind the conscience, or the obligation of man to obey God."

Hence St. Alphonsus says: "To reject the divine teaching of the Catholic Church is to reject the very basis of reason and revelation, for neither the principles of the one nor those of the other have any longer any solid support to rest on; they can then be interpreted by every one as he pleases; every one can deny all truths whatsoever he chooses to deny. I therefore repeat: If the divine teaching authority of the Church, and the obedience to it, are rejected, every error will be endorsed and must be tolerated." (Appendix to his work *Council of Trent.*) "Indeed, by denying the very foundation of religion, or rejecting revealed truth," says Brownson, "we deprive reason itself of its strength, and obscure its light. It ceases to be able to hold with a firm grasp the truth that lies in its own order, as is evinced by the immense intellectual superiority of Catholics over Protestants. Compare an Irish or Spanish peasant with an English or Protestant-German peasant, the learned Benedictines of St. Maur or the Bollandists, with your most erudite Protestant scholars and critics, or the great mediæval doctors with your most lauded Protestant theologians. The difference in mental lucidity, acuteness, and strength is so great as to render all comparison almost ridiculous."

"The age" says Dr. O. A. Brownson, "boasts of its liberality; but its boasted liberality is the result of its indifferentism to dogmatic theology, and its lack of firm belief in any positive or affirmative truth at all. The sects have ceased to cut each other's throats, for the differences between them are not worth quarrelling about, since they are all animated by one and the same spirit, and are moving in one and the same direction. Yet, wherever the age is in earnest, it is as intolerant as any preceding age. There may be individuals who honestly detest intolerance in every way or shape, but these are chiefly to be found among Catholics who take seriously the popular doctrine of religious liberty, and go out of their way to disclaim all solidarity with the past history of their Church, and to protest against the spirit, if not the very letter, of the Syllabus. The Church teaches the truth, and all truth is intolerant, and refuses to tolerate even the semblance of error. The popularity or the unpopularity of a principle or doctrine has nothing to do with its truth or with one's obligation to stand by it. Where Catholics are in a minority, as with us, worldly prudence may seem to counsel the advocacy of what is called, but falsely so called, the freedom of conscience, that is, the right of every man to form or to choose for himself his own religion and abide by it; but a higher prudence, divine prudence, counsels adherence to Catholic principle, to that which is true always and everywhere. Neither the principles nor the doctrines of the Church change or undergo any modification with the changes or variations of time or place. No man has the right before God, however he may before the state, to hold any religion but the one only true Catholic religion, and no one can adhere to any other but at his own peril.

"Yet, with all their boasted liberality, Protestants assert only the liberty to deny the truth, and if their intolerance to Catholicity has changed its form, it has not diminished in its intensity. Their hatred of the Church has in no degree abated. Protestant nations do not now persecute Catholics, as they did in the beginning, from fear of the intervention of foreign Catholic governments, for, strictly speaking, there are no longer any Catholic governments on earth; yet their dread of the Church and hostility to everything Catholic are as great as ever, and precisely because the term *Catholic* is directly opposed to their denial of objective truth, and their resolution of religion into a subjective sentiment or emotion, varying with place and time, and from individual to individual. They feel this; they feel that Catholicity is the assertion of Catholic truth, and therefore that the Church differs from them, not simply in degree, as more or less, but in kind, and directly contradicts their whole order of thought. Hence the intolerance of Protestants to Catholicity is not inspired by love of truth or by zeal for the word of God, but by their want of faith, and wish to feel themselves free from all obligation to believe and hold fast the truth, to follow either reason or revelation, contented with their own opinions, whatever they may be, and satisfied to live and die in their religious indifferentism, or simple religious subjectivism. This they cannot do so long as confronted with the Catholic Church. They must destroy her or not be able to enjoy with a quiet conscience their own beliefs or no beliefs.

"The hostility to the Church does not arise from her special doctrines or dogmas, or from any intellectual conviction that they are false or unreasonable, but from the fact that she teaches that truth is objective, independent of the believer, and is obligatory, and no one has or can have the right before God to resist it. Protestants hate the Church for two reasons: 1. because she claims to teach infallibly by the divine assistance, and 2. because she maintains that truth is Catholic and binds both reason and conscience. The claim of the Church to teach by divine authority through the Pope and Councils was the principal object of hostility in the beginning. This was an absolute necessity of the position assumed by the reformers. But, we have seen, as time went on, it became necessary, in order to sustain their position against the pressure of the Catholic argument, to deny not only the authority of the Church, but also the authority of truth itself, and then to hold themselves under no obligation to regard it, and free to resist it whenever they chose. The presence and influence of the Church are opposed to this interior freedom from truth, which unbelievers call freedom of mind, and Protestants religious liberty, and both make war on her, and war to the knife, because she does not and cannot favor it. They, unbelievers, and Protestants, form an alliance against her, and seek, by all the arts and devices in their power, her total destruction from the face of the earth; for both instinctively feel that either she or they must perish.

"It is worthy of remark that in the war which Protestants and infidels have hitherto waged against the Church neither has nor pretends to have any truth or principle to oppose to her. They do not fight for the truth, nor for any affirmative or Catholic principle that she denies or neglects, but for what they call the rights of the mind, which, translated into plain English, means the emancipation of the human mind from the authority of truth, and therefore from God who is truth, or, in simpler terms still, the liberty to treat truth and falsehood as of equal value, as equally indifferent, or to deny all real distinction between them, and therefore between right and wrong. Neither reason nor revelation can tolerate this sort of liberty—intellectual and moral license rather; and the very existence and presence of the Church condemns it. Hence the irreconcilable antagonism between the Church and the sects. Yet is there a notable difference between the temper and motives of the two parties. The Church is always calm and collected, for she knows that she has the truth; she indulges in no passion, resorts to no violence, to no cruelty or harshness against her enemies, for she knows that they are only harming themselves, not her; and hence she is moved in her resistance to their blind rage only by that divine charity which seeks to save souls, not to destroy them. She is moved by love for her enemies, and seeks at all times, by all the means in her power, to do them good,—good for time and for eternity. Her temper towards them is that of infinite tenderness and compassion. But the temper of her enemies towards her is that of hatred, and hatred without cause; they are not moved by charity, by love of souls; for, if they believe in salvation at all, they believe that souls can be saved in the Church at least as well as out of it, and hence, the dupes of their own hateful passions, there is no extreme of violence or cruelty to which, where they have the power, they will not go, if they judge it necessary or useful to their cause. We see the proofs of it in the anti-Catholic legislation and measures of Prussia, of Switzerland, of protestantized Italy, revolutionary Spain, and the miserable republics south of us on this continent, where the influence of our own republic has been most hostile to religion and the peace and order of society.

"All these things prove, first, that the Protestant party do not, as they pretend, oppose the Church for purely political reasons, for she has no political power or connection; and, second, that they really, here and everywhere, oppose her because she is Catholic in her teaching, asserts truth as binding on the intellect and the conscience, in direct contradiction to their doctrine of the indifference of truth and falsehood, or that every man has the natural right to be of any religion, if not Catholic, or of no religion, as he pleases.

"There are, no doubt, Protestants in large numbers who hold the principal Christian mysteries as taught by the Church and handed down by tradition; but they, as we have said, hold them, not as Catholic truth, but as opinions, which do not bind the intellect or conscience, and which they are free to hold or reject as suits their pleasure, their convenience, or their caprice. In the popular language of the day, they are called simply *religious opinions*, not dogmas, and rarely articles of faith. Some may hold them to be essential doctrines of Christianity, but Christianity itself is held to be an opinion, or an interior sentiment, not a law which no one has the right to dispute, and which every one is bound to obey. It is only one among many religions, none of which are wholly false or wholly true.

"There are, we like to believe, among Protestants, many individuals who are far superior to their Protestantism, who have not yet learned to distrust reason, who hold that truth is obligatory, that religion is the law of conscience, who are honest, upright, kind-hearted, and benevolent according to their light, and who mean to be true Christian believers. These can be reasoned with and be more or less affected by argument; but they are not genuine Protestants. They may not very well understand the doctrines retained from the Church by the early reformers, but they believe them to be revealed truths, which it would be sinful in them to deny, not mere opinions which one is free to hold or not hold according to his pleasure. These serve to keep up a show of religion in the several Protestant sects, but they are not governed by the Protestant spirit, and if carried away by the Protestant movement, they are not its leaders. They are the laggards in the onward march of Protestantism. You find some of them in Geneva, who in earnest condemn the measures adopted by the Council against Bishop Mermillod and the Catholic clergy; some, like Herr von Gerlach, in Prussia, who resist with all the means in their power the legislation demanded by the government against the Church and her faithful pastors; and a small number even in this country who openly oppose the iniquity of taxing Catholics for the support of schools to which their consciences forbid them to send their children. It is not these, as men, as individuals, that we denounce, for many of them we honor and esteem, but the Protestantism with which they are associated.

"That Protestants, that so-called orthodox Protestants at least, profess to hold, and claim as belonging to their Protestantism, many things that are also held by Catholics, nobody denies; but these things are no part of Protestantism, for the Church held and taught them ages before Protestantism was born. They are part and parcel of the one Catholic faith, and belong to Catholics only. Protestants can rightfully claim as Protestant only those things wherein they differ from the Church, which the Church denies, and which they assert; that is, what is peculiarly or distinctively Protestant. We cannot allow them to claim as theirs what is and always has been ours; we willingly accord them their own, but not one whit more. All which they profess to hold in common with us is ours, not theirs. Adopting this rule, which is just and unimpeachable, nothing in fact is theirs but their denials, and as all their denials are, as we have seen, made on no Catholic principle or truth, they are pure negations, and hence Protestantism is purely negative, and consequently is no religion, for all religion is affirmative.

"Nor is this all. We have seen that the Protestant denials, in both their logical and historical developments, lead to the denial of all dogmatic religion, of all objective truth, and reduce the truths of reason and of revelation to mere personal opinions, and therefore involve the denial of those very doctrines which Protestants profess to hold in common with us. The immense majority of Protestants will give up these doctrines, or consent to hold them simply as opinions with no objective authority, sooner than desert the Protestant movement or reject the denials which are the essence of Protestantism, if we may speak of the essence of a negation, which has no being in itself or elsewhere. A few of the laggards may be occasionally captured, but most of them will quicken their pace and close up with the main body. Individual conversions, indeed, are made, which in the aggregate are considerable, but which are little more than the dust in the balance compared with the whole number of Protestants, and are by far outnumbered by the Catholics who lapse, here and elsewhere, into Protestantism or infidelity.

"It is obvious, then, that to carry on a controversy with Protestants, as if they were Christians simply erring as to some portions of the Christian faith, can effect nothing. They cannot be convinced by argument, for they hold firmly nothing which can serve as the basis of an argument. It seems to us much more important to strip them of all Christian pretensions, to deprive them of their prestige and the power of seduction which their Christian profession gives them, by showing them up in their utter nakedness as downright infidels, than to labor to make them accept the Catholic doctrines they avowedly reject. Infidels they are, and it is of no little importance to let it be seen that no man can be a Protestant and be at the same time a Christian or follower of our Lord and Saviour Jesus Christ. We owe this to uninstructed or imperfectly instructed, and especially to our worldly-minded Catholics, who are exposed to Protestant influences and seductions, and who would recoil with horror from open and undisguised infidelity or denial of the Lord who has bought us, and yet be tempted to fraternize with Protestants who pretend that they are Christians, and hold the essentials of the Christian faith, if they find that Catholics themselves concede that Protestants are Christians, though heterodox Christians. We owe it also to those who, in the ranks of Protestants, feel themselves bound to be Christians, and would fain be Christians. Both classes should be made to understand, what is true, that Protestantism is not Christianity, is not religion, but is, when pushed to its last consequence, the denial of revelation, the denial of reason, the denial of God, the author of reason, and only a disguised atheism, or subtle form of universal negation or nihilism. Every honest Protestant should, as far as possible, be made to understand this, so that he may understand the risk he runs if he remains in the ranks of Protestants; and every Catholic should be made to understand it, so that he may see clearly that, if he yields to the seduction of Protestantism, he severs himself completely and entirely from Christ our Lord, and insures his eternal perdition.

"We know nothing more reprehensible than the mambypambyism babbled by sentimental Catholics about the good faith of 'our separated brethren.' There may be persons in good faith amongst Protestants, but, if so, they do not lack opportunities of showing it, and of coming out from the Babylon in which they have been reared. Men cannot be saved without Christ, for there is no other name given under heaven whereby they can be saved. Without faith it is impossible to please God, and he that cometh to God must believe that he is, and is the remunerator of them that seek him ; and how can those be saved by Christ who adhere to the party that rejects him and makes war on him ? And how can they have faith or believe in God who commune with those who resolve all faith, all belief, all truth, indeed, into a mere opinion, or an inward sentiment, varying with each individual ? If Catholicity is Christian, if reason is authoritative in its own province, nothing is more certain than that Protestantism is in no sense Christian, and that persons living and dying Protestants cannot be saved. It is a stultification of common sense to maintain the contrary, and besides, it practically neutralizes all our efforts to convert Protestants, and to bring them to a living and saving faith in Christ.

"We know what theologians say of invincible ignorance and we do not contradict them. Invincible ignorance excuses from sin in that whereof one is invincibly ignorant ; but it gives no faith, no virtue ; and without faith, without positive virtue, no man can be saved. The man who holds implicitly the Catholic faith, but errs through invincible ignorance with regard to some of its *consectaria,* and even dogmas, may be saved ; but how can a man be said to hold implicitly the Catholic faith, who holds nothing, or rejects every principle that implies it ? It is not safe to apply to Protestants, who really deny everything Catholic, a rule that is very just when applied to sincere but ignorant Catholics, or Catholics that err through inculpable ignorance. Protestantism does not stand on the footing of ordinary heterodoxy, it is no more Christian than was Greek and Roman paganism.

"No doubt, this will be complained of as illiberal, as quite too severe ; but the only question we have to ask is :

Is it true? Is it the law? If it is the law of God, it is true; if it is what the Church teaches, we have nothing to do with the question of its liberty or illiberality, of its severity or its leniency. All we have to guard against is against asserting it in a harsh or illiberal spirit, in a severe and cruel temper, or with any uncharitableness towards those who expose themselves to the terrible consequences of rejecting Christ and his law, or who refuse to suffer him to reign over them. We may love and pray for them, but to seek to alter the divine constitution of his kingdom is to incur ourselves the guilt of rebellion. There is but one right way; and while it is our duty to walk in it, it is also our duty to do our best to show it to those who are out of it, and induce them to come into it. It were a sin against charity to leave them to think that they can be saved out of it, or by any other way. It would alter nothing in the law, which is independent alike of them and of us, were we to do so. A man may be as liberal as he pleases with what is his own, but to give away what is another's is an injustice. God is just and merciful, and he loves all the works of his hands, for never would he have made anything, if he had hated it. Christ so loved even sinners that he gave his life for them, and it is a want of faith in him to doubt the wisdom or justice, the goodness or mercy of his law. The Church cannot save those who reject her, but she weeps as a loving mother over those who are out of the way, and go to sure destruction. Charity is higher and broader than blind sentimentality. It loves all men, but it loves them in God." (Review, Oct. 1873)

Every well instructed Catholic knows and understands this great truth of our religion, and would feel highly indignant at the suggestion of the least thing contrary to it.

About five years ago, if we remember well, a Protestant preacher of New Orleans acted like the Protestant Bishop Coxe. He selected, from Familiar Explanation of Christian Doctrine, the same detached sentences quoted by Coxe, to prove by them the idolatry and error of the Catholic religion. He had his long discourse inserted in a Protestant newspaper of New Orleans. His object was to prevent Protestant ladies from taking part in a fair the profits of which were to go towards paying off the debts of some Catholic churches. In reply to this malicious article Judge McGloin, a learned and devout Catholic of New Orleans, inserted in the same newspaper an elaborate article in which he clearly proved, from good Catholic authors, that the explanation which we had given of the Catholic Doctrine in question was perfectly correct.

CHAPTER V.

REFUTATION OF THE FALSE ASSERTIONS OF REVERENDS S. O. CRONIN AND YOUNG.

How S. O. comments on the following questions and answers contained in *Familiar Explanation*.

"*Question.* Have Protestants any faith in Christ? *Answer.* They never had. *Q.* Why not? *Ans.* Because there never lived such a Christ as they imagine and believe in. *Q.* In what kind of a Christ do they believe? *Ans.* In such a one of whom they can make a liar with impunity, whose doctrines they can interpret *as they please, and who does not care what a man believes, provided he be an honest man before the public.* (Italics ours). *Q.* Will such a faith in such a Christ save Protestants? *Ans.* No sensible man will assert such an absurdity. *Q.* What will Christ say to them on the day of judgment? *Ans.* I know you not, because you never knew me. *Q.* Are Protestants willing to confess their sins to a Catholic bishop or priest, who alone has power from Christ to forgive sins? 'Whose sins you shall forgive they are forgiven them.' *Ans.* No; for they generally have an utter aversion to confession, and therefore their sins will not be forgiven them throughout all eternity. *Q.* What follows from this? *Ans.* That they die in their sins and are damned."

The comment which Bishop Coxe has made on these questions and answers is said to have given occasion to "the most prominent priest of the U. S. to put his own comment on the same questions and answers.

There are rules for interpreting Holy Scripture; there are rules for interpreting laws and the last will of a man; and there are rules for interpreting an author's doctrine. One of these rules is to understand well the *status quæstionis* and give it in plain words. This the most prominent priest of the U. S. has purposely ignored.

Another rule to interpret an author's doctrine is that, if an author has published a small work, and has written at large on the same subject, we must interpret his small work according to what he says in his large work and in the latest edition of his work. Now, what bishop, what priest, what Catholic editor of a newspaper does not know that the Rev. M. Muller, C.SS.R., has published nine large volumes in explanation of Catholic Doctrine. Who can believe that S. O. is not aware of this fact ? Did not then charity and justice plainly tell him that, in explaining Father Müller's small volume on Christian Doctrine, he must follow the Explanation of Christian Doctrine which Father Müller has given in his large work of Christian Doctrine ?

Another rule of interpreting an author's doctrine is to explain it in connection with the context. That the Protestant Bishop Coxe has dishonestly left out all the proofs which we have given in Explanation of Christian Doctrine from pp. 12 to page 86 ; that he has dishonestly taken up sentences detached from the proofs preceding them, from pp. 87 to 97, and following them from pp. 98 to 116, to show that there is no salvation possible out of the Roman Catholic Church ; that he has misinterpreted them, we can easily account for, because he even knows how to misquote Holy Scripture and misinterpret its meaning. All heretics have done this. Need we wonder at his dishonesty in misquoting and misinterpreting sound doctrine of a Catholic author ? No Catholic wonders at this, because we all know that heresies have been maintained for some time by the same false principles from which they have sprung. We know that there are many Protestants who live in *vincible* or *culpable* ignorance of the true religion—of the true Church of Christ. Being unwilling to give up their false, human religion, they are glad to find even frivolous reasons to quiet their uneasy consciences and to remain as they are. Protestant preachers, too, know this from their own experience. Hence they quote texts from Holy Scripture to make them feel easy, such as the most prominent priest of the U. S. quotes in their favor when he says: " They (Protestants) say with us, in the language and meaning of the Apostle : ' There is no other Name (Jesus Christ) under heaven given to men, whereby we must be saved.' " In like manner, Protestant preachers will misquote and misinterpret certain Catholic authors' doctrines detached from the context, and draw from them frivolous reasons whereby to quiet the uneasy consciences of certain members of their congregations in regard to the true religion. Knowing that dishonest preachers have, in this way, taken hold of some answers detached from the context in our *Familiar Explanation of Christian Doctrine* of the first edition, we have, more than a year ago, changed, in the second edition, those answers, though true in the sense they were given. But alas! that the dishonesty, the twisticalness and tortuosity of the minds of Protestant preachers should have been imitated by a brother priest, that he thus should have confirmed culpably and inculpably ignorant Protestants in their wrong belief; that he thus should have made Catholics, who are weak in faith, still weaker in it, and have strengthened liberal Catholics in their wrong views, is something that baffles almost all belief.

Now, to show plainly and understand well his grave errors, we must state clearly the point in question. This point is :—

"*Out of the Roman Catholic Church there is no salvation.*" *Heretics are out of the Roman Catholic Church; therefore, if they die as heretics, they are lost forever.*

Here the question arises, "Who is a *heretic*?"

The word "*heretic*" is derived from the Greek, and means to choose or adhere to a certain thing. Hence a baptized person, professing Christianity, and choosing for himself what to believe and what not to believe as he pleases, in obstinate opposition to any particular truth which he knows is taught by the Catholic Church as a truth revealed by God, is a heretic.

To make a person guilty of the sin of heresy, three things are required:

1. He must be baptized and profess Christianity. This distinguishes him from a Jew and idolater;
2. He must refuse to believe a truth revealed by God, and taught by the Church as so revealed;
3. He must obstinately adhere to error, preferring his own private judgment in matters of faith and morals to the infallible teaching of the Catholic Church. Hence it follows that the following persons are guilty of the sin of heresy:—

1. All those baptized persons who profess Christianity and obstinately reject a truth revealed by God and taught by the Church as so revealed;
2. Those who embrace an opinion contrary to faith, maintain it obstinately, and refuse to submit to the authority of the Catholic Church;
3. Those who wilfully doubt the truth of an article of faith, for, by such a wilful doubt, they actually question God's knowledge and truth, and to do this is to be guilty of heresy;
4. Those who know the Catholic Church to be the only true Church, but do not embrace her faith;
5. Those who could know the Church, if they would candidly search, but who, through indifference and other culpable motives, neglect to do so;
6. Those Anglicans who know the true Church, but do not become Roman Catholics, thinking that they approach very near the Catholic Church, because their prayers and ceremonies are like many prayers and ceremonies of the Catholic Church, and because their creed is the Apostles' Creed. These are heretics in principle, for "the real character of rank heresy," says St. Thomas Aquinas, "consists in want of submission to the divine teaching authority in the Head of the Church."

Heresy, therefore, is a corruption of the true faith. "This corruption," says St. Thomas Aquinas, " takes place either by altering the truths which constitute the principal articles of faith, or by denying obstinately those which result therefrom. But, as the error of a geometrician does not affect the principles of geometry, so is the error of a person which does not affect the fundamental truths of faith, no real heresy."

Should a person have embraced an opinion which is contrary to faith, without knowing that it is opposed to faith, he is, in this case, no heretic, if he is disposed to renounce his error as soon as he comes to know the truth.

But it is false to say that only those truths are of faith which have been defined by the Church, and that therefore he only is a heretic who denies a defined truth.

A man steals a large sum of money from his neighbor. Now is that man no thief so long as the court has not pronounced him guilty of theft?

Jesus Christ has revealed to his Church a certain number of truths. She knows what those truths are. She has always believed and taught them as revealed truths. "Every revealed truth," says Cardinal Manning, "is definite and precise; nevertheless all are not defined; but the Church defined many of these truths in precise terms only when it was fit or necessary to do so; and this fitness, or necessity, arose when a revealed truth was obscured, or contested, or denied out of vincible or invincible ignorance. Those who, out of invincible ignorance, denied certain revealed truths, were excused from heresy until the Church delivered them from the ignorance of these truths by declaring and defining them in precise terms. The definition, however, adds nothing to its intrinsic certainty, for this is derived from divine Revelation; the definition adds only the extrinsic certainty of universal promulgation by the doctrinal authority of the Church, imposing obligation upon all the faithful."

No doubt, Luther, Calvin, and other heresiarchs of the sixteenth century were considered by the Church as heretics even before she had defined those truths which were denied by those impious men; and those denied truths were articles of faith, and believed as such just as firmly before as after their definition by the Council of Trent. "So, in like manner," says Cardinal Manning, "the existence of God has always been an article of faith, and yet it was defined, only a few years ago, in the Vatican Council. Hence, all those truths are articles of faith, which are taught by the Church as revealed truths, no matter whether or not they are defined." (For instance, the Church teaches the Assumption of the Blessed Mother of God, body and soul, into heaven, in the institution of the feast, of the Assumption of the Blessed Virgin Mary, in her Office and holy Mass of this feast, as clearly as she could teach it by defining this truth.) "Any one, therefore, who knows that the Church teaches a truth as revealed, is bound in conscience to believe it as an article of faith; if he does not so believe it, he is a heretic before God." (*Vat. Counc.* by CARDINAL MANNING)

Any one, then, who sufficiently knows the truths of the true religion and denies even but one of them, commits one of the greatest sins. To reject what we know has been revealed by God is not only to cut ourselves off from all the blessings of religion, but it is to call in question the fact that the Lord of heaven and earth is a God of Truth, and he who calls in question this Truth, offers to God the greatest insult. We believe the truths of faith because God has revealed them and proposes them by his infallible Church for our belief. Now, to believe some of these truths and reject one or more of them is as much as to say : I believe that God told the truth in this point, but not in that other. This is a horrible blasphemy. Wilful heresy, therefore, in regard even to but one sacred truth of religion, destroys all faith, attacking as it does the authority of God, who revealed the truth. If a man who poisons the food of his fellow-men is most damnable in the sight of God, how much more damnable are not those who poison the souls of men by the seed of heresy.

To take away the life of the body is a mortal sin. Now, is it not a greater crime to rob the soul of its life—the grace of God, and lead it to everlasting perdition by false doctrines? Hence it is that Holy Scripture condemns the sin of heresy in the strongest terms.

"A man," says St. Paul, "that is a heretic, after the first and second admonition, avoid; knowing that he who is such an one is subverted, and sinneth, being condemned by his own judgment." (Tit. iii. 10.) And again he says: "Though we, or an angel from heaven, preach a Gospel to you besides that which we have preached to you, let him be anathema," that is, accursed. (Gal. i. 8, 9.) St. Paul also classes sects or heresies among the works of the flesh, and says that those who do such things shall not obtain the kingdom of God. (Gal. i. 29.)

But not every one who lives in heresy is guilty of the sin of heresy. Hence we distinguish two kinds of heretics: Those who are, and those who are not, guilty of the sin of heresy. We made this distinction of heretics in our little work *Familiar Explanation of Christian Doctrine*, as S. O. testifies when he says: 1. It is evident that the author of *Explanation* "had in mind a *wilful, obstinate, obdurate, God-defying, truth-rejecting, unrepentant heretic*;" 2. when, from *Familiar Explanation*, he quotes the following question and answer:—

"*Q.* What are we to think of the salvation of those who are out of the pale of the Church without any fault of theirs, and who never had any opportunity of knowing better? *Ans.* Their inculpable ignorance will not save them; but if they fear God, and live up to their conscience, God in his infinite mercy will furnish them with the necessary means of salvation, even so as to send, if needed, an angel to instruct them in the Catholic faith, rather than let them perish through inculpable ignorance."

According to this distinction of heretics we divide the doctrine of the Church on heretics into two parts. In part I. we will speak of those who are true heretics, that is, of those who are guilty of the sin of heresy and die in it; and in part II. we will speak of those who are not guilty of the sin of heresy.

Part I.

There is No Salvation out of the Roman Catholic Church for those who die without being united to her.

§ 1. S. O. begins to Comment on the above Questions and Answers.

S. O. emphatically declares that,

"*Such expositions of the Church's doctrine as applicable to modern Protestants have, to my own knowledge, done a great deal of harm to honest, well-meaning, conscientious people, and give an entirely false idea of the belief of Protestants There is nothing to be gained by misrepresenting our own doctrines, and just as little by misrepresenting the doctrines of those who do not believe all that we do.*"

Is there not much ignorance contained in the above words of S. O.? To misrepresent our own *Catholic doctrines* is to misrepresent the truths that lead to salvation; it is to misrepresent God who revealed them; it is to misrepresent the Church of Christ that teaches them; and to do all this is a terrible crime.

Now, what can S. O. mean by misrepresenting Protestant doctrines? Very likely this: It is very wrong to make the devil blacker than he is, and to call him the author of Protestantism; it is very wrong to say that Protestant belief is only a human belief and availeth nothing unto salvation; that this faith is no *absolute, divine* faith in Christ and his religion; in a word, it is very wrong to represent Protestantism such as it is.

Nothing, he says, is to be gained by misrepresenting God and the devil, the teachers from God and those from the devil, truth and falsehood, divine and human faith, true and false Christianity.

But is there nothing to be lost by misrepresenting God and his religion? Is there nothing to be gained in representing Protestant belief such as it is? Alas! S. O. seems not to see the loss in the former, nor the gain in the latter way of acting! It will, therefore, be an act of charity to continue to show him, in the sequel of this treatise, the bad consequences of misrepresenting God and his religion, and the good results of representing clearly the devil and his counterfeit religion.

§ 2. S. O. CONTINUES TO SPEAK EX CATHEDRA.

"And in the hope," he says, *"of counteracting the false impressions conveyed by such teaching, I desire to submit the foregoing questions and replies to a fair examination.* Let us tell the truth," he says, "and shame the devil."

To understand well the examination to which that great priest of the Church is going to submit some questions and replies of ours, it must be remembered that we had given several clear proofs for the truth that there is no salvation out of the Roman Catholic Church, namely:

Christ has solemnly declared that only those will be saved, who have done God's will on earth, as explained, not by private interpretation, but by the infallible teaching of the Roman Catholic Church.

"Not every one," says Christ, "who saith to me, Lord, Lord, shall enter the kingdom of heaven; but he that doth the will of my Father who is in heaven, he shall enter the kingdom of heaven." (Matt. vii. 21.)

The will of the heavenly Father is that all men hear and believe his Son, Jesus Christ.

"This is my well beloved Son. Him you shall hear."

Now, Jesus Christ said to his Apostles and to all their lawful successors:

"He that heareth *you* heareth *me*, and he that despiseth *you* despiseth *me*, and he that despiseth me, despiseth *him*, the heavenly Father, that sent *me*."

Now all those who do not listen to Jesus Christ speaking to them through St. Peter and the Apostles, in their lawful successors, despise God the Father; they do not do his will, and therefore heaven will never be theirs.

What non-Catholic engages a servant who tells him:

"I will serve you on condition that you give me three hundred dollars a month and let me serve you according to my will, not according to yours"?

How, then, could God the Father admit one into his Kingdom, who has always refused to do his will,—who, instead of learning to do the will of God, the full doctrine of Christ, through the Catholic Church, was himself his own teacher, his own lawgiver, his own judge, in all religious matters!

"Go and teach all nations: teach them to observe *all things whatsoever* I have commanded you. He that believeth not all these things shall be condemned."

Our divine Saviour says:

"No one can come to the Father, except through me."

If we then wish to enter heaven, we must be united to Christ—to his body, which is the Church, as St. Paul says. Therefore, out of the Church there is no salvation.

Again Jesus Christ says:

"Whoever will not hear the Church, look upon him as a heathen and a publican," a great sinner. Therefore, out of the Church there is no salvation.

Holy Scripture says:

"The Lord added daily to the Church such as should be saved." (Acts, ii. 47.)

Therefore the Apostles believed and the holy Scriptures teach that there is no salvation out of the Church.

Hence the Fathers of the Church never hesitated to pronounce all those forever lost who die out of the Roman Catholic Church: "He who has not the Church for his mother," says St. Cyprian, " cannot have God for his Father;" and with him the Fathers in general say that, " as all who were not in the ark of Noe perished in the waters of the Deluge, so shall all perish who are out of the true Church." St. Augustine and the other bishops of Africa, at the Council of Zirta, A. D. 412, say: "Whosoever is separated from the Catholic Church, however commendable in his own opinion his life may be, he shall, for the very reason that he is separated from the union of

Christ, not see life, but the wrath of God abideth on him." Therefore, says St. Augustine, "a Christian ought to fear nothing so much as to be separated from the body of Christ (the Church). For, if he be separated from the body of Christ, he is not a member of Christ; if not a member of Christ, he is not quickened by his Spirit." (Tract. xxvii. in Joan., n. 6, col. 1992, tom. iii.)

"In our times," says Pius IX., "many of the enemies of the Catholic faith direct their efforts toward placing every monstrous opinion on the same level with the doctrine of Christ, or confounding it therewith; and so they try more and more to propagate that impious system of the indifference of religions. But quite of late, we shudder to say it, certain men have not hesitated to slander us by saying that we share in their folly, favor that most wicked system, and think so benevolently of every class of mankind, as to suppose that not only the sons of the Church, but that the rest also, however alienated from Catholic unity they may remain, are alike in the way of salvation, and may arrive at everlasting life. We are at a loss, from horror, to find words to express our detestation of this new and atrocious injustice that is done to us." (Allocution to the Cardinals, held on Dec. 17, 1847.) We may also add here that Pope Leo XIII., in his Encyclical Letter to the Archbishops and Bishops of Bavaria, teaches, as Pastor of the Universal Church, that "submission to the Pope is necessary to salvation."

"How grateful then," says St. Alphonsus, "ought we to be to God for the gift of the true faith. How great is not the number of infidels, heretics, and schismatics. The world is full of them, and, if they die out of the Church, they will all be condemned, except infants who die after baptism." (Catech. first command. No. 10 and 19.) Because, as St. Augustine says, where there is no divine faith, there can be no divine charity, and where there is no divine charity, there can be no justifying or sanctifying grace, and to die without being in sanctifying grace, is to be lost forever. (Lib. I. Serm. Dom. in monte, cap. V.)

This faith, as we have already seen, the Church teaches very plainly in the profession of faith which she requires converts to make before they are received into the Church; the very first article reads as follows: "I, N. N., having before my eyes the holy Gospel which I touch with my hand, and *knowing that no one can be saved without that faith which the holy, Catholic, Apostolic, Roman Church holds, believes and teaches,* against which I grieve that I have greatly erred," etc.

So it is evident that there is no salvation out of the Church. We gave several of these proofs for this great truth in *Familiar Explanation*. Coxe, the Protestant bishop, and S. O. have *dishonestly* suppressed them, and the latter has impudently asserted that we have misrepresented the Catholic Doctrine; he, therefore, also asserts that this Doctrine, which we have proved by the words of Our Lord, of his Apostles, and of the Fathers of the Church, has been misrepresented by our Lord himself, by his Apostles, and the Fathers and Doctors of the Church. What great piety, this!

But, you know, a little volume, like *Familiar Explanation*, giving so many plain reasons to show that salvation out of the Church is impossible, is a bad hand, which should not fall into the hands of non-Catholics, because the perusal of it might induce them to join the Roman Catholic Church.

In answer to Q. 19. we put ten popular reasons together for one argument to show that no salvation is possible for those who culpably adhere to Protestant principles and die in them. These reasons are: 1. Because true Protestants or true heretics have no *divine* faith; 2. Because they make a liar of Jesus Christ, of the Holy Ghost, and of the Apostles; 3. Because they have no faith in Jesus Christ; 4. Because they fell away from the true Church of Christ; 5. Because they are too proud to submit to the Pope, the Vicar of Christ; 6. Because they cannot perform good works whereby they can obtain heaven; 7. Because they do not receive the Body and Blood of Christ; 8. Because they die in their sins; 9. Because they ridicule and blaspheme the Mother of God and the Saints of heaven; 10. Because they slander the Spouse of Jesus Christ, the Catholic Church.

We proved each of these assertions; but Bishop Coxe and S. O. dishonestly again suppressed eight of these proofs, because they would have been so many bad hands for non-Catholics, who, after the perusal of these reasons, might have made up their minds to join the Catholic Church, in spite of all difficulties. What an excellent way to tell the truth by suppressing and concealing it from the public! What a ridiculous way to shame the devil! What an honorable way to shame themselves!

To prevent non-Catholics from getting the little volume containing such clear proofs for the truth of our religion, they made an attack upon some reasons we gave to show that true Protestants have no faith in Christ.

S. O. has taken up some of those reasons to show that we have misrepresented both Catholic and Protestant belief. Let us see again how he has told the truth and shamed the devil and especially himself. It must be remembered that he had to show that salvation out of the Church is possible, for we have proved by many reasons that it is impossible. As he has solemnly declared that we have misrepresented this Catholic doctrine, he should have proved from Holy Scripture, from the General Councils of the Church, and from the writings of the Fathers, that his assertion is true; for his anonymous authority is worth nothing. He has proved none of his assertions, nor is he able to disprove our doctrine, for by saying the contrary he would be a heretic. Is not this a nice way to tell the truth, to shame the devil and especially himself?

§ 3. S. O. EXAMINES AND EXPLAINS THE QUESTION AND ANSWER:

"*Q.* Have Protestants any faith in Christ? *Ans.* They never had."

To this answer S. O. replies:—

"I ask, then, what do all Protestants, save those called Unitarians, believe about Jesus Christ? They believe precisely what the Catholic Church teaches, namely, that He is true God and true man, the Person of the Word of God incarnate, conceived of the Holy Ghost and born of the Virgin Mary; that He is the Messiah, the Redeemer; that by His infinite merits alone is the salvation of mankind possible or obtainable." S. O. asserts that Protestants believe precisely what the Catholic Church teaches about Christ; but let it be remembered that they do not believe those truths *because the Catholic Church teaches them;* if they believe them, it is because they choose to believe them. Our faith in Christ is *absolute* and *divine;* that of Protestants is *all human*. But our would-be theologian probably never understood the difference between divine and human faith, or he would have made the distinction that we make, and then he could not have said what he says of Catholic and Protestant faith in Christ. So let us teach him the difference.

§ 4. WHAT CATHOLIC FAITH IS.

No one can go to heaven unless he knows the way to heaven. If we wish to go to a certain city, the first thing we do is to ask the way that leads to it. If we do not know the way, we cannot expect to arrive at that city. So, too, if we wish to go to heaven, we must know the way that leads to it. Now, the way that leads to it is the knowing and doing of God's will. But it is God alone who can teach us his will; that is, what he requires us to believe and to do, in order to be happy with him in heaven.

The end for which man was created—his everlasting union with God—says the Vatican Council, is far above the human understanding. It was, therefore, necessary that God should make himself known to man, and teach him the end for which he was created, and what he must believe and do in order to become worthy of everlasting happiness.

"If you wish to judge well of a grand edifice, you must

study in detail its form and dimensions; you must examine minutely its style of architecture and strive to comprehend the architect's design. All this will cause you much trouble and impatience, and still your knowledge of the edifice will not be complete.

"But, if the architect himself explains to you his plan, and, in addition to the knowledge you already have of the building, gives you sufficient information of its first cause, then you will be able to give a full, distinct description of the whole edifice.

"In like manner, a learned man may strive on all occasions, and by all natural means in his power, to know the first cause of the grand edifice of creation, its plan and object. All this will give him much trouble, and yet his knowledge of the work of creation will be very incomplete so long as he has not learned its first cause, and plan, and object from the divine Architect himself." (St. Thomas Aquinas.)

Now, God himself, in his infinite mercy, came to tell us why he had created us; he came and taught us the truths which we must believe, the commandments which we must keep, and the means of grace which we must use to work out our salvation.

To know God's will is to know the true religion or the true way to heaven. As God is but one, so his holy will is but one, and therefore his religion is but one and the same. In order that we might learn, with infallible certainty, this one true religion, Almighty God appointed but one infallible teaching authority—the Roman Catholic Church—and commanded all to hear her and believe her infallible doctrine, under pain of exclusion from eternal life.

Now, God is infinite truth itself. He knows things only as they are, and can speak them only as he knows them. As sovereign Author and Lord of all things, he has an absolute authority over all men,—an authority which he can exercise either directly by himself, or through an angel, or a prophet, or one or more of his reasonable creatures. God, therefore, has a right to command, under pain of eternal damnation, the human understanding to believe certain truths; he has a right to command the human will to perform certain duties, and the senses to make certain sacrifices. Nothing can be more reasonable than to submit to such a command of God. This submission of the understanding and the will to God's revelation is called *faith*, which, as St. Paul says, "bringeth into captivity every understanding to the obedience of Christ." (II. Cor. x. 5.) As soon, then, as man hears the voice of his Maker, he is bound to say: *Amen, it is so;* I believe it, no matter whether I understand it or not. The Lord of heaven and earth is the *Infallible* Truth itself. He can neither deceive nor be deceived. He is the *wherefore* and the *why* of my belief.

Hence St. Basil says: "Faith, always powerful and victorious, exercises a greater ascendancy over minds than all the proofs which reason and human science can furnish, because faith obviates all difficulties, not by the light of manifest evidence, but by the weight of the infallible authority of God, which renders them incapable of admitting any doubt."

"There is," says Thomas Aquinas, "more certainty in faith than in human science and all the other intellectual virtues. We must consider the certainty of a thing in its cause, or the object that receives it. The cause of our faith is God, the source and origin of all truth, So, by this principle, no certainty is comparable to that of faith.

"It may be said that he who knows perceives better than he who believes. Does it hence follow that natural knowledge has more certainty than faith? No; for a thing is to be considered rather by its cause than by the disposition of him who receives it.

"Human science and art are only contingencies, but the object of faith is the knowledge of eternal truths. Prudence and knowledge proceed from reason and experience; but faith comes by the operation of the Holy Ghost. All our sensitive organs and intellectual faculties are liable to err; but faith is infallible, for it is founded on the word of God:

'Because you received it from us, not as the word of men, but as the true word of God.'" (Thess. ii. 13.)

Now, Jesus Christ, the Son of God, has revealed our religion and invested all the truths of his revelation in an infallible Teaching Body—the Holy Roman Catholic Church, through which he has made it known, and continues to make it known, to all nations, to the end of time, in a manner most easy and infallible. She is the heir to the rights of Jesus Christ. She is the faithful depositary of the spiritual treasures of Jesus Christ. She is the infallible Teacher of the doctrines of Jesus Christ. She wields the authority of Jesus Christ. She lives by the life and spirit of Jesus Christ. She enjoys the guidance and help of Jesus Christ. She speaks, orders, commands, concedes, prohibits, defines, looses, and binds in the name of Jesus Christ. In the light of divine faith, which the Catholic has received in baptism, he believes the divine authority of the Church, and therefore he believes and obeys her in all things; and in believing and obeying her, he believes and obeys Almighty God himself, who said to the Apostles and their lawful successors in the Catholic Church: "He that heareth you, heareth me, and he that despiseth you, despiseth me." (Luke, x. 16.) The faith of the Catholic, therefore, is divine, because it is based on divine authority. He knows and believes that Jesus Christ speaks to him through his Church, and therefore he believes all the truths she teaches him, with the utmost firmness and simplicity, with an unwavering conviction of their reality. The fact that Jesus Christ has said it, has done it, has taught it to his infallible Church, and commanded her to teach it to all nations, is for him the weightiest of all reasons to believe it. The famous word of the Pythagoreans, "The master has said it," was with them a foolish idolatry, believing, as they did, that no one could be deceived. Applied, however, to Jesus Christ, it is a first principle, a sacred axiom for every Catholic. The heavens and the earth shall pass away, but "the truth of the Lord remaineth forever." (Ps. cxvi. 2.) The good Catholic silences every objection to his faith by saying: " The Son of God, Jesus Christ, has revealed it to us by his Church, and we have no more questions to ask." Hence St. Thomas Aquinas says:—

" The principles and rule of faith depend on the authority and doctrine of the one, holy, Catholic, and Apostolic Church. So, out of the true Church there is no faith or salvation. When the light of faith and grace flashes upon the soul, then man firmly believes all that God has revealed and proposes for our belief by his Church. Hence an act of faith differs from all the other acts of the human intellect as to what is true or false."

This is the reason why the Church allows none of her children to call into question her divine mission. The light of faith which shines upon the mind of a Catholic so utterly consumes doubt, that hereafter he cannot entertain it except by his own great fault.

"Faith," says St. Alphonsus, "is a virtue, or a gift, which God infuses into our souls in baptism, by which gift we believe the truths which God himself has revealed to the Holy Church, and which she proposes to our belief.

" By the *Church* is meant the Congregation of all who are baptized and profess the true faith under a visible Head, that is, the Sovereign Pontiff.

" I say, *the true faith*, to exclude heretics, who, though baptized, are separated from the Church.

" I say, *under a visible Head*, to exclude schismatics, who do not obey the Pope, and on that account easily pass from schism to heresy. St. Cyprian well says: 'Heresies and schisms have no other origin than this—the refusal to obey the Priest of God, and the notion that there can be more than one priest at a time presiding over the Church, and more than one judge at a time filling the office of Vicar of Christ.'

" We have all the revealed truths in the Sacred Scriptures and in the Traditions gradually communicated by God to his servants. But how should we be able to ascertain what are the true Scriptures and the true Traditions, and what is their true meaning, if we had not the Church to teach us? This Church Jesus Christ established as the pillar and ground of truth. To this Church our Saviour himself has promised that she shall never be conquered by her enemies. 'The gates of hell shall not prevail against her'. (Matt. xvi. 18). The gates of hell are the heresies and heresiarchs that have caused so many deluded souls to wander from the right path. This Church it is that teaches us, through her pastors, the truths which we must believe. Hence St. Augustine says: 'I would not believe the Gospel were I not moved by the Authority of the Church. The cause, then, which imposes on me the obligation to believe the truths of faith is, because God, the Infallible Truth, has revealed them, and because the Church proposes them to my belief. Our rule of faith, therefore, is this: My God, because thou who art the Infallible Truth, hast revealed to the Church the truths of faith, I believe all that the Church proposes to my belief." (First Command. n. 4, 5, 6).

Such is the faith which God prescribes in the first commandment. It is only by such faith that he is truly honored and worshipped; for, by such faith we acknowledge him as the Sovereign Being of infinite Perfections, made known to us by revelation, and as the Sovereign Truth, who can neither deceive nor be deceived.

When the famous and valiant Count de Montfort was told that our Lord in the Sacred Host had appeared visibly in the hands of the priest, he said to those who urged him to go and see the miracle: "Let those go and see it who doubt it; as for myself, I believe firmly the truth of the mystery of the Holy Eucharist, as our Mother the Holy Church teaches it. Hence I hope to receive in heaven a crown more brilliant than the crowns of the angels; for they being face to face with God, have not the power to doubt."

Look at the martyrs who, from being pagans, became Christians. They did not die for the sake of a religious opinion; they died for the sake of religion, because they were certain and convinced of its truth. The martyrs saw the truth, and how could they but speak what they had seen?

They might shudder at the pain, but they could not help seeing the truth of their religion. Threats could not undo the heavenly truths, and therefore could not silence their confession of them. "Truth," says St. Thomas Aquinas, "is the good of the intellect, the life of the intellect, whilst falsehood is the evil, the death of the intellect. As long as man remained innocent, it was impossible for man's intellect to believe that to be true which was really false. As in the body of the first man there could not be the presence of any evil, so, in like manner, in his soul there could not be the belief in anything false." Hence we easily understand why even innocent Catholic children have an intuition of truth without fear and confusion, and talk of God and his mysteries as if they had conversed with angels, while they display a clear knowledge of the whole circle of revealed truths, in comparison with which knowledge the wild guesses and perpetual contradictions of the most famous and learned pagans, or unbelieving philosophers or sectaries, are but inarticulate cries.

One day a little Irish girl was weeping to find herself in a Protestant school, to which she had been carried by force, and where it was considered a useful employment of time to blaspheme the Mother of God. "How do you know she is in heaven?" said a grim Protestant spinster to the little girl. The child knew very well that Our Lady is the Queen of heaven, and enthroned by the side of her divine Son, but had never asked herself *how* she knew it, nor met any one before who was impudent enough to deny it. She winced for a moment, as if she had received a blow, then flinging back the long hair which fell over her face, this child of a Galway peasant fiercely answered: "How do I know she is in heaven? Why, you Protestants don't believe in purgatory. If she is not in heaven she must be in hell. It's a pretty son who would send his mother to hell!" Such an answer will surprise no Catholic; it may astonish a Protestant. Other children say like words a hundred times. The gift of faith is a light of the Holy Ghost, which enlightens the minds of the faithful, even of children, to know and to believe that what the Church teaches is a holy and divine doctrine.

Without this inestimable gift of grace—the light of divine faith—it is impossible to be saved, as we have shown in our *Familiar Explanation*. But Coxe and S. O. have dishonestly suppressed this truth and concealed it from their fellow-men.

§ 5. What Protestant Belief in Christ is.

Of ourselves we can do only what is not above our natural strength. Whenever we are to do something above our natural strength, we need the help of another. Man is endowed with great natural gifts,—with the gifts of understanding, will, and memory. By means of these gifts, man can do great things: he can learn languages, build churches, palaces, great cities, steamboats, railroads; he can count days, dates, distances, and money. By the natural power of his reason, man can understand various kinds of truths about this world, about human society, about the realms of space, about matter, about the soul. By his natural reason, man can inquire, argue, and draw conclusions, about religious truth. His thoughts and words, however, about religious truths will not extend beyond mere reasoning.

Cardinal Newman tells us that, some years ago, there was much talk in the world of a man of science, who was said to have found out a new planet. How did he find it out? Did he watch night after night, wearily and perseveringly, in the chill air, through the tedious course of the starry heavens, for what he might find there, till at length, by means af some powerful glass, he discovered, in the dim distance, this unexpected addition to our planetary system? Far from it. It is said that he sat at his ease in his library, and made calculations on paper in the daytime: and thus, without looking once up at the sky, he determined, from what was already known of the sun and the planets, of their number, their positions, their motions, and their influences, that, in addition to them all, there must be some other body in that very place where he said it would be found, if astronomers did but turn their instruments upon it. Here was a man who read the heavens, not with eyes, but by reason. In like manner, reason and conscience may lead the natural man to discover, and in a measure, pursue, objects which are, properly speaking, supernatural and divine. The natural reason is able, from the things which are seen, from the voice of tradition, from the existence of the soul, and from the necessity of the case, to infer the existence of God.

A man without eyes may talk about forms and colors. A blind man may pick up a good deal of information of various kinds, and be very conversant with the objects of sight, though he does not see. He may be able to talk about them fluently, and may be fond of doing so; he may even talk of seeing as if he really saw, till he almost seems to pretend to the faculty of sight. He speaks of heights, and distances, and directions, and the dispositions of places, and shapes and appearances, as naturally as other men; and yet he is not duly aware of his own pitiable privation. How does this come about? It is partly because he hears what other men say about these things, and he is able to imitate them, and partly because he cannot help reasoning upon the things he hears, and drawing conclusions from them; and thus he comes to think that he knows what he does not know at all.

"Now, this will explain the way in which the natural man is able partly to understand, and still more to speak upon, supernatural subjects. There is a large floating body of Catholic truth in the world. It comes down by tradition from age to age; it is carried forward by preaching and profession from one generation to another, and is poured about into all quarters of the world. It is found in fulness and purity in the Church alone; but portions of it, larger or smaller, escape far and wide, and penetrate into places which have never been under the teaching of divine grace. Now, men may take up and profess these scattered truths, merely because they fall in with them. These fragments of revelation, such as the doctrine of the Holy Trinity. or of the Atonement, are the religion which they have been taught in their childhood; and therefore they retain them, and profess them, and repeat them, without really *seeing* them as the Catholic sees them, but as receiving them merely by word of mouth, from imitation of others. In this way it often happens that a man, external to the Catholic Church, writes sermons and instructions, draws up and arranges devotions, or composes hymns which are faultless, or nearly so, which are the fruit, not of his own illuminated mind, but of his careful study, sometimes of his accurate translation, of Catholic originals. The natural heart can burst forth, by fits and starts, into emotions of love toward God. The natural imagination can depict the beauty and glory of the divine attributes.

"Catholic truths and rites are so beautiful, so great, so consolatory, that they draw one on to love and admire them with a natural love, as a prospect might draw one on, or a skilful piece of mechanism. Hence men of lively imagination profess this doctrine or that, or adopt this or that ceremony or usage, for their mere beauty's sake, not asking themselves whether they are true, and having no real perception or mental hold of them. Thus, too, they will decorate their churches, stretch and strain their ritual, and attempt candles, vestments, flowers, incense, and processions, not from faith but from poetical feeling.

"Moreover, the Catholic creed, as coming from God, is so harmonious, so consistent with itself, holds together so perfectly, so corresponds part to part, that an acute mind, knowing one portion of it, would often infer another portion, merely as a matter of just reasoning. Thus an accurate thinker might be sure that, if God is infinite and man finite, there must be mysteries in religion. It is not that he feels the mysteriousness of religion, but he infers it; he is led to it as a matter of necessity; and, from mere clearness of mind and love of consistency, he maintains it.

"Learned men, outside the Church, may compose most useful works on the evidences of religion, or in defence of particular doctrines, or in explanation of the whole scheme of Catholicism. In these cases reason becomes the handmaid of faith. Still it is not faith; it does not rise above an intellectual view or notion; it affirms, not as grasping the truth, not as seeing, but as "being of opinion," as "judging," as "coming to a conclusion."

"The natural man, then, can feel; he can imagine, he can admire, he can reason, he can infer. In all these ways he may proceed to receive the whole or part of Catholic truth; but he cannot see, he cannot love. His religious sentiments may be right and good in themselves, but not in him. His heretical sentiments on other points are a proof that he does not see what he speaks of.

"The natural conscience may ascertain and put in order the truths of the great moral law, nay, even to the condemnation of that concupiscence which it is too weak to subdue, and is persuaded to tolerate.

"The natural will can do many things really good and praiseworthy; nay, in particular cases, or at particular seasons, when temptation is away, it may seem to have strength which it has not, and to be imitating the austerity and purity of a saint. One man has no temptation to hoard; another has no temptation to gluttony and drunkenness; another has no temptation to ill-humor; another has no temptation to be ambitious and overbearing. Hence human nature may often show to advantage; it may be meek, amiable, kind, benevolent, generous, honest, upright, and temperate; and so a man may talk of Christ and heaven, too, read Scripture, and 'and do many things gladly,' in consequence of reading, and exercise a certain sort of belief, however different *from that faith which is imparted to us by grace.*

"The natural man, therefore, before he is brought under the grace of divine birth, can but inquire, reason, argue, and conclude about religious truth, but he does not, and he cannot see it." (Cardinal Newman, on Grace). He does not and he cannot have such faith in Christ as is necessary for salvation. Hence we said that they (Protestants) never had any divine faith in Christ. "He who does not believe all that Christ has taught," says St. Ambrose, denies Christ himself." (In Luc. c. 9.) "It is absurd for a heretic, says St. Thomas Aquinas, "to assert that he believes in Jesus Christ. To believe in a man is to give our full assent to his word and to all he teaches. True faith, therefore, is absolute belief in Jesus Christ and in all he has taught. Hence he who does not adhere to all that Jesus Christ has prescribed for our salvation has no more the doctrine of Jesus Christ and of his Church, than the Pagans, Jews, and Turks have." "He is" says Jesus Christ, "a heathen and publican." As S. O. has impudently asserted that we have misrepresented Protestant doctrine, no doubt, he would not feel in the least ashamed even to tell St. Thomas Aquinas in his face, that he misrepresents Protestant faith, when he says that it is absurd for a heretic to say he believes in Jesus Christ, etc.

S. O. tells again the readers of the *C. U.* and *T.* that "They (Protestants) say with us, in the language and meaning of the Apostle: 'There is no other *name* under heaven given to men, whereby we must be saved.'"

This applies only to Catholics who have the true religion of Christ, and do the will of his heavenly Father; for Christ has solemnly declared: "Not every one who saith to me Lord, Lord, shall enter the kingdom of heaven; but he that doth the will of my Father who is in heaven, he shall enter the kingdom of heaven." (Matt. vii. 21.)

As Protestants have no absolute faith in Jesus Christ, neither can they have any absolute faith in these words of Christ. We say these words in truth, because we have divine faith, and a Protestant has only human faith in them. Here is the difference between Protestant and Catholic belief, as we shall soon more clearly explain.

"This," he says, "being the undeniable truth," (that is, that the faith of Catholics and Protestants in Christ is the same) "what must we think of the *reason* given why they are said never to have had *any* faith in Christ! Let us hear it again: '*Q.* Why not? *Ans.* Because there never lived such a Christ as they imagine and believe in.' This answer put into the Catholic's mouth is false, for Protestants do believe in just such a Christ as did live and did die for us all, just such a Christ as we believe and know to have lived, suffered, and died.'"

Let S. O. read over again the above answer of St. Thomas and St. Ambrose. We repeat again, that Protestants have no *absolute* or *divine* faith in Christ, and therefore the above answer put in a Catholic's mouth is perfectly true. But, as it is a good work to instruct the ignorant, let us dwell for a few moments on the words of S. O. He is not ashamed to tell us Catholics "that Protestants believe in just such a Christ as we Catholics believe and know to have lived, suffered, and died." Now we Catholics believe in a Christ in whom we have absolute, divine faith; and this absolute, divine faith we have not only in Christ himself, but also in all he has done for our salvation, and teaches us through his one, holy, Catholic, and Apostolic Church. Now a Protestant can have no *divine* faith in Christ nor in his teaching. For, "to reject but one article of faith taught by the Church," says St. Thomas Aquinas, "is enough to destroy faith, as one mortal sin is enough to destroy charity; for the virtue of faith does not consist in merely adhering to the Holy Scriptures, and in revering them as the Word of God; it consists principally in submitting our *intellect* and *will* to the divine authority of the true Church charged by Jesus Christ to expound them. 'I would not believe the Holy Scriptures,' says St. Augustine, 'were it not for the divine authority of the Church.' 'He, therefore, who despises and rejects this authority, cannot have true faith. If he admits some supernatural truths, they are but simple opinions, as he makes them (the truths) depend on his private judgment." (De Fide, q. v., art. 3.)

"Indeed, a religion," says Cardinal Manning, "which men put together for themselves, a Christianity which men make by picking and choosing a doctrine here and a doctrine there, a form of belief which is made by the selection of texts from Holy Scripture, are all human. The fragments out of which such religions are made may be taken out of the word of God; nevertheless, they have ceased to be the word of God as soon as any human intellect and human hand has taken them to pieces, and put them together, and for this reason : Suppose that any man should take the four Gospels, and out of them select certain texts, and put them together, could that be a fifth gospel ? No; the Gospel of St. Matthew was written by St. Matthew, that of St. Mark by St. Mark, that of St. Luke by St. Luke, that of St. John by St. John, and any man who endeavored to make a fifth gospel would make a gospel of his own and not of any Evangelist, because he would not know the sense, meaning, and coherence of the texts so as to make that gospel an inspired book. These texts were dictated to inspired writers by the Spirit of God, and it would only be a fragmentary Christianity made out of the fragments of the truths; it would simply be a religion of human institution, and no truth which comes from man can be the matter of our faith."

But some Protestants, for instance, the Anglicans, think that they approach very near to the Catholic Church. They will tell you that their prayers and ceremonies are like many prayers and ceremonies of the Catholic Church, that their creed is the Apostles' Creed. But, in principle, they are very far off. "Thus," says Mr. Marshall, "they profess to believe *in one Church*, which has unfortunately become half a dozen ; *in unity*, which ceased to exist long ago for want of a centre; *in authority*, which nobody needs obey, because it has lost the power to teach ; *in God's presence with the Church*, which does not keep her from stupid errors ; *in a divine constitution*, which needs to be periodically reformed; *in a mission to teach all nations*, while she is unable to teach even herself; *in saints*, to whom Anglicans would be objects of horror and aversion ; and *in sanctity* of truths which their own sect has always defiled. What foolish belief. Even an untutored Indian Chief, by the aid of his rude common-sense, and the mere intuition of natural truth, does not fail to see the folly of Protestant belief, and confounds it before those Protestant missionaries who come to convert his tribe to Protestantism. Elder Alexander Campbell, in a lecture before the American Christian Missionary Association, relates the folllwing: Sectarian missionaries had gone among the Indians to disseminate religious sentiments. A council was called, and the missionaries explained the object of their visit. 'Is not all the religion of white men in a book?' quoth a chief. 'Yes,' replied the missionaries. 'Do not all white men read the book?' continued the chief. Another affirmative response. 'Do they all agree upon what it says?' inquired the chief, categorically. There was a dead silence for some moments. At last one of the missionaries replied; 'Not exactly; they differ upon some doctrinal points.' 'Go, then, white man,' said the Chief, 'call a council, and when the white men all agree, then come and teach the red men.' How the absurdity of Protestantism is so easily perceived and confounded even by the rude child of the forest!" Hence it is that the famous convert and American Reviewer says: "What Protestants call their religion is only a disguised secularism which is amply provided for by the secular press, the instincts of nature, and the anti-Catholic sentiment of the country." (Brownson's Review, January, 1873.)

It is, therefore, quite absurd to speak of Protestantism as of a religion or Church; and it is scandalously absurd for S. O. to assert that the Protestant faith in Christ is the same as that of Catholics! The truth is one; errors are many; the Church, the pillar and ground of truth, is one; sects are many, that deny the truth and the Church's infallible authority to teach truth. Every sensible man, then, seeing a class of men drawn into a whirlpool of endless religious variations and dissensions, is forced to say: "This is only an ephemeral sect, without substance and without any divine authority; it is a plant not planted by the hand of Almighty God, and therefore it will be rooted up; it is a kingdom divided against itself, and therefore it will be made desolate; it is a house built on sand, and therefore it cannot stand; it is a cloud without water, which is carried about by the winds; a tree of autumn, unfruitful, twice dead, by want of divine faith, and therefore it will be plucked up by the roots; a raging wave of the sea, foaming out its own confusion; a wandering star, to which the storm and darkness are reserved forever; a withered branch cut off from the body of Christ, the One, Holy, Roman Catholic Church, which alone is established by Christ on earth as his "pillar and ground of truth," in *one* fold, watched over by his own chief shepherd, ever immovable amid the storms of hell; with unshaken faith, amid the variations of philosophical systems, the infernal persecutions of the wicked, the revolutions of empires, the attacks of interest, of prejudice, of passion, the dissolving labors of criticism, the progress of physical, historical, and other sciences, the unrestrained love of novelty, the abuses which sooner or later undermine the most firmly-established human institutions. The faith of this Church alone is divine, because she alone teaches divinely revealed truths with divine authority.

This is clear to every unprejudiced and well-reflecting mind. Mr. T. W. M. Marshall relates the following, in one of his lectures:

"A young English lady, with whom I became subsequently acquainted, and from whose lips I heard the tale, informed her parents that she felt constrained to embrace the Catholic faith. Hereupon arose much agitation in the parental councils, and a reluctant promise was extorted from the daughter that she would not communicate with any Catholic priest till she had first listened to the convincing arguments with which certain clerical friends of the family would easily dissipate her unreasonable doubts. These ministers were three in number, and we will call them Messrs. A., B., and C. The appointed day arrived for the solemn discussion, which one of the Ministers was about to commence, when the young lady opened it abruptly with the following remark: 'I am too young and uninstructed to dispute with gentlemen of your age and experience, but perhaps you will allow me to ask you a few questions?' Anticipating an easy triumph over the poor girl, the three ministers acceded with encouraging smiles to her request. 'Then I will ask you,' she said to Mr. A., 'whether regeneration always accompanies the sacrament of baptism.' 'Undoubtedly,' was the prompt reply; 'that is the plain doctrine of our Church.' 'And you, Mr. B.,' she continued, —'do you teach that doctrine?' 'God forbid, my young friend,' was his indignant answer, 'that I should teach such soul-destroying error! Baptism is a formal rite, which,' etc., etc. 'And you, Mr. C.,' she asked the third, 'what is your opinion?' 'I regret,' he replied with a bland voice, for he began to suspect they were making a mess of it, 'that my reverend friends should have expressed themselves a little incautiously. The true doctrine lies between these extremes'—and he was going to develop it, when the young lady, rising from her chair, said: 'I thank you, gentlemen; you have taught me all that I expected to learn from you. You are all ministers of the same Church, yet you each contradict the other, even upon a doctrine which St. Paul calls one of the *foundations* of Christianity. You have only confirmed me in my resolution to enter a Church whose ministers all teach the same thing.' And then they went out of the room, one by one, and probably continued their battle in the street. But the parents of the young lady turned her out of doors the next day, to get her bread as she could. They sometimes do that sort of thing in England.

"Another friend of mine, also a lady, and one of the most intelligent of her sex, was for several years the disciple of the distinguished minister who has given a name to a certain religious school in England. Becoming disaffected toward the Episcopalian Church, which appeared to her more redolent of earth, in proportion as she aspired more ardently toward heaven, she was persuaded to assist at a certain Ritualistic festival, which, it was hoped, would have a soothing effect upon her mind. A new church was to be opened, and the ceremonies were to be prolonged through an entire week. All the Ritualistic celebrities of the day were expected to be present. Her lodging was judiciously provided in a house in which were five of the most transcendental members of the High Church party. It was hoped that they would speedily convince her of their apostolic unity, but, unfortunately, they only succeeded in proving to her that no two of them were of the same mind. One recommended her privately to pray to the Blessed Virgin, which another condemned as, at best, a poetical superstition. One told her that the Pope was, by divine appointment, the head of the Universal Church; another, that he was a usurper and a schismatic. One maintained that the 'Reformers' were profane scoundrels and apostates; another, that they had, at all events, good intentions. But I need not trouble you with an account of their various creeds. Painfully affected by this diversity, where she had been taught to expect complete uniformity, her doubts were naturally confirmed. During the week she was invited to take a walk with the eminent person whom she had hitherto regarded as a trustworthy teacher. To him she revealed her growing disquietude, and presumed to lament the conflict of opinions which she had lately witnessed, but only to be rewarded by a stern rebuke; for it is a singular fact that men who are prepared at any moment to judge all the saints and doctors, will not tolerate any judgment which reflects upon themselves. It was midwinter, and the lady's companion, pointing to the leafless trees by the roadside, said, with appropriate solemnity of voice and manner: 'They are stripped of their foliage now, but wait for the spring, and you will see them once more wake to life. So shall it be with the Church of England, which now seems to you dead.' 'It may be so,' she replied; 'but what sort of a spring can we expect *after a winter which has lasted three hundred years* ?' You will not be surprised to hear that this lady soon after became a member of a Church which knows nothing of winter, but within whose peaceful borders reigns eternal spring."

Alas! S. O. has not been ashamed to assert that we have misrepresented Protestant belief, though we have said of it only what St. Thomas Aquinas and all the great Doctors of the Church have said of it!

§ 6. More False Oracles of S. O.

"It is," he says, "neither true nor honest to say that the Protestant believes *as he pleases*. The fact is, he believes *what he believes his Creator and God wishes him to believe.* He is in error as to the divine will. This we know."

This is a down-right falsehood, and a great insult to God. God wishes every Protestant to believe all that Christ teaches him through his Church, and he wishes him to believe it with *divine* faith; and S. O. avows this truth by saying: "He (the Protestant) is in error as to the divine will. This we know." Is it not strange how this priest contradicts himself almost in the same breath!

"But," continues S. O. to say, "he (the Protestant) is *guilty* because 'he is *wrong*' is to say more than God has ever authorized any human being to say." Well, was not St. Paul a human being? Was he not authorized by the Holy Ghost to say: "For whosoever have sinned without the law, shall perish without the law." (Rom. ii. 12.) If those Protestants who live in inculpable ignorance of the true religion are not guilty of the sin of heresy, does it follow that they are not guilty of sins against their conscience? But this needs a good explanation, which we will give later on; it needs a better one than the most prominent priest of the U. S. gives by saying: "To think that we Catholics are *the only honest people* is to be guilty of the most contemptible kind of pharisaism. The true Catholic never thinks in that foolish way. He thanks God that he is right and knows that he is right and prays that all may be led to a knowledge of the truth. He does not find it in his theology or in his heart to damn anybody or wish anybody to be damned."

By *honest people*, S. O. here means people that have the

true faith; for he says, "He (the Catholic) thanks God that he is right, and knows that he is right, and prays that all may be led to a knowledge of the truth." It is therefore false to say that "To think that we Catholics are the only true believers, is to be guilty of the most contemptible kind of pharisaism." The true Catholic is bound in conscience to think in that way, because he knows that the Catholic religion is the only true religion. How foolish to say the contrary. But when S. O. says: "He (a Catholic) does not find it in his theology or in his heart to damn anybody or wish anybody to be damned," he is right; but in order to be honest, he should have added, immediately after these words, " nor does the Rev. M. Muller, C.SS.R., teach anything of the kind in his *Explanation of Christian Doctrine.* But a true, educated Catholic does not find in his theology nor in his heart the great falsehoods which S. O. tells when he solemnly asserts that "Protestants believe *all* that the Catholic believes of the facts of his (Christ's) divine life, miracles, passion, death, and resurrection."

What a scandalous assertion this! If it came from the lips of a Protestant, we would declare it a down-right lie, but coming, as it does, from the lips of S. O., it is a terrible scandal. Is there any fact of Christ's divine life more evident than the establishment of his—the Roman Catholic Church? Do Protestants believe this divine fact?

"Reason, it is true," says the Roman Catechism, "and the senses, are compelled to asceitain the existence of the Church, that is, of a society of men devoted and consecrated to Jesus Christ; no faith is necessary to understand a truth which is acknowledged by Jews and Turks; but do Protestants believe the privileges and dignity of the Church as Catholics believe them? By no means, because they have not the light of faith, which alone enables us to say I *believe the Catholic Church.*"

Again, has not God ordained from the beginning of the world that men should give him the honor of adoration by offering sacrifice to him. Has this law ever been abolished by God, in the Old Testament, or by Jesus Christ in the

New Law ? Has he not, on the contrary, confirmed this law by the institution of the unbloody sacrifice of his Body and Blood in Holy Mass, which is to be offered up to the end of the world ? And has not Jesus Christ, for this purpose, established a new order of priesthood at the Last Supper ? Are not the seven sacraments, the visible means of grace, so many facts of Christ's divine life ? Do Protestants believe all these and many other facts of Christ's divine life ? Ah ! that most prominent priest of the U. S. knows only too well that Protestants do not believe these facts. How can he then so impudently tell such a lie to the readers of the *B U.*, aye, to all Catholics, whose faith in these facts, he says, is also that of Protestants ? Do Catholics deny these facts ? In the very instant that a Catholic would deny any of these facts, he would be a Protestant, a heretic, and cut off as a rotten member of the Church of Jesus Christ.

The above assertion of S. O. is a true insult to the Catholic faith, which is an *absolute, divine*, faith, a gratuitous gift of the Holy Ghost, while Protestant belief is all human, only an opinion alterable at pleasure, without foundation; it reminds one of the Brahmin's theory of the support of the earth. The Hindoo says : "The world rests on the back of an elephant, the elephant rests on the back of a turtle." But what does the turtle rest on ? So it is with the *Protestant Brahmins*. They will tell you, with all the coolness of Hindoo hypocrisy and pretension, that religion depends on the written word of God, and they make the word of God depend on private interpretation ; but they do not say what the "turtle" stands on. This is the dilemma in which all are caught who rest religion on a human or an atheistical basis. They cut religion loose from its assigned divine Teacher—the Roman Catholic Church, and set it a-going on human authority. But the trouble is, they have no support for this "turtle."

For the benefit of S. O. we repeat here the words of Dr. O. A. Brownson.

"That Protestants, that so-called orthodox Protestants at

least, profess to hold, and claim as belonging to their Protestantism, many things that are also held by Catholics, nobody denies; but these things are no part of Protestantism, for the Church held and taught them ages before Protestantism was born. They are part and parcel of the one Catholic faith, and belong to Catholics only. Protestants can rightfully claim as Protestant only those things wherein they differ from the Church, which the Church denies, and which they assert; that is, what is peculiarly or distinctively Protestant. We cannot allow them to claim as theirs what is and always has been ours; we willingly accord them their own, but not one whit more. All which they profess to hold in common with us is ours, not theirs. Adopting this rule, which is just and unimpeachable, nothing in fact is theirs but their denials, and as all their denials are, as we have seen, made on no Catholic principle or truth, they are pure negations, and hence Protestantism is purely negative, and consequently is no religion, for all religion is affirmative."

§ 7. S. O. DECLARES TRUTH TO BE RANT AND ABUSE. HE CONTINUES TO QUOTE FROM "EXPLANATION:"

"*Q.* In what kind of a Christ do they believe? *Ans.* In such a one of whom they can make a liar with impurity."

"What possible meaning," he says, "can such language and such an assertion convey to the mind of any one, Catholic or Protestant? It is *rant and abuse,* and nothing less. The idea of any one believing in or wishing to believe in one whom, as his Saviour, he can make a liar of with impunity, is too absurd to deserve a moment's consideration."

Softly, softly, S. O. When we gave the above answer, we also gave the proofs for it. But you and Coxe have dishonestly suppressed these proofs, in order to be able to call our answer *rant* and *abuse,* and to say that it is too absurd to deserve a moment's consideration. A man like you, who sees no difference between divine and human faith, will answer as you do. Do you, then, mean to say that, when St. John, the Apostle and Evangelist, wrote, "He that believeth not the Son (Jesus Christ), maketh him a liar" (I. John, v. 10.), the Holy Ghost told through him *rant and abuse*, and that these words of the Holy Ghost are too absurd to deserve a moment's consideration ?

"Not to believe all that Christ has said," says Cornelius a Lapide, "is as much as to say that Christ is a liar, and this is an awful blasphemy." Here we add the proofs which you have passed over in silence.

Jesus Christ says: "Hear the Church." "No;" say Luther and all Protestants, "do not hear the Church, protest against her with all your might!"

Jesus Christ says: "If any one will not hear the Church, look upon him as a heathen and a publican." "No," says Protestantism, "if any one does not hear the Church, look upon him as an apostle, as an ambassador of God."

Jesus Christ says: "The gates of hell shall not prevail against my Church." "No," says Protestantism, "'Tis false; the gates of hell have prevailed against the Church for a thousand years and more."

Jesus Christ has declared St. Peter, and every successor to St. Peter—the Pope—to be his Vicar on earth. "No," says Protestantism, "the Pope is Anti-Christ."

Jesus Christ says: "My yoke is sweet, and my burden light." (Matt. xi. 30.) "No," said Luther and Calvin, "it is impossible to keep the commandments."

Jesus Christ says: "If thou wilt enter into life, keep the commandments." (Matt. xix. 17.) "No," said Luther and Calvin, "faith *alone*, without good works, is sufficient to enter into life everlasting."

Jesus Christ says: "Unless you do penance, you shall all likewise perish." (Luke, iii. 3.) "No," said Luther and Calvin, "fasting, and other works of penance are not necessary in satisfaction for sin."

Jesus Christ says: "This is my body." "No," said Calvin, "this is only the figure of Christ's Body, it will become his body as soon as you receive it."

Jesus Christ says: "I say to you, that whosoever shall

put away his wife, and shall marry another, committeth adultery; and he that shall marry her that is put away, committeth adultery." (Matt. xix. 9.) "No," say Luther and all Protestants, to a married man, "you may put away your wife, get a divorce, and marry another."

Jesus Christ says to every man: "Thou shalt not steal." "No," said Luther to secular princes, "I give you the right to appropriate to yourselves the property of the Roman Catholic Church."

There are about three hundred millions of Catholics living at present all over the world. Ah! how they feel shocked at these insults which Protestants offer to Jesus Christ. Even little children are shocked by them.

A Calvinist nobleman was once disputing about the real presence with the father of St. Jane Frances de Chantal. Frances was at that time only five years of age. Whilst the dispute was going on she advanced and said to the nobleman: "What, sir! do you not believe that Jesus Christ is really present in the Blessed Sacrament, and yet he has told us that *he is present?* You then make him a liar. If you dared attack the honor of the king, my father would defend it at the risk of his life, and even at the cost of yours; what have you then to expect from God for calling his Son a liar?" The Calvinist was greatly surprised at the child's zeal, and endeavored to appease his young adversary with presents; but full of love for her holy faith, she took his gifts and threw them into the fire, saying: "Thus shall all those burn in hell who do not believe the words of Jesus Christ."

> "God gives the frail and feeble tongue
> A doom to speak on sin and wrong."

S. O. says that Protestants believe that Christ is "true God" and true Man. If they believe that he is true God, why is it that they do not believe all his words and all that he has done for our salvation? Why is it that they do not honor him as God, but refuse to believe his whole doctrine? How have they treated Jesus Christ in the Blessed Sacrament? It is too horrible to relate. Can it be expected that those who so terribly have dishonored Jesus Christ in the Blessed Sacrament will, as they should, honor, and treat, and believe Jesus Christ in heaven? How have they honored Him in those who take his place on earth, of whom Christ says: "He who heareth you, heareth me; and he who despiseth you, despiseth me, and he who despiseth me, despiseth Him (God the Father) who sent me." (Luke, x. 16.) Glance again over chapter III., and you will find how Jesus Christ has been treated by Protestants in the Pope, the bishops, and the priests of the Roman Catholic Church.

To establish the sacrilegious doctrine of his primacy over the English Church, Henry VIII. had put to death two cardinals, three archbishops, eighteen bishops and archdeacons, five hundred priests, sixty superiors of religious houses, fifty canons, twenty-nine peers, three hundred and sixty knights, and an immense number both of the gentry and people. He confiscated to the crown, and distributed among his favorites, the property of six hundred and forty-five monasteries and ninety colleges, one hundred and ten hospitals, and two thousand three hundred and seventy-four free chapels and chantries.

And how have they treated Jesus Christ in the poor members of his Body? "Amen, I say to you, as long as you did it to one of these, my least brethren, you did it to me." (Matt. xxv. 40.)

For over three hundred years the Irish people have suffered, struggled, and died for the faith. They suffered poverty with all its bitterness, they endured exile with all its sorrows, they suffered outrage and even death itself, rather than lose their God. The minions of hell enacted the fiendish penal laws, and soon that country, so rich and fruitful in colleges and convents, became one vast, dreary wilderness. In tracts of country, thirty, forty, fifty miles in extent, the smoke from an inhabited house, as English chroniclers themselves declare, was nowhere to be seen. The people had disappeared and left only skeletons in the land. The living were to be met only in the glens and dark caves of the mountains. There they dragged out a wretched existence, feeding on the weeds and garbage of the earth. Like shadows they moved about, haggard and wan, starving and wounded, and they endured the cruel pangs of hunger, till God, in his mercy, took them to a better world. Again and again were these harrowing scenes repeated. Ireland became prosperous again in spite of the most galling oppression; and the people of Ireland were again starved and massacred for their faith, and those that survived were shipped off to the British West Indies, and sold there as slaves. The British fleet was ordered around the coast. Over eighty thousand of the most influential and most distinguished of the Irish Catholics were packed on board, and their bones have long since rotted in the soil of the English sugar-plantations of Jamaica.

The last effort of tyranny is still fresh in the minds of many—I mean the late famine years. There are, no doubt, some of our readers who have witnessed the appalling scenes of that gloomy period, and once witnessed, they can never, never be forgotten. Ah! no. Like living fire, these horrid scenes burn into the memory, and leave there a horrid scar—a mark that can never be effaced. There were thousands and thousands wasting away and dying of hunger. They were falling and dying as the leaves fall in autumn. The food that was sent to the poor people from America was kept in the harbors until it rotted. And there, in the sight of the famishing people, the wealthy Protestant, the overfed wives and daughters of the sleek, oily Protestant parsons, had plenty of food for their cattle; they had food in abundance for their pet birds or their lapdogs, whilst the poor starving Catholics wished to even eat the husks of the swine, and it was not given them.

A few years before the gloomy reign of terror, there lived near a certain town in Ireland a poor, honest farmer with his wife and children. They were poor, indeed, but yet they were contented and happy. Never did the poor or the stranger pass their door without partaking of their hospitality; and what they had, they gave with a willing heart. But the famine year came on. The good farmer was unable to pay the tithes. His little property was distrained. The police entered his farm; they seized his unreaped corn; they took away his crops; they drove his cattle to the pound. The poor unhappy man himself was expelled from that little spot of earth on which he was born, where he had lived so long, and where he had hoped to die. He was turned into the public road with his wife and children. No roof, no food, no clothing—he was cast, in beggary and nakedness, into the cold, heartless world. He sought for a shelter for his little ones. He sought for employment, but could find none. He was a Catholic. His neighbors around were bitter Protestants of the blackest dye. They offered him shelter, food, and clothing, but on one condition —that he would apostatize.

O God! who shall tell the agony of that poor, heart-broken father? No hope to cheer him save the hope of death; no eye to pity him save the all-merciful eye of God! He saw his poor wife dying before his eyes. He saw her wasting day by day—slowly pining away while praying and weeping over her starving children; he heard his famished children crying for food, and their piteous cries rent his very soul. Oh! he could help them, he could provide them food, clothing, and a pleasant home— but then he must apostatize, he must renounce his holy faith! Oh! what a sore trial, what a cruel martyrdom! His loving wife died before his eyes—died of hunger. She died with words of patience, words of hope upon her lips. The poor husband wrung his hands in anguish. He bent over the lifeless form of his wife. Dark night was thickening around him—thickening even within him; he felt the cruel pangs of hunger gnawing at his very vitals. And were he not upheld by his holy faith, he would have yielded to despair. But the cries of his children aroused him. He forgot for a moment his own sufferings. He took his two weak, starving babes in his trembling arms, and hurried away with tottering steps. He begged from house to house, from door to door; he begged for a crumb of bread for his poor, starving little ones, but no one gave him a morsel of food. They offered him food, and clothing, and shelter if he would only apostatize, if he would give his children to be brought up in their false creed. "But," cried the heart-broken father, "oh! how could I give my children to be brought up in the false creed and deny their holy faith? Oh! how could I sell their souls to the Evil One for a mess of pottage?" After some time the unhappy man felt a heavy load weighing like lead upon his trembling arm. He looked. One of his poor babes had ceased moaning. It was dead—cold and stiff in death. The heart-broken father sat down beneath a tree by the wayside and prayed, but he could not weep. Ah! no; his eyes were dry, his heart was withered. In wild, passionate tones he called on heaven to witness his agony—he called God to witness that he did not wish the death of his children, that he would gladly lay down his life to save his family, but he could not—oh! no! no!—he could not deny his holy faith; he could not sell their souls to the devil. He tried once more to obtain some food for his remaining child, but in vain, and at last the poor innocent sufferer gasped and died too in his arms. Ah! whose heart can remain unmoved at the sufferings of the Irish Catholic? Whose heart, at the same time, does not rejoice at their constancy in the faith.

Our Lord Jesus Christ, when hanging on the cross, excused those who had crucified him. "Father, forgive them, for they know not what they do." (Luke xxiii. 34.) They did not know that Christ was their God. "For," says St. Paul, "if they had known it, they would never have crucified the Lord of Glory." (I. Cor. ii. 8.) But the most prominent priest of the U. S. solemnly assures us that Protestants believe in the divinity of Christ. How, then, is such faith compatible with such treatment of Christ? Alas! we repeat, what a shame for S. O. to tell Catholics and Protestants that their faith in Christ is all the same!

§. 8. S. O. CONTINUES TO DECLARE FALSE WHAT IS TRUE.

He continues to quote part of our Answer:—"Whose (Christ's) doctrines they can interpret *as they please.*"

"This again is false," he says; "Protestants do not believe they can interpret the doctrines of Christ *as they please,* and any one who asserts it misrepresents Protestant teaching."

Before our would-be theologian said that our answer was false, he should have shown that Protestants have a rule and an infallible authority by which they must go in interpreting Christ's doctrines, and that they never interpreted Christ's doctrines as they pleased. But he knows he cannot furnish any proofs for the truth of his assertions.

Whence, then, we ask, has Protestantism and all other isms risen? Is it not from the private interpretation of Holy Scripture, and Christ's doctrines? Has not Protestantism introduced the principle that "there is no divinely-appointed authority to teach infallibly; let every man read the Bible and judge for himself"? Is not this a historical fact? Monseigneur de Cheverus, in his sermons, often dwelt on the necessity of a divine teaching authority, to render unwavering the faith of the unlearned as well as of the ignorant. To convince Protestants of this necessity, he often repeated, in his discourses to them, these simple words: "Every day, my dear brethren, I read the holy Scripture like yourselves; I read it with reflection and prayer, having previously invoked the Holy Ghost, and yet, at almost every page, I find many things that I cannot understand, and I find the great necessity of some speaking authority, which may point out to me the meaning of the text, and render my faith firm." And his hearers immediately made the application to themselves. "If Monseigneur de Cheverus," said they, "who is more learned than we, cannot comprehend the Sacred Scripture, how is it that our ministers tell us that the Bible is to each of us a full and clear rule of faith, easily understood of itself, and requiring no aid in understanding its meaning?"

From the time of the apostles to the present day, there have risen unlearned men, as well as men accomplished in every kind of learning, who undertook to interpret the Bible according to their own private opinions. The consequence was, that the ignorant were led into errors, for want of knowledge, and the learned, through pride and self-sufficiency. Instead of interpreting Scripture according to the teaching of the Church, and learning from her what they should believe, they have tried to teach the Church false and perverse doctrines of their own. They avail themselves of the Scriptures to prove their errrors. They say that they have the Scriptures on their side, which are the fountain of truth. But these deluded men do not consider that the truth is found, not by reading, but by understanding, the holy Scriptures. This arrogance in interpreting the Bible according to their fancy proceeds from pride. But God resists the proud, and withholds from them the light of faith. In punishment for their pride and want of submission to the teaching of his Church, he permits such men to fall into all kinds of errors, absurdities, and vices; he permits the Holy Scriptures, which are a great fountain of truth, to become to them a great fountain of errors, so that to them may be applied the words of our divine Saviour, "You err, not knowing the Scriptures;" (Matt. xxii. 29.) and of St. Peter, "They wrest the Scriptures to their own destruction." (II. Pet. iii. 16.)

The Adamites pretended to find in the Book of Genesis that they were as pure as our first parents, and need not be ashamed of being naked any more than Adam and Eve before the fall. Arius pretended to find, in forty-two passages of the Bible, that the Son of God was not equal to the Father. Macedonius maintained that from holy Scripture he could prove that the Holy Ghost was not God; and Pelagius asserted, on the authority of holy Scripture, that man could work out his salvation without the grace of God. Luther asserted that he found in Isaias that man was not free; and

Calvin tried to prove from Scripture that it is impossible for man to keep the commandments. There is no error so monstrous, no crime so heinous, no practice so detestable, which perverse men have not endeavored to justify by some passage of Scripture. St. Augustine asks, " Whence have risen heresies and those pernicious errors that lead men to everlasting perdition ? " and he answers: " They have risen from this: that men understand the Scriptures wrongly, and then maintain presumptuously and boldly what they thus understand wrongly." (In Joan. tr. xviii.) Thus, "the Gospel," as St. Jerome observes, "is, for them, not the Gospel of Christ any longer, but the Gospel of man, or of the devil: for the Gospel consists, not in the words, but in the *sense*, of Scripture, wherefore, by false interpretion, the Gospel of Christ becomes the gospel of man, or of the devil." " My thoughts, saith the Lord, are not as your thoughts, neither are your ways my ways ; for, as the heavens are exalted above the earth, even so are my ways exalted above your ways, and my thoughts above your thoughts." (Isa. l. 8, 9.) Who, then, shall, by his *private* reason, pretend to know, to judge, to demonstrate, to interpret, the unsearchable ways of God and the incomprehensible, divine mysteries hidden in the Holy Scripture ? " How can I understand it, if no one explains it to me ? " (Acts, viii.)

To sum up what has been said : In the order of time, the Catholic Church precedes the Scripture. There was no time when a visible and speaking divine authority did not exist, to which submission was not due. Before the coming of Jesus Christ, that authority among the Jews was in the synagogue. When the synagogue was on the point of failing, Jesus Christ himself appeared; when this divine personage withdrew, he left his authority to his Church, and with her his Holy Spirit. All the truths which we believe to be divine, and which are the objects of our faith, were taught by the Church, and believed by millions of Christians, long before they were committed to writing, and formed what is called the New Testament. And those truths would have remained to the end of the world, pure and unaltered, had that primitive state continued; that is, had it never seemed good to any of the apostolic men, as it did to St. Luke, to commit to writing what they had learned from Christ. He did it, he says, that Theophilus, to whom he writes, might *know the verity of these words in which he had been instructed.*

A Catholic, therefore, never forms his faith by reading the Scriptures; his faith is already formed before he begins to read; his reading serves only to confirm what he always believed; that is, it confirms the doctrine which the Church had already taught him. Consequently, if these books had not existed, the belief in the facts and truths of Christianity would have been the same; and it would not be weakened if those books were no longer to exist.

As the Catholic Church made known to the Christians those facts and truths long before they were recorded in writing, she alone could afterward rightly decide, and infallibly state, what books did, and what did not, contain the pure doctrine of Christ and his apostles; she alone could and did know what books were, and what were not, divinely inspired; she alone could and did make that inspiration an object of faith; she alone can, with infallible authority, give the true meaning, and determine the legitimate use, of the Holy Scriptures.

Although the Scripture, the true word of God, is not to us *a rule of faith*, taken *independently* of the teaching authority of the pastors of the Church, the successors of the apostles, yet it is not inferior to the Church in excellence and dignity. It is inspired, holy, and divine. Hence, it is the custom of the Church to erect a throne in the middle of councils, on which she places the Sacred Books as presiding over the assembly, occupying, as it were, the first place, and deciding with supreme authority. When celebrating Mass, she wishes that the faithful, during the reading of the Gospel, should all rise, and remain standing, to show their reverence for the sacred truths. We venerate the Scriptures as a sacred *deposit* bequeathed to us by the kindest of parents, containing truths of the highest moment, practical lessons of saving morality, and facts of history relating to the life of our divine Saviour, and the conduct of his disciples, eminently interesting and instructive. For all this we are very grateful.

Besides, the Scriptures come forward with a powerful aid, to support, by the evidence of the contents, both the divine authority of the Church, and the divine truths of the faith which we have received from her, applying that aid to each article, and giving a lustre to the whole. So Theophilus, when he read that admirable narration which St. Luke compiled for him, was more and more confirmed in the *verity of things in which he had been instructed.* (St. Luke, i. 1-4.)

For those, however, who reject the divine authority of the Church, the holy Scriptures can no longer be authentic and inspired writings—they are for them no longer the word of God; for they have no one who can tell them, with divine certainty, what books are, and what are not, divinely inspired; they have no one who, in the name of God, can command them to believe in the divine inspiration of the writers of those books. Explaining them, as they do, according to their fancy, and translating them in a way favorable to their errors, they have, in the Scriptures, not the Gospel of Christ, but that of man or the devil, calculated only to confirm the ignorant in their errors, and the learned in their pride and self-sufficiency. We read, in the Gospel of St. Matthew and of St. Luke, that Satan hid himself under the shade of the Scripture when he tempted our divine Saviour. He quoted passages from holy Scripture, in order to tempt him to ambition and presumption. But he is answered: "Begone, Satan; it is written, Thou shalt not tempt the Lord thy God." Satan, being overcome, left *for a time.* But not long after, under the mask of Arius, Nestorius, Pelagius, Luther, Calvin, John Knox, Henry VIII., and a host of other heresiarchs, he renewed his attacks on Jesus Christ, in the person of the Catholic Church. This demon is heresy, which hides itself under the shade of

Scripture. Were Satan to utter blasphemies, he would be known at once, and men would flee from him in horror. So he deceives them under the appearance of good; he repeats passages from holy Scripture, and men naturally listen to him, and are apt to believe and follow him. But the good Catholic answers him: "Begone, Satan! It is written, he that will not hear the Church, let him be to thee as a heathen and the publican." (Matt. xviii. 16.) This is the great, the infallible, and the only rule of faith, that leads to him who gave it,—Jesus Christ.

The heretics and Catholics to whom St. Dominic preached the Gospel put together in writing the strongest arguments in defence of their respective doctrines. The Catholic arguments were the work of St. Dominic, who confirmed the Catholic doctrine by many passages of Holy Scripture. The heretics, too, quoted Holy Scripture in confirmation of their doctrine. It was proposed that both writings should be committed to the flames, in order that God might declare, by his own interposition, which cause he favored. Accordingly, a great fire was made, and the two writings were cast into it: that of the heretics was immediately consumed to ashes, whilst that of the Catholic remained unhurt, after it had been cast into the fire three times, and taken out again.

This public miracle happened at Fanjaux; the fruit of it was the conversion of a great number of heretics of both sexes. The same kind of miracle happened at Montreal. St. Dominic drew up in writing a short exposition of the Catholic faith, with proof of each article from the New Testament. This writing he gave to the heretics to examine. Their ministers and chiefs, after much altercation about it, agreed to throw it into the fire, saying that, if it burned, they would regard the doctrine which it contained as false. Being cast thrice into the flames, it was not damaged.

Let us unceasingly thank Almighty God for the grace of being children of the Catholic Church. St. Francis de Sales exclaims: "O dear Lord! many and great are the blessings thou hast heaped on me, and I thank thee for them. But how shall I be ever able to thank thee for enlightening me with thy holy faith? O God! the beauty of thy holy faith appears to me so enchanting, that I am dying with love of it; and I imagine I ought to enshrine this precious gift in a heart all perfumed with devotion." St. Teresa never ceased to thank God for having made her a daughter of the holy Catholic Church. Her consolation at the hour of death was to cry out: "I die a child of the holy Church, I die a child of the holy Church."

All this being undeniably true, by what right, then, does S. O. call false what is a well-known fact and an undeniable truth? And does not he himself say: "The Protestant doctrine of the rule of faith,—each one's private interpretation of the written word of God,—is unquestionably erroneous"? Does he not give himself the lie in these words? Can he understand anything else by private interpretation than the Catholic Church understands by it? He tries to make believe that no sensible Protestant believes that he can interpret Holy Scripture as he pleases, just as little as he believes that a private citizen has a right to interpret the laws of the State as he pleases; that he has to go by the decisions of the Supreme Court. Of course, every Protestant understands that he must go by the decisions of the Supreme Court. But does it follow therefrom that Protestants do not interpret the Bible as they please? What poor logic this!

From the fact that no Protestant as a private citizen has a right to interpret the laws of the State, but must follow the decisions of the Supreme Court, Protestants should, of course, understand that Almighty God did not leave his laws and written word to be interpreted by private individuals, but by the Roman Catholic Church, the supreme authority appointed by Jesus Christ to teach all men infallibly his doctrine, and interpret infallibly the written and unwritten word of God. But Protestants have rejected this divine teaching authority, and interpret the Bible by private interpretation. S. O. avows this to be wrong, but excuses Protestants for doing what is wrong, because "what seems so clear to us is not so clear to others who exist in a condition so different from ours that they cannot see things as we see them." Why can they not? It is because they have no divine faith, and have rejected Christ and his teaching when they rejected the divine teacher—the Roman Catholic Church; and therefore we conclude again, that no one can be saved in such a faith.

§ 9. S. O. DECLARES WHOLLY UNTRUE WHAT HE CANNOT UNDERSTAND.

He goes on to say : " The reply of the book continues : —' A Christ who does not care what a man *believes provided he be an honest man before the public.*'

" I cannot conceive how the author could have brought himself to pen that sentence. It is wholly untrue, beginning, middle, and end. The personality the author sets up as the Christ of Protestants is a caricature which the author should not have associated with the Holy Name."

Softly, S. O., softly ; you have probably read two treatises, *My Clerical Friends* and *Church Defence* written by a celebrated English Convert. The able and pleasing writer has, by the strength and solidity of his reasoning, turned all church pretensions of the Anglicans into perfect ridicule.

His Eminence Cardinal Wiseman has left them not an inch of ground to stand on, and has blown their church pretensions to the winds.

"It is not difficult," says Brownson, "to turn Anglicans and their church pretensions into ridicule, and we confess that we have hardly ever been able to treat either seriously. As to the High Church party, his Eminence Cardinal Wiseman has left nothing to be said; he has left them not an inch of ground to stand on, and has blown their church pretensions to the winds. As for Low-Churchmen, or the Evangelicals—the Exeter Hall people—they hold from Calvin, and have no church pretensions at all. They are to be placed in the same category with Presbyterians, Dutch Reformed, Congregationalists, and Methodists, who place the essence of religion in emotion, and count dogma of no great importance, perhaps of none. They are unmistakably Protestants, and alternate between fanaticism and indifference." You see, nothing but a caricature of Christ is left to these people.

Indeed, is not a caricature of a man left, after his arms, feet and head have been cut off? Would you not have a caricature of a Christ, if you were to deny either his divinity, or his humanity, or his human soul and will? Would you not have a caricature of baptism, if you baptized with wine, or in only the name of the Father, or only in the name of the Son, or only in the name of the Holy Ghost? Well, has not Protestantism lopped off the head from Christ's Body, which is the Catholic Church? Has it not lopped off the Body and Blood of Christ in the Holy Eucharist; the divine Christian sacrifice offered in the Mass; confession of sins, most of the sacraments; the invocation of the saints? Has it not tried to annihilate, if possible, the Head and Body of Christ—the Catholic Church, etc.? What has Protestantism left of Christ and his doctrine, except a caricature of Christ and a caricature of his religion? Hence St. Thomas says: "True faith is absolute faith in Christ and all his doctrine. Pagans and Jews, in publicly denying his divinity, are real infidels; but the heretic adopts or rejects the precepts of the Gospel according to his own private judgment, with full liberty of conscience. *So this kind of doctrine*, founded on private judgment, fantasy, and interest of individuals, *is but a hideous carcass, a frightful skeleton of religion*, and is no more the doctrine of Jesus Christ and his Church than that of Jews, Pagans, or Turks." (Rev. E. O'Donnell's Comp. Theol. S. Thomas, vol. 2. chapt. iii.) O great St. Thomas, and Angelic Doctor of the Church! Had S. O. lived at the time when you published those words, he would have called them *wholly untrue, beginning, middle*, and *end*. He would never have forgiven you for calling Protestant doctrine a *hideous carcass, a frightful skeleton of religion*, and for saying that it is no more the doctrine of Christ and his Church than that of Jews, Pagans, or Turks. In the days of St. Thomas Aquinas it would also have been very difficult to find an editor of a newspaper who, like the Rev. Father Cronin, would have cheerfully endorsed the doctrine of S. O.

Alas! he cannot see the difference between divine and human faith—between the faith of Catholics and that of Protestants, how could he see and understand the consequences of Protestant belief? He never learned logic enough to draw right conclusions from right premises. Not being able to see that our answer is a very natural conclusion from its premises—the belief of Protestants in Christ, he impudently calls it *wholly untrue, beginning, middle, and end.* How far the beginning of the answer goes, where the middle of it begins, and how far it goes, and where the end of it begins, he does not tell, nor does he give the least reason why the beginning of the answer is wholly untrue, nor does he prove that the middle and end of it are false. All proud ignorant men give such answers, when they are unable to give a better one. It is an answer that a Protestant preacher may give, but is not expected from S. O. If this is not for him the way to tell the truth, and shame the devil, it is most assuredly the best way to shame himself.

As we have explained to him the premises of our answer, we must now also make clear to him the conclusion— the answer drawn from its premises. He says quite correctly that "the personality the author (Rev. M. Muller, C. SS. R.) sets up as the Christ of Protestants is a *caricature* which the author should not have associated with the Holy Name." Well, is there any worse caricature of Christ than the personality of Antichrist, as described in Holy Scripture? And yet, how often does not Holy Scripture associate this caricature of Christ with the Holy Name when speaking of the true Christ? But be it remembered that, as the apostasy of the Gentiles from the Patriarchal faith brought forth the worst caricatures of the true God, —idols and idol-worship, so, in like manner, the apostasy of Protestants from the true Catholic faith in Christ will

finally bring forth the worst caricature of the true Christ—
the personality of Antichrist.

A body which has lost the principle of its animation becomes dust. Hence it is an axiom that the change or perversion of the principles by which anything is produced is the destruction of that very thing. If you can change or pervert the principles from which anything springs, you destroy it. For instance, one single foreign element introduced into the blood produces death; one false assumption admitted into science destroys its certainty; one false principle admitted into faith and morals is fatal. The so-called Reformers started wrong. They would reform the Church by placing her under human control. Their successors have, in each generation, found they did not go far enough, and have, each in turn, struggled to push it further and further, till they find themselves without any Church life, without faith, without religion, and beginning to doubt if there be a God. It is a well-known fact that, before the so-called Reformation, infidels were scarcely known in the Christian world. Since that event they have come forth in swarms. It is therefore historically correct that the same principle that created Protestantism three centuries ago has never ceased, since that time, to spin it out into a thousand different sects, and has concluded by covering Europe and America with that multitude of free-thinkers and infidels who place these countries on the verge of ruin.

The individual reason taking, as it does, the place of faith, the true Protestant, whether he believes it or not, is an infidel in germ, and the infidel is a Protessant in full bloom. In other words, infidelity is nothing but Protestantism in the highest degree. Hence it is that Edgar Quinet, a great herald of Protestantism, is right in styling the Protestant sects *the thousand gates open to get out of Christianity*.

No wonder, then, that thousands of Protestants have ended and continue to end in framing their own formula thus: "I believe in nothing." And here I ask, what is

Out of the Catholic Church there is No Salvation. 119

easier, from this state of religion and infidelity, than the passage to idolatry?

This assertion may seem incredible to some at this day, and may be considered an absurdity; but idolatry is expressly mentioned in the Apocalypse as existing in the time of Antichrist And, indeed, our surprise will much abate, if we take into consideration the temper and disposition of the present times. When men divest themselves, as they seem to do at present, of all fear of the Supreme Being, of all respect of their Creator and Lord; when they surrender themselves to the gratification of sensuality; when they give full freedom to the human passions, and direct their whole study to the pursuits of a corrupt world, with a total forgetfulness of a future state; when they give children a godless education, and have no longer any religion to teach them, may we not say that the transition to idolatry is easy? When all the steps to a certain point are taken, what wonder if we arrive at that point? Such was the gradual degeneracy of mankind in the early ages of the world, that brought on the abominable practices of idol-worship.

Of course, it will be said that we have the happiness of living in the most enlightened of all ages; our knowledge is more perfect, our ideas more developed and refined, the human faculties more improved and better cultivated, than they ever were before; in fine, that the present race of mankind may be reckoned a society of philosophers, when compared to the generations that have gone before. How is it possible, then, that such stupidity can seize upon the human mind as to sink it into idolatry?

This kind of reasoning is more specious than solid. For, allowing the present times to surpass the past in refinement and knowledge, it must be said that they are proportionately more vicious. Refinement of reason has contributed, as every one knows, to refine upon the means of gratifying the human passions.

Besides, however enlightened the mind may be supposed to be, if the heart is corrupt, the excesses into which a man will run are evidenced by daily experience.

Witness our modern spiritism (spiritualism). What else is our modern spiritualism than a revival of the old heathen idol-worship ?

Satan is constantly engaged in doing all in his power to entice men away from God, and to have himself worshipped instead of the Creator. The introduction, establishment, persistence, and power of the various cruel, revolting superstitions of the ancient heathen world, or of pagan nations in modern times, are nothing but the work of the devil. They reveal a more than human power. God permitted Satan to operate upon man's morbid nature, as a deserved punishment upon the Gentiles for their hatred of truth and their apostasy from the primitive religion. Men left to themselves, to human nature alone, however low they might be prone to descend, never could descend so low as to worship wood and stone, four-footed beasts, and creeping things. To do this needs satanic delusion.

Paganism in its old form was doomed. Christianity had silenced the oracles and driven the devils back to hell. How was the devil to re-establish his worship on earth, and carry on his war against the Son of God and the religion which he taught us ? Evidently only by changing his tactics and turning the truth into a lie. He found men in all the heresiarchs who, like Eve, gave ear to his suggestions, and believed him more than the Infallible Word of Jesus Christ. Thus he has succeeded in banishing the true religion from whole countries, or in mixing it with false doctrines. He has prevailed upon thousands to believe the doctrines of vain, self-conceited men, rather than the religion taught by Jesus Christ and his Apostles. It is by heresies, revolutions, bad secret societies, and godless State school education, that he has succeeded so far as to bring thousands of men back to a state of heathenism and infidelity. The time has come for him to introduce idolatry, or his own worship. To do this he makes use of spiritualism. Through the spirit-mediums he performs lying wonders. He gives pretended revelations from the spirit-world, in order to destroy or weaken all faith in divine revelation. He thus strives to re-establish in Christian lands that very same devil-worship which has so long existed among heathen nations, and which our Lord Jesus Christ came to destroy. The Holy Scriptures assure us that all the gods of the heathens are devils (" *Omnes dii gentium dæmonia.*"—Ps.) These demons took possession of the idols made of wood or stone, of gold or silver; they had temples erected in their honor; they had their sacrifices, their priests; and their priestesses. They uttered oracles. They were consulted through their mediums in all affairs of importance, and especially in order to find out the future, precisely as they are consulted by our modern spiritualists at the present day.

In modern spiritualism the devil communicates with men by means of tables, chairs, tablets, or planchette; or by rapping, writing, seeing and speaking mediums. It is all the same to the devil, whether he communicates with men and leads them astray by means of idols, or by means of tables, chairs, planchette, and the like.

Assuredly, if the philosopher is not governed by the power of religion, his conduct will be absurd and even despicable to the most ignorant individual of the lowest rank.

Socrates, Cicero, Seneca, are said to have been acquainted with the knowledge of one Supreme God; but they had not courage to profess his worship, and in their public conduct basely sacrificed to stocks and stones with the vulgar. When men have banished from their heart the sense of religion, and despise the rights of justice, (and is this not the case with numbers?) will many of them scruple to offer incense to a statue, if by so doing they serve their ambition, their interest, or whatever may be their favorite passion? Where is the cause for surprise, then, if infidelity and irreligion be succeeded by idolatry? That pride alone, when inflamed with a constant flow of prosperity, may raise a man to the extravagant presumption of claiming for himself divine honors, we see in the example of Alexander, the celebrated Macedonian conqueror, and of several emperors of Babylon and ancient Rome. From suggestions of that same principle of pride, it will happen that Antichrist, elevated by a

122 *Out of the Catholic Church there is No Salvation.*

continued course of victories and conquests, will set himself up for a god. And as at that time the propagation of infidelity, irreligion, and immorality will have become universal, this defection from faith, disregard for its teachers, licentiousness in opinions, depravity in morals, will so far deaden all influence of religion, and cause such degeneracy in mankind, that many will be base enough even to espouse idolatry, to yield to the absurd impiety of worshipping the worst caricature of Christ, Antichrist, as their Lord and God; some out of fear for what they may lose, others to gain what they covet.

Then will it be evident to all that infidelity, and even idolatry, existed in the Protestant principle of private judgment, as the oak exists in the acorn, as the consequence is in the premise; or, in other words, that this principle was but the powerful weapon of Satan to carry on his war against Christ; of the sons of Belial to fight the keepers of the law; of false anti-social liberty to destroy true and rational liberty—to make worshippers of the devil out of the worshippers of God.

§ 10. S. O. AVOWS THAT OUR CONCLUSION IS CORRECT, BUT TELLS MORE D—D LIES.

S. O. continues to quote from our *Explanation of Christian Doctrine* and to comment on it.

"*Q.* Will such a faith in such a Christ save Protestants? *Ans.* No sensible man will assert such an absurdity."

"The answer is correct, for such a faith in such a Christ would bring about such a salvation as every sensible man would be perfectly willing to resign to such an author."

We have shown in our *Explanation* that the Roman Catholic Church only is the true Church of Jesus Christ; that Christ's doctrine is to be found only in this true Church; that only the members of this Church have *absolute divine* faith in Christ and in all that he has done for our salvation; that only in this divine faith salvation is possible, because it is the foundation of justification; we have shown that Protestants have rejected all *divine* faith in Jesus Christ and in his doctrine; that, by rejecting Christ's Church, they have rejected Christ himself and his doctrine, and that therefore, we say, it is an absurdity for people to believe that they can be saved in their faith, which is but a human invention which has led and still leads to the worst kinds of abominitions. But as S. O. seems to have so much faith and confidence in the faith of Protestants in Christ, all Catholics are perfectly willing not to disturb him in his honest belief and in his invincible ignorance. But at the same time we protest against the lies he tells in his continuation of the above answer, namely:

"It is strange how some pious and good people consider it their religious duty and pleasure to see to it that their dissenting neighbors are properly and comfortably damned. They remind one of certain persons immortalized in Hudibras, who:—

> ' Compound for sins they are inclined to
> By damning those they have no mind to,"

or words to that effect."

Here S. O. most impudently asserts that some pious and good people (Catholics, especially the Rev. M. Muller, C. S. S. R., the author of *Explanation of Christian Doctrine*) consider it their *religious duty* and *pleasure!* to see to it that their dissenting neighbors are properly and comfortably damned!"

Did ever a more infamous calumny come from the lips of a heretic against Catholics! Alas! the Rev. Editor of the *B. C. U.* and *T.* solemnly assures us that the above words come neither from a Jew nor from a heretic; he solemnly assures us that they were written by the most prominent priest in the U. S., and he has cheerfully endorsed them and had them printed for the benefit of the readers of the *C. U.* and *T.*

See, how, in plain words, S. O. gives himself the lie in a palpable and shameful manner by quoting from our *Explanation* the following answer:—

124 *Out of the Catholic Church there is No Salvation.*

"*Q.* What are we to think of the salvation of those who are out of the pale of the Church without any fault of theirs, and who never had any opportunity of knowing better ? *Ans.* Their inculpable ignorance will not save them ; but if they fear God and live up to their conscience, God, in his infinite mercy, will furnish them with the necessary means of salvation, even so as to send, if needed, an angel to instruct them in the Catholic faith, rather than let them perish through inculpable ignorance."

Alas! what a shame for S. O. to fall from one abyss of lies and false assertions into another !

§ 11. S. O. DECLARES THAT THE FINAL SENTENCE OF THE ETERNAL JUDGE ON THE LAST DAY WILL FALL ONLY UPON BAD CATHOLICS—FROM HIS OWN ARGUMENT IT IS PROVED THAT PROTESTANTS TOO ARE INCLUDED IN THAT SENTENCE.

He quotes again :—

"*Q.* What will Christ say to them on the day of judgment ? *Ans.* I know you not, because you never knew me."

"It is not, " he says, " special pleading for me to take the author at his word, since his argument is that Protestants do not *know* the true Christ, and to say that at the day of judgment no man will be condemned by Christ *because* he never knew Him. *No man will be condemned on account of his ignorance*, neither Protestant, nor heathen, nor, I may add, Catholic either. He can be condemned only because, when knowing Christ, he has refused to accept Him, to believe in Him, to do his will and keep his commandments. Instead of our Lords' saying that to Protestants, who never knew the truth of his doctrines as taught by the Catholic Church, it is those Catholics he threatens to disown who, knowing Him, have denied Him by their sinful lives,—who, knowing the will of the Lord, did it not. " And he shall say to you : I know you not whence you are, depart from me, all ye workers of iniquity. " (St. Luke, xiii. 26.-27). "

As it is not special pleading for S. O. to take the Author of *Explanation* at his word, because the Author's argument is that Protestants do not *know* the true Christ, it will, anyhow, be special pleading for the author of *Explanation* to take S. O. at his word, since his argument has been all along that Protestants *do know* the true Christ and believe precisely what the Catholic Church teaches concerning Christ. If S. O. then declares that the above sentence affects "those Catholics who, knowing Christ, have denied him by their sinful lives,—who, knowing the will of the Lord, did it not," he must also, for the very same reason, declare that those Protestants, too, are included in the sentence of the eternal judge, who, knowing Christ, have denied him by their sinful lives—who, knowing the will of the Lord, did it not.

As S. O., like Protestants, uses his own private interpretation of Holy Scripture, at least of the above sentence of the eternal judge, contrary to what the Vatican Council declared on this subject, we here add what St. Augustine (Serm. 23.) says concerning those words of Christ, "I know you not." "If he who knows all things," says this great Doctor of the Church, declares '*I know you not,*' he means to say, "I reprobate you," because I never knew you as belonging to my fold by absolute, divine faith in all my words and in all I have done for your salvation, and so you have always remained separated from me, and therefore I reprobate you."

S. O. will do well to reflect on this interpretation of the above final sentence of Christ. We also submit to his examination the following words of Christ, which he and all his Protestant friends will hear on the day of doom.

"He that shall be ashamed of me and of my words in this adulterous and sinful generation, the Son of Man also will be ashamed of him, when he shall come in the glory of his Father, with the holy angels." (Mark. viii. 38.) In this text it is stated in the plainest terms that to be ashamed, not only of Christ, but also of his words, that is, of his doctrine, of his religion, and consequently of his Church,—the depositary of that faith,—is a mortal sin, and will entail on the soul eternal damnation. But if *to be ashamed* of Christ and his doctrine will condemn the soul to hell, how much more the *denying* of Christ and of his, the holy Catholic, Church! Is not S. O. to a certain degree ashamed of Christ and of his doctrine when he says so much in favor of Protestant belief, and so very little in favor of Catholic faith; when he declares that we have misrepresented Catholic and Protestant doctrines; when he asserts that the proofs we gave and which are given by the best theologians for the truth that there is no salvation out of the Church, are false, etc., etc. ? Is it not to deny, to a certain degree, Christ and his doctrine, when he declares that the faith of Protestants in Christ is precisely the same as that of Catholics? Is not this as much as to say: The devil's religion is as good as that of God; falsehood is as good as truth; counterfeit Christianity is as good as true Christianity; human faith is as good as divine faith; the way to hell is as good as the way to heaven?

O happy Protestants ! A little while ago, S. O. said of you, that " you believe precisely what the Catholic Church teaches, namely, that Jesus Christ is true God and true man, etc.; that Protestants believe all that the Catholic Church believes of the facts of his divine life, miracles, passion, death and resurrection. This is an undeniable truth." And now he says, " that you never knew the truth of Christ's doctrines as taught by the Catholic Church; " and what he called an *undeniable* truth, he here denies in plain words. He also says of you that "the Protestant doctrine of the rule of faith,—each one's private interpretation of the written Word of God, is unquestionably erroneous, and immediately after he says that you do not believe in this rule. He says that Protestants are in error as to the divine will. This we know ; but on account of this error, they are not guilty before God ; and then again he partly denies this assertion by saying that wilful, obstinate, truth-rejecting Protestants are guilty." What a consolation for Protestants to learn these infallible oracles from S. O., to be assured by him that the words of Christ, "I know you not whence you are, all ye workers of iniquity," will be addressed, not to Protestants, but only to Catholics; to learn from him for certain that "*no man* will be condemned on account of his ignorance, neither Protestant, nor heathen, nor Catholic either." Although all Catholic theologians teach that *culpable* ignorance of the means of salvation and of our great duties is a mortal sin, yet he emphatically assures every Protestant, every heathen, and every Catholic that "*no man* will be condemned on account of his ignorance." If your ignorance has been inculpable, so much the better, because, *though you should commit sins against your conscience,* yet you will not be condemned, because no one is condemned on account of such inculpable ignorance! What dazzling theological light beams forth for modern Protestants from the infallible oracles of S. O! How consoling for them to be quite sure that in this case, as in every other, he has displayed his customary omniscience. Catholic theology, dogmatic and moral, logic, history of the Catholic Church and of society, as every one can see, are his strong points. He might possibly err in other matters, but not in these. The less fortunate ancestors of modern Protestants had no such guide. What little help they could get from the writings of St. Augustine and other Fathers of the Church, they had; but the *surer* and *more luminous* teaching of S. O., communicated through the *Catholic U.* and *T.* of Buffalo, was reserved for the Protestants of the present generation. The sun of that journal has not been long above the horizon. It arose to receive and to reflect upon its readers the electric theological rays of one of the greatest oracles that ever lived—who looks upon himself as an apostle of enlightenment and measures the success of his enlightenment by the success he hopes to have in persuading, not only Catholics, but especially Protestants, and even the heathen, to believe that the Rev. M. Muller, C.SS.R., has in his *Explanation* misrepresented Catholic and Protestant belief—God and the devil.

§ 12. S. O. Declares the Honest life of Protestants a Standing Reproach to bad Catholics.

"Many Protestants," says S. O., "by reason of their honest, upright, and charitable lives, are a standing reproach to bad Catholics."

We teach, indeed, and we firmly believe, that there is no salvation out of the Catholic Church; yet we do not teach that all who are members of the Catholic Church will be saved. "Certainly, in our cities and large towns," says Dr. O. A. Brownson, "aye, even in small villages of our great country, may be found many so-called liberal or nominal Catholics, who are no credit to our religion, to their spiritual Mother,· the Church. Subjected as they were, in the land of their birth, to the restraints imposed by Protestant or quasi-Protestant governments, they feel, on coming here, that they are loosed from all restraint; and forgetting the obedience that they owe to their pastors, to the prelates whom the Holy Ghost has placed over them, they become insubordinate, and live more like non-Catholics than Catholics. The children of these are, to a great extent, shamefully neglected and suffered to grow up without sufficient moral and religious instruction, and to become the recruits of our vicious population. This is certainly to be deplored, but can easily be explained without prejudice to the truth and holiness of the Catholic religion, by adverting to the condition to which those individuals were reduced before coming to this country; to their disappointments in a strange land; to their exposure to new and unlooked-for temptations; to the fact that they were by no means the best of Catholics, even in their native countries; to their poverty, destitution, ignorance, insufficient culture, and a certain natural shiftlessness and recklessness, as well as to the great lack of Catholic schools, churches, and fervent priests. As low and degraded as this class of the Catholic population may be, they are not so low as the corresponding class of non-Catholics in every nation; at the worst, there is always some germ that, with proper care, may be nursed into life, that may blossom and bear fruit. Their mother, the Church, never ceases to warn them to repent and be cleansed from their sins by the sacrament of penance. If they do not heed the voice of their mother, but continue to live in sin to the end of their lives, their condemnation will be greater than that of those who were born in an inheritance of error, and whose minds have never been penetrated by the light of truth. 'That servant,' says Jesus Christ, 'who knew the will of his Lord, and did not according to his will, shall be beaten with many stripes.' (Luke, xii. 47.)"

No doubt, it is, generally speaking, far more easy to reconcile with God a disedifying Catholic, who has not renounced the faith, than to get a Protestant so far as to renounce his errors, and prejudices, and secret sins that he may be addicted to, and to do all that is necessary to obtain forgiveness. How many Catholics have there been, who, for several years, led disedifying lives, and afterwards became models of virtue, even great saints. A disedifying Catholic, no doubt, displeases God on account of his sins, but not on account of his faith. A Protestant, however, cannot please God, as long as he remains without divine faith, without which it is impossible to please God, says the Holy Ghost in Holy Scripture. And if faith, without good works, is dead to a certain degree, it should be remembered that good works performed without divine faith are also dead.

What right, therefore, has S. O. to say that, by reason of their honest, upright, and charitable lives, many Protestants are a standing reproach to bad Catholics. It would have been more honorable for him, it would have done more good to Protestants, if he had said that the millions of Catholics in Ireland and other countries, who have died for their faith in the persecutions they had to suffer from Protestants, are a standing reproach to all kinds of Protestants; that the lives of virginity and self-sacrifice that so many saintly Catholics lead, especially thousands of holy sisters, brothers, and priests, is a standing reproach to Protestants as long as they live in heresy.

§ 13. S. O.'s Pharisaical Language.

"This *Explanation*," says S. O., "is a book which wounds the sincere Protestant who is honestly seeking the truth, and causing him to turn hopelessly and despairingly from the true spouse of Christ his Redeemer."

There is nothing in which the great Apostle of the Gentiles seems more to glory than in his ardent zeal for the salvation of souls, and in the sincerity of his heart in delivering to the world the sacred truths of eternity pure and uncorrupted. He was not ashamed of these divine truths; he rejoiced when he was called to suffer for them; he had no worldly interest in view in preaching them; he sought not the esteem and favor of men in delivering them; his only view was to promote the honor of his blessed Master, and to gain souls to him, and therefore he had no idea of using flattering words, or of accommodating the doctrine of the Gospel to the humors of men.

He knew that the truths revealed by Jesus Christ are unalterable; that "heaven and earth shall pass away, but his words shall never pass away;" and that, therefore, to corrupt these sacred words, though but in one single article, would be "a perverting the Gospel of Christ." (Gal. i. 7), a sin so grievous, that the Holy Ghost, by his mouth, pronounces a curse upon any one, though an angel from heaven, who shall dare to be guilty of it. Hence he describes his own conduct in preaching the Gospel as follows: "Ye know, from the first day that I came into Asia, in what manner I have been with you for all the time. . . . How I have kept back nothing that was profitable to you, but have preached it to you, and taught you publicly, and from house to house." (Acts xx. 18, 20.) "We had confidence in our God, to speak to you the Gospel of God in much carefulness; . . . not as pleasing men, but God, who proveth our hearts; for neither have we used at any time the speech of flattery, as you know, nor taken occasion of covetousness; God is witness. Nor sought we glory of men, neither of you, nor of others." (I. Thess. ii. 2, 4.) " For we are not as many, adulterating the Word of God; but with sincerity, but as from God, in the sight of God, we speak in Christ." (II. Cor. ii. 17.) " We renounce the hidden things of dishonesty, not walking in craftiness, nor adulterating the Word of God, but by manifestation of the truth commending ourselves to every man's conscience in the sight of God; . . . for we preach not ourselves, but Jesus Christ our Lord." (II. Cor. iv. 2, 5.) "Do I speak to please men? If I yet pleased men I should not be a servant of Christ." (Gal. i. 10.) Now, "Christ sent me to preach the Gospel, not in wisdom of speech, lest the cross of Christ should be made void; for the word of the cross to them, indeed, that perish, is foolishness; but to them that are saved, that is, to us, it is the power of God. . . . And it pleased God by the foolishness of our preaching to save them that believe. . . . For the foolishness of God is wiser than men, and the weakness of God is stronger than men . . . . and the foolish things of the world God hath chosen, that he may confound the wise; and the weak things of the world hath God chosen that he may confound the strong, . . . that no flesh should glory in his sight." (I. Cor. i. 17.) " But I am not ashamed of the Gospel; for it is the power of God unto salvation to every one that believeth." (Rom. i. 16.) And therefore, "I, when I came among you, came not in loftiness of speech or of wisdom, declaring to you the testimony of Christ; and my preaching was not in the persuasive words of human wisdom, but in showing of the Spirit, and in power; that your faith might not stand on the wisdom of men, but on the power of God." (I. Cor. ii. 1.)

The Church of Christ, animated by the same divine spirit of truth which inspired this holy Apostle, has at all times regulated her conduct according to the model set before her in his own words and example. "Earnestly contending for the faith once delivered to the saints" (Jude, ver. 3.) her continual care is "to keep that which is committed to her trust" pure and undefiled, "avoiding all profane novelties of words" (I. Tim. vi. 20.), that the sacred *words* of God, "once put into her mouth, may never depart from her, from henceforth and for ever." (Isa. lix. 21.) She therefore knows not what it is to temporize in religion, in order to please men, nor to adulterate the Gospel of Christ to humor them; she declares the sacred truths revealed by Jesus Christ in their original simplicity, without seeking to adorn them with the persuasive words of human wisdom, much less to disguise them in a garb not their own. Truth, plain and unadorned, is the only weapon she employs against her adversaries, regardless of their censure or their approbation. "This is the truth," she says, "revealed by God; this ye must embrace, or ye can have no part with him." If the world look upon what she says as foolishness, she is not surprised, for she knows that "the sensual man perceiveth not the things that are of the Spirit of God; for it is foolishness to him, and he cannot understand" (I. Cor. ii. 14.), but that "the foolishness of God is wiser than men"; and pitying this blindness, she earnestly prays God to enlighten them, "with modesty admonishing them, . . . if, peradventure, God may give them repentance to know the truth." (II. Tim. ii. 25.)

If ever there was a time when this conduct of the Church was necessary, the present age seems particularly to demand it. At present the gates of hell seem opened, and infidelity of every kind stalks lawless on the earth; the sacred truths of religion are reviled and denied, the Gospel adulterated by countless contradictory interpretations; its original simplicity disfigured by loftiness of speech and the persuasive words of human wisdom. A thousand condescensions and compliances are admitted and received, by which the purity of faith and morals greatly suffers, and the "narrow way that leads to life," is converted into the "broad road that leads to destruction." This observation applies particularly to that latitudinarian opinion, so common nowadays, that *a man may be saved in any religion*, *provided he lives a good moral life according to the light he has;* for, by this, the faith of Christ is made void, and the Gospel rendered of no avail. A Jew, a Mahometan, a heathen, a deist, an atheist, are all comprehended in this scheme, and if they live a good moral life, have an equal right to salvation with a Christian! To be a member of the Church of Christ is no longer necessary; for whether we belong to her or not, if we live a good moral life, we are in the way of salvation! What a wide field does this open to human passions! What license does it give to the caprice of the human mind! It is therefore of the utmost consequence to state and to show plainly the revealed Catholic truth that "there is no salvation out of the Catholic Church."

A strong, vigorous, and uncompromising presentation of this Catholic truth must be made against those soft, weak, timid, liberalizing Catholics, who labor to explain away all the points of Catholic faith offensive to non-Catholics, and to make it appear that there is no question of life and death, of heaven and hell, involved in the differences between us and Protestants. This truth is hated by many, we know, and yet it is a truth revealed by God to his Church for our salvation.

St. Thomas asks the question: "Can man hate truth?" and he answers: "Truth in general never provokes hatred, but it can in a particular manner. As to good, which is always desirable, no one could resist its attractions or hate it; but it is not the same in regard to truth. Truth, in general, is always in harmony with our nature, but it may happen in certain cases that it is not agreeable to our feelings and prejudice. Hence St. Augustine says: 'man likes the splendor and beauty of truth, but he cannot bear its precepts and remonstrances.' The great Apostle says likewise: 'Am I then become your enemy, because I tell you the truth?'" (Gal. iv. 16.)

St. Thomas also asks the question: "Should Christ *have preached to the Jews without offending them?*"

The salvation of the people is preferable to the caprice and bigotry of individuals. If their perversity and fanaticism is huffed at what the true minister of God preaches, he must not be daunted and troubled on that account, for the Word of God is free, in spite of tongue and sword. If the truth scandalizes the wicked, says St. Gregory, it is better to suffer their scandal than to discontinue the doctrine of grace and truth. Who were those who took offence at our Saviour's doctrine? A small number of fanatic Scribes and Pharisees, full of hypocrisy and wickedness, who, through malice and jealousy, opposed the divine doctrine, which alone could save and sanctify the people. "Let them alone," said our divine Saviour, "they are blind, and if the blind leads the blind they shall both fall into the pit." (Matt. xv. 14.)

"At the time of the Vatican Council," says Cardinal Manning, "there were some who thought that the Catholic doctrine of the infallibility of the Pope should not be defined, lest schismatics and heretics should be repelled yet further from the Church. But their reason was not good. The reason that prevailed for the definition of the dogma in question was that Catholics have a right to be taught by the Council what they are to believe in so weighty a matter, lest the pernicious error of the time should in the end infect simple minds and the masses of the people unawares. Hence it was that the Fathers of Lyons and of Trent deemed themselves bound to establish the doctrine of the truth, notwithstanding the offence that might be taken by schismatics and heretics. For if these seek the truth in sincerity, they will not be repelled, but, on the contrary, drawn towards us, when they see on what foundations chiefly repose the truths taught by the Catholic Church. But should any of them feel repelled by stating the truth, they are only such as seek a pretext for not joining the Catholic Church. (See Postulatum of Vat. Counc.)

If we desire that all those who are not members of the Catholic Church should cease to deceive themselves as to the true character of their belief, and propose to them considerations which may contribute to that result, it is certainly not from enmity to their persons, nor from indifference to their welfare. As long as they remain victims of a delusion as gross as that which makes the Jew still cling to his abolished synagogue, and which only a miracle of grace can dispel, some of them will probably resent the counsels of their truest friends; but why should they take us for enemies. "The Christian," says Tertullian, "is the enemy of no one," not even of his persecutors. He hates heresy because God hates it; but he has only compassion for those who are caught in its snares. Whether he exhorts or reproves them, he displays not malice, but charity. He knows that they are, of all men, the most helpless; and when his voice of warning is most vehement, he is only doing what the Church has done from the beginning. His voice is but the echo of hers. We are told that, before the Council of Nice, she had already condemned thirty-eight different heresies; and in every case she pronounced anathema upon those who held them. And she was as truly the mouthpiece of God in her judicial as in her teaching office.

The Church is, indeed, uncompromising in matters of truth. Truth is the honor of the Church. The Church is the most honorable of all societies. She is the highest standard of honor, because she judges all things in the light of God, who is the source of all honor. A man who has no love for the truth, a man who tells a wilful lie or takes a false oath, is considered dishonored. No one cares for him, and it would be unreasonable to accuse one of intolerance or bigotry because he refuses to associate with a man who has no love for the truth. It would be just as unreasonable to accuse the Catholic Church of intolerance, or bigotry, or want of charity, because she excludes from her society, and pronounces anathema upon, those who have no regard for the truth, and remain wilfully out of her communion.

If the Church believed that men could be saved in any religion whatever, or without any at all, it would be uncharitable in her to announce to the world that out of her there is no salvation. But as she knows and maintains that there is but one faith, as there is but one God and

Lord of all, and that she is in possession of that one faith, and that without that faith it is impossible to please God and be saved, it would be very uncharitable in her and in all her children, to hide Christ's doctrine from the world. To warn our neighbor when he is in imminent danger of falling into a deep abyss, is considered an act of great charity. It is a greater act of charity to warn non-Catholics of the certain danger in which they are of falling into the abyss of hell, since Jesus Christ, and the Apostles themselves, and all their successors, have always most emphatically asserted that out of the Church there is no salvation.

This answer, we think, is plain enough for S. O. The heretical animus, which characterizes his *Queer Explanation* throughout, is calculated only to keep honest Protestants as far from the Catholic Church as ever.

PART II.

Of Those Heretics who are not guilty of the sin of Heresy.

Before we speak in detail of this class of heretics we must explain what is meant by LAW and CONSCIENCE.

§ 1. NATURAL LAW. (According to St. Thomas Aquinas.)

God governs and directs the material world and all irrational creatures according to the laws of his omnipotence and wisdom, having provided every creature with means proportioned to the end which it has gradually to fulfil in time and place. "Thy Providence, O Father, governeth all." (Wisd. xiv. 3.) "God, with a certain law and compass, enclosed the depth; he compassed the sea with its bounds, and set a law to the waters, that they should not pass their limits." (Prov. viii. 27–30.) As to *rational* creatures—angels and men—God wishes to govern them by the law of goodness and justice.

The law of God's goodness for men is that they shall always glorify God by doing his holy will; that all their homage and adoration are due to him alone, and are never to be given to any creature; that they are to honor, reverence, and love those who gave them birth and brought them up; that they are not to kill one another, nor live like brutes, nor rob one another, but that every one is to treat his fellow-men as he wishes to be treated by them. To this law of divine goodness, God added for mankind the law of his justice; that is, if any one refuses to obey this law of divine goodness, he shall be subjected to the torments which God's justice has decreed for all rebellious creatures.

This law of his goodness and justice God impressed upon mankind from the very beginning. "See," says St. Paul, "the goodness and severity of God: towards them, indeed, that are fallen, the severity · but towards thee, the goodness of God, if thou abide in goodness." (Rom. xi. 22.)

This law of God's goodness and justice is also called *Natural Law*—Law of Nature, because it is naturally impressed on the mind and heart of every rational being, and makes him know the difference between good and evil.

As man possesses the gift of reason, or, as it is sometimes called, "the light of nature," no man is left in utter ignorance of God and of his will—of the Natural Law. "God has not left himself without testimony" (Acts, xiv. 16), even among the heathens, who, if they do not have full light and knowledge, may yet, as St. Paul told the Athenians, "feel after him, or find him" (Acts, xvii. 27.) "For when the Gentiles," he says, "who have not the law, do by nature those things that are of the law, these, not having the law, are a law unto themselves, who show the works of the law written in their hearts, their conscience bearing witness to them." (Rom. ii. 14, 15.) This *light of nature* is a participation of the eternal law or wisdom of God. "The light of thy countenance, O Lord, is signed upon us," says the Royal Prophet (Ps. iv.), thus indicating that the light of reason, which makes us distinguish between good and evil, right and wrong, is nothing else than the impression of divine light on the soul of man.

As all men have this light of nature as a rule of right and wrong, no man can plead utter ignorance of right and wrong. Hence it is that we find, even in the heathen nations, the obligations of the natural law respected. This eternal, natural law of right and wrong is called *moral* law, because natural law, or sound reason, is the rule and standard of good morals; it is the rule to guide men in all their actions; it tells them what is good and bad, what they must do or avoid.

All men, without exception, know the light of nature, the first and general principles of right and wrong. But all do not know the necessary conclusions deduced from these principles. A geometrician in Paris comes to the same conclusion as another in London or in any other part of the world, that, for instance, three angles of a triangle are equal to two right angels, etc. Practical reason draws similar conclusions, if we do not lose sight of general principles; but by deviating from these principles, reason varies with circumstances. For instance, if a sum of money was intrusted to you, reason commands you to give it back to the owner. But if you knew he wanted it for the purpose of committing some bad action, as vengeance against his neighbor or country, then reason forbids you to give it to him for such a wicked deed. Still, some may think and act differently, and be, therefore, mistaken in losing sight of general principles, as others fall into error in overlooking the first principles. Natural law, therefore, is invariable for all, as long as they do not lose sight of the first principles of right and wrong.

As Natural Law comprises the first principles of right and wrong, these principles are unchangeable. It is self-evident that that which is natural cannot but be. For instance, the law of nature obliges us to worship God and love him. God, then, after having given us life and reason, never changes what is naturally necessary for his creature, namely, to adore and love his creator. Hence the natural law imperatively enjoins upon us the duties of gratitude and love towards God, from which nothing can exempt us.

§ 2. THE WRITTEN LAW.

"The laws of nature," says St. Thomas Aquinas, "and all principles of justice and morality, were almost effaced in the time which elapsed between Adam and Moses. At the time of Abraham, all nations had fallen into idolatry. They were plunged into all sorts of vices. Almost all shut their eyes to the light of reason. They were like one who is falling into an abyss. The deeper he falls, the less day-light he sees. God permitted the wicked to fall into this state of universal ignorance and impiety, in order to humble their pride and arrogance. Always full of pride and perversity, they pretend that their private reason alone is sufficient for them to know their duties, and their natural powers to practise them. So, after that sad experience of their ignorance and impiety, God, in his mercy, came to their assistance by giving them the written law in the person of Moses, as a remedy for their blindness and obstinacy. The natural law is imperfect. Hence a divine law is absolutely necessary to direct us in the way of eternal beatitude. We cannot attain to a supernatural end by natural or human means. We need a divine law to direct our thoughts and actions towards that end. The judgment of men is inconsistent and changeable. They need an infallible law to direct and rectify their judgment, in order to know with certainty what they must do and avoid in order to obtain everlasting happiness. So Almighty God added to the natural law a higher law, relating to a higher end, in the form of the Mosaic and evangelical law."

"The Law," says St. Paul, "was given through the agency of angels by the hand of a mediator." (Gal. iii. 19.) And St. Stephen said to the Jews: "Ye have received the law by the ministry of angels." (Acts, vii. 53.) St.

Dionysius the Areopagite says that the angels are commissioned to bring all messages from heaven to earth, that is from God to man.

The principal object of divine law is to render man holy. "Be ye holy, as I am holy," says the Lord. This holiness consists in perfect love of God and man. This charity is the accomplishment of the Law. It is, then, by the practice of virtue that we become holy and resemble God. Hence it was necessary that the Old Law should contain different moral precepts regarding the virtues necessary for the perfect happiness of man. These moral precepts are all contained in the ten commandments. These commandments are a full explanation of the natural law. They are of a divine institution. They were communicated by the ministry of angels to Moses, who proclaimed them all to the Hebrew people; but he added other precepts, ordinances, and ceremonies for the punctual observance of the commandments.

The three first prescribe our duties towards God; that is, to worship him by faith, hope, and charity; and the seven last prescribe our duties towards all our fellow-men.

§ 3. THE NEW LAW OR THE LAW OF GRACE.

The whole human race, says St. Thomas Aquinas, was destined to live successively during three distinct periods. The first period was that of the Old Law, the second that of the New Law, and the third and last that of the kingdom of eternal glory. St. Paul says that the Old Law (the many ceremonial precepts) was abolished on account of its weakness and unprofitableness, for it brought nothing to perfection; but it brought into us a better hope, by which we draw nigh to God. (Heb. vii. 8.) He says again: "That the Old Law and commandment are indeed holy, just and good." Now we say that a doctrine is good when it is conformable to truth, and we say that a law is good when it is consistent with reason. Such was the Old Law; for it repressed concupiscence, which militates against reason, and it forbade all transgressions contrary to human reason and the divine Law. It acted as a physician does in restoring a patient to health by salutary prescriptions.

The chief end of man is eternal glory; but it is only by divine grace that we can merit it. The Old Law could not confer it. "The Law was given by Moses; grace and truth came by Jesus Christ." (John, i. 17.) But the Old Law was good, because it was a preparation for the Law of Grace, for the coming of the Messiah, either by giving testimony of him, or by preserving among the Jews the knowledge and worship of the true God. "Before that faith came, we were kept under the Law for that faith which was to be revealed." (Gal. iii. 23.)

However, notwithstanding the imperfection of the Old Law, the Jews had sufficient means of salvation by faith in the Redeemer to come. Jesus Christ, ardently expected, was the Saviour of the Patriarchs, of the Prophets, and of all the holy souls of the Old Law; as Jesus Christ, truly come, is the Saviour of the Apostles, martyrs, and all the holy souls of the New Law.

The Law of Jesus Christ then, or the Law of Grace, was substituted for the Old Law. This Law is called new for several reasons.

The Law of Grace is *new* in its *author*. The Old Law was given by the ministry of angels, but the New Law, by the only begotten Son of God. Hence, to prove the pre-eminence of the New Law above the Old Law, St. Paul says: "God had spoken in times past to our fore-fathers by the prophets, but he has spoken to us by his Son, whom he hath appointed heir of all things." (Heb. i. 1-2.)

The Law of Christ is *new* in its *efficacy*. The Old Law did not confer the grace of justification; it only prefigured and promised it in view of the New Law, which supplied the insufficiency by substituting reality for figures, and the gift of graces for promises. Thus the Law of Christ is the perfect accomplishment and realization of the Mosaic Law.

The law of Christ is *new* in its *rewards*. Moses, as we read in the beginning of the Book of Exodus, conveyed the Hebrew people from Egypt, for the conquest of foreign nations, and promised them a land flowing with milk and honey.

The Law of the Gospel proposes and promises, first of all, celestial and eternal happiness and glory. Jesus Christ began to preach the Gospel with these humble and holy words; "Do penance; the kingdom of heaven is approaching."

The Law of Christ is *new* in the *perfection* it requires. The law ought to direct all human acts for the observance of justice and the punishment of all crimes. But the Mosaic law punished only external acts, whilst the law of the Gospel restrains even internal acts. The one repressed the actions of the hands, whilst the other repressed even the sinful thoughts and passions of the heart.

The Law of Christ is *new* in the *motive of its operation*. The Old Law operated only by fear and punishment, whilst the Law of Grace operates by perfect justice and charity. "For the Law of the spirit of life in Christ Jesus hath delivered me from the law of sin and death," says St. Paul. (Rom. viii. 2.) In the Old Testament, says St. Augustine, the law was given in an external form to terrify the wicked, whilst, in the New Testament, it is given by the infusion of divine charity for our justification. The Old Law of words was written on tables of stone, whilst the Law of Grace is engraved on the living tables of the hearts of the faithful. Hence the New Law is a law of grace, infused into the souls of the just, and proceeds from faith in Christ, who added counsels thereto for all who aspire to virtue and perfection.

By its divine authority, the New Law has the power to prescribe outward works and prohibit certain others. As it has made us children of light, we must perform works of justice and charity and avoid those of sin and darkness. "For you were heretofore darkness, but now light in the Lord; walk then as children of light." (Eph.v. 8.) The New Law is a law of grace and sanctity. But in order to know that we possess this divine gift of grace and sanctity, visible signs are necessary, and the sacraments are such signs of grace. He who has received the gift of grace must manifest it in words and actions; for the law of Christ orders us to profess our faith, and never to deny it on any occasion. (Matt. x. 32-33.)

The New Law, being a law of grace, charity, and liberty, adds counsels to precepts, which are not absolutely obligatory. The precepts of the New Law are of a moral, indispensable obligation, whilst the counsels are of a discretionary character, and left to our own choice. "Ointment and perfumes rejoice the heart, and the good counsels of a friend are sweet to the soul." (Prov. xxvii. 9.) Now, Christ being the essence of all wisdom and charity, his evangelical counsels are the most useful and salutary to all Christians.

Man is placed in this world between heavenly beatitudes and temporal enjoyments; so that, the more he is attached to the one, the more he renounces the other. However, it is not necessary to deprive himself of all the goods of this world to attain eternal happiness; but by depriving himself of the goods of this world, he places himself in a safer way to work out his salvation. The riches and enjoyments of this world seduce us by the attraction of three kinds of of concupiscence. Hence, the new law, in order to bring us to evangelical perfection, proposes poverty as an infallible remedy to overcome the concupiscence of the eyes; chastity, to resist that of the flesh; and obedience, to conquer the pride and vanity of life. The counsels of the Gospel are thus a moral discipline which leads to sanctity and perfection. Hence St. Paul, after having counselled virginity, adds: "And this I speak for your profit, not to cast a snare upon you, but for that which may give you power to attend upon the Lord without impediment."

A certain traveller was obliged to pass through a vast forest in the darkness of the night. In order not to lose the way to his country, he carried a lamp in his hand, in the light of which he could always clearly see the way he had to travel to reach his home in safety.

144 Out of the Catholic Church there is No Salvation.

In this world, we all travel towards our true country, which is heaven. We have to travel through the vast forest of this world, in the darkness of the night, that is we have to travel through the darkness of the temptations of the devil, of the flesh, and of the errors of false religions and the perverse principles of wicked men.

Now, in order that we may not lose our way to heaven, God has given us a lamp in the light of which we can always see the way we must go to enter the kingdom of heaven. This lamp is especially the New Law, the true religion of Christ. "The commandments of God," says the Holy Scripture, "is a lamp, and his law is a light." (Prov. vi. 23.) The law of Jesus Christ is called a lamp, a light, because it shows to every one the way to heaven; it tells him what he must do and what he must avoid in order to please God and be saved. "Keep my commandments and my law as the apple of thine eye, and thou shalt live." (Prov. viii. 2).

The law of Christ, therefore, is one of the greatest gifts for every man. "I will give you," says the Lord, "a good gift," the gift of my commandments, "forsake not my law." (Prov. iv. 2.)

As the Law of Grace is perfect in every manner, it cannot be succeeded by any other law. It will therefore last to the end of the world.

§ 4. Conscience in General.

God was not satisfied with showing to man the way to heaven—which is the keeping of the commandments of Jesus Christ,—he, moreover, has given to every one an invisible companion, who stays with him day and night, to the end of his life. Some give to this companion the name of conscience; others call him the oracle or voice of God in the nature and heart of man, as distinct from the voice of revelation. A certain poet says : " Whatever creed be taught, or land be trod, Man's conscience is the oracle of God." Yes, the voice of conscience holds of God, and not of man; it is planted in us, before we have had any training, though such training is necessary for its strength, growth, and due formation; it is found even in the untutored savage.

When Columbus discovered America, the chieftain of an Indian tribe one day said to him; "I am told that thou hast lately come to these lands with a mighty force, and subdued many countries, spreading great fear among the people; but be not, therefore, vain-glorious. Know that, according to our belief, the souls of men have two journeys to perform after they have departed from the body: one, to a place dismal and foul, and covered with darkness, prepared for those souls who have been unjust and cruel to their fellow-men; the other, pleasant and full of light, for such as have promoted peace on earth If, then, thou art mortal and dost expect to die, and dost believe that each one shall be rewarded according to his deeds, beware that thou wrongfully hurt no man, nor do harm to those who have done no harm to thee." (Irving's "Columbus," chap. v., p. 443.)

From this short oration of a heathen it is evident that there is a voice of conscience even in the savage, telling him what is right and wrong.

This faithful companion knows how far every one is acquainted with the law of God. He knows our desires, our words, our actions, and the omission of our duties. Now his office is to apply our knowledge of the law to every thing we desire, say, and do, in order to see whether our desires, words, and actions are in conformity with the law of God, or in opposition to it.

Hence St. Thomas says: "Conscience is not a power, but an act of the soul by which we apply, to a particular action, the first principles of right and wrong. If we apply these principles to the commission or omission of an act, our conscience is witness of it. 'For thy conscience knoweth that thou hast also often spoken evil of others.' (Eccles. vii., 23.) If we apply those principles to what ought or ought not to be done for the moment, our conscience excites

146 *Out of the Catholic Church there is No Salvation.*

us to do it or dissuades us from doing it. If we apply those principles to a past transaction, to know whether it was good or bad, our conscience accuses or excuses us."

Conscience, or the sense of right and wrong, which is the first element in religion, is so delicate, so fitful, so easily puzzled, obscured, perverted; so subtle in its argumentative methods, so impressible by education, so biassed by pride and passion, so unsteady in its flight, that this sense of right and wrong is at once the highest of all teachers, yet the least clear and luminous in most men. Hence it is that we meet with different kinds of conscience.

1. *The right or true conscience.*

A right or true conscience is one which, according to sound principles, dictates what is right and wrong. For instance: Before we published our little work *Familiar Explanation of Christian Doctrine*, we requested the Rev. Francis J. Freel, D. D., then the beloved Pastor of the Church of St. Charles Borromeo, in Brooklyn, N. Y., and the Rev. A. Konings, C.S S.R., one of the best theologians of this country, to examine the manuscript and see whether it was all correct in every point of doctrine. Knowing their theology well, these two theologians could judge well of the doctrine I had explained.

Here is what they wrote about the Explanation of Christian Doctrine:—

CHURCH OF ST. CHARLES BORROMEO,
SYDNEY PLACE,
BROOKLYN, August 28, 1874.

Rev. dear Father Muller:

I have carefully read and examined your excellent manuscript, entitled *Familiar Explanation, etc.* As far as I can judge, it is a clear, *sound, orthodox,* exposition of Catholic doctrine, in a form of question and answer, which cannot fail to be extremely useful for the right understanding of the truths, commandments, and sacraments of our holy religion. Particularly useful seem to be the parts which explain the True Faith, the True Church, the Infallibility of the Pope, and, well, I should have to mention every chapter, from the beginning to the end. It is another *great Godsend* for these days of unbelief and corruption.

I am your humble servant in the Sacred Hearts of Jesus and Mary,

FRANCIS J. FREEL, D.D.

ILCHESTER, HOWARD CO., MD.,
September 12, 1874.

Rev. dear Father Müller.:

I have most carefully read and examined your excellent manuscript, "Familiar Explanation of Christian Doctrine." I took the liberty to make a few alterations. I do not hesitate for a moment to pronounce this work of yours one of the most useful for our time and country. It is written in the true spirit of St. Alphonsus. Its *theology is sound and solid*, its spirit most devout, and its language simple and popular. I was particularly pleased with those chapters which treat on the Church, Papal Infallibility, Indifference to Religion, Prayer, and Grace. Your book cannot but prove most useful to those who are learning and to those who teach the Christian Doctrine. Its diligent and frequent perusal cannot fail to confirm converts in their faith, and supply Catholics with quite popular and solid arguments to refute the fallacious objections of non-Catholics. I feel confident that both the clergy and laity will hail with delight the publication of a book so well calculated to remedy the two great evils of our time and country—want of faith and true piety.

Congratulating you on having so successfully accomplished one of the most difficult works,

I am your devoted confrère,
A. KONINGS, C.S.S.R.

148 *Out of the Catholic Church there is No Salvation.*

The Rev. Dr. Freel and the Rev. A. Konings, then, gave these testimonials according to their *right* or *true conscience*.

2. *The certain conscience.*

A *certain* conscience is one which is clear and absolute in its dictates, so that, in obeying it, we feel morally certain that we are right.

When, upon the above favorable criticisms of *Explanation*, the Most Rev. J. Roosevelt Bailey, Archbishop of Baltimore, gave us the Imprimatur for the little volume, his conscience was morally certain; and also our conscience was morally certain when we placed the manuscript into the hands of the printer.

By moral certainty, is meant such a one as prudent and enlightened men think it reasonable to act upon in matters of importance. It is the highest kind of certainty we can ordinarily gain in matters of daily conduct.

The Church requires no other certainty in giving permission for the publication of a work treating of faith and morals. (See Third Plenary Council of Baltimore, p. 120, No. 220). The Rev. B. Neithart, C.S.S.R., also had this moral certainty when he wrote to us, "Were it in my power, I would assuredly procure thousands of copies of this work, and distribute them broadcast over the entire land; nor would I rest till this little volume came into every household, and was thumbed by every hand—Catholic, Protestant, or infidel."

The conscience of the Rt. Rev. Thomas L. Grace, Bishop of St. Paul, was morally certain of the truth he told, when he wrote to us on Dec. 12, 1881:—

"*Rev. dear Father:*— I received the book you were so kind to send me, 'The Greatest and the First Commandment.' I am reading it. What I have already said of the other books of the series, I repeat now *with greater emphasis of this one and of all,* namely: These books are not merely elementary, nor are they dryly dogmatic; they give reasons and authorities, explain and illustrate, and, written in a plain and easy style, they well deserve to be entitled—Catholic Theology popularized. The science of theology, or the philosophy of religion, has been sealed except to the clergy and the highly educated among laymen. Few of the latter, however, care to go through the drudgery of study in a language foreign to them, and with forms and a terminology requiring long practice to make familiar. Yet the greatest need of the Church in the present day is to have Catholics thoroughly instructed in the principles of their religion and the reasons for their faith. I conceive this to be your motive in writing these books—to supply the means by which this most needed knowledge may be placed within the reach of every earnest Catholic. It is this that constitutes the super-eminent excellence of these books. But not only do they instruct *with utmost thoroughness and precision*, they are deeply edifying; and what is of greater consideration, they are pleasing and attractive by their style and manner. *I mean no mere commendation in writing this.* These books, to be available for their real value, must be known to our Catholic people, which, I regret to say, is not the case." Many other learned prelates, and priests, and the Catholic Press of our country have spoken of my works in the same manner, as can be seen from the recommendations of my works, placed in front of the last volume of *God the Teacher of Mankind.*

Since the publication of this large work, we have, by Benziger Brothers, published the third improved edition of our Catechisms, and the second improved edition of *Familiar Explanation of Catholic Doctrine.* His Eminence, J. Cardinal Gibbons, writes of these catechisms and *Familiar Explanation:* "They are strongly marked by *soundness of doctrine*, simplicity and plainness of language, a spirit of faith and devotion, and precision in expressing and defining Catholic truths." Rest assured that the Cardinal wrote this with moral certainty of the truth. It is also with the same moral certainty that many other learned prelates, priests, and the Catholic Press have testified to the orthodoxy of our Doctrine, as S. O. may read in front of our ninth volume of *God the Teacher of Mankind.*

3. *There is also the timorous or tender conscience,*

which fears not only sin, but also whatever can have the least shadow and smallest appearance of sin. Happy the conscience which is so disposed!

Splendid examples of tenderness of conscience, which have not been as yet recorded in any Catholic book, are S. O., and the Rev. Editor of the *B. U.* and *T.* See how careful they have been never to mention the name of the author of Familiar Explanation of Christian Doctrine, nor to drop from their pen one word of praise either in regard to the author, the Rev. M. Muller, C.SS.R., or in regard to any of his works, as he might be strongly tempted to vain glory, and to expose him to such a dangerous temptation would not be right for their tender conscience, which, by such an imprudent act, might lose considerable of its tenderness.

In the light of their tender conscience they also foresaw, that, if the name of the author, or of any of his works, was mentioned to the public, both many of the clergy and of the laity would be scandalized at what they said of his little volume, and that they would not believe it, knowing the author, as they do, to be a truly orthodox writer. In order, therefore, that their tender conscience might not be tormented day and night by such a scandal, and in order, also, that they might not lose their own reputation with the public, they acted in perfect conformity to the principles of their tender conscience. What an unspeakable happiness to be blessed with so tender a conscience!

4. *The doubtful conscience.*

A doubtful conscience is one which is, as it were, hanging in a balance, and being in suspense, uncertain whether a thing is lawful or not, whether an action is forbidden or allowed. On both sides it sees plausible reasons, which make an impression, but amongst these reasons there is none that draws down the weight, and is sufficient to ground a determination. Thus wavering between these different and opposite reasons, it remains undetermined, and dares not make a decision for fear of being deceived, and of falling into sin. Now, it is never allowed to act with a doubtful conscience. When we do something, we must be morally sure that what we are doing is lawful. To do something, and have, at the same time, a reasonable doubt about the lawfulness of our action, is to commit sin, because we expose ourselves to the danger of sin. If we act in such a doubt about the lawfulness of our action, we show ourselves indifferent as to whether we break a law or not, and consequently make ourselves guilty of the sin to the danger of which we expose ourselves. Hence St. Paul says: "Anything that is not according to conscience, is a sin." (Rom. xiv. 13.)

We must, then, seek for light and instruction, if we can; or, if it is necessary to act without delay, and we have neither means nor time to consult and procure information to clear the doubt and settle our conscience, after begging God to enlighten us, we must consider and examine what seems most expedient in his sight under the present circumstances, then take our determination and proceed; yet always reserving the intention of procuring information, and correcting the mistake afterwards, if anything was not according to law. This is no longer acting in doubt, as the prospect of doing what seems most expedient takes away the doubt: we may, it is true, be deceived, but we cannot sin.

Now, doubts may arise in our mind as to whether we have complied with a certain law that must be complied with. It is a law, for instance, to be validly baptized. Now, if there arises a reasonable doubt about the validity of a person's baptism, that person must be baptized again to make sure of the compliance with the law. It is a certain law that, in order to be saved, a man must profess the true faith, live up to it, and die in it. Now if a non-Catholic for good reasons doubts the truth of his religion, he is not allowed to continue to live and die in this doubt. He must, to the best of his ability, inquire about the true religion, and after having found it, he is obliged to embrace it, in order to comply with the law of professing the true divine faith and worship. It is a law that we must confess all our mortal sins which we do remember after a careful examination of conscience. Now, if after confession we have a reasonable doubt as to whether we have confessed a certain mortal sin, we are bound to confess that sin, in order to make sure of having complied with the law of confessing all our mortal sins. If we have borrowed money from our neighbor and afterwards have a reasonable doubt as to whether we have returned it, we are still bound to pay it. In the time of war, an officer, or soldier, who doubts as to whether the war is just, is bound to obey his general, because it is a certain law that no one, much less a superior, is to be accused of unjust commands and actions, as long as there are not quite evident reasons to prove the contrary. There is a law which says, "Thou shalt not kill." If a hunter, then, seeing something stir in a brush-wood, doubts whether it is a man or an animal, he is not allowed to fire before he is sure that it is not a man. Or should a physician, when prescribing medicine, reasonably doubt that the medicine might kill his patient, he is not allowed to prescribe such a medicine.

Whenever, then, a law exists for certain, and we doubt whether we have complied with it, we can remove the doubt only by doing what is commanded; and if the law forbids something, and we reasonably doubt that what we are about to do might violate the law, we are bound not to perform such an action; for every certain law requires a positively certain obedience.

But there may also arise in our minds doubts about the real existence of a law, that is, about its promulgation or its obligation in a certain case. There is one: he doubts whether a certain war is just. This doubt (called a speculative doubt) brings on another, whether it is lawful to take part in such a war. This last doubt is called a practical doubt, because there is question about doing something that may be against a certain law. To act under such a practical doubt is, as we have said above, to become guilty of sin.

In order not to expose ourselves to the danger of committing sin, we must be morally certain that what we are doing is lawful. This certainty, however, need not be such as to exclude even every speculative doubt. For instance, one doubts whether the dish which is placed before him on a Friday is not flesh-meat. So far, this doubt is but a speculative doubt, suggesting the question as to whether or not this particular case comes under the law of abstinence. But should he before whom the dish is placed not wish to order another dish, the practical doubt arises whether it is lawful for him to eat a dish which may be forbidden by the law of abstinence. It is evident that this person, if he is conscientious, is not allowed to eat the dish before he is morally sure that the eating of it is not forbidden by the law of abstinence.

What, then, is he to do if he cannot find out whether the dish is real flesh-meat or not? whether the law of abstinence in this case is binding on him or not? Many such cases may occur, in which we entertain speculative doubts whether a law exists for such a case, or such a person, or under such a circumstance of time or place, and we may not be able to decide whether the law exists or not. But from the fact that such a speculative doubt continues, it does not follow that we can leave the matter alone and act as we please. Such conduct would, no doubt, expose us to the danger of violating a law that may really exist. To acquire moral certainty for the lawfulness of our action, we must see whether there are reasons which prove that a law really exists, or does not exist, in this or that case.

Now, in trying to find out such reasons, we may find some that may seem to prove the real existence of the law, whilst others may seem to prove that the law does not exist. It may happen that the reasons *pro* and *con.* are equally or almost equally strong, and it may also happen that the reasons *pro* are considerably stronger than the reasons *con.*, or *vice versa*. Those reasons which are considerably stronger may increase in strength and weight (become so strong and weighty) so much as to make those opposed to them sink in weight and strength. Now the question arises, how weighty these reasons must be to induce us to judge with moral certainty that the law is uncertain and, consequently, is not binding. If the reasons proving that the law does not exist are as strong or nearly as strong as those which prove the existence of the law, then we have moral certainty, says St. Alphonsus, to believe that the law does not exist; but if the reasons proving the existence of the law are considerably stronger than those proving the contrary, then we ought to believe that the law exists.

This teaching is undoubtedly quite reasonable. In business matters, every sensible man adheres to that one of two opinions which is best grounded. In scientific matters, those opinions which are but little grounded are also but little cared for.

From what has been said, it is easy to understand what rigorism and laxism is. It is rigorism to pronounce in favor of the existence of the law in spite of very weighty reasons proving the contrary. This doctrine was condemned by Alexander VIII. Those who teach such a doctrine are called *strict Tutiorists*. It is still rigorism, though not quite so bad, to maintain that we must pronounce in favor of the existence of the law, even if the opinion that the law does not exist is better grounded. Those adhering to this opinion are called *less strict Tutiorists*. Finally, it is still rigorism to maintain that the reasons proving that the law does not exist must be considerably stronger than those proving the contrary, in order to pronounce in favor of liberty or the non-existence of the law. Those adhering to this opinion are called Probabiliorists. But each of these three opinions must be rejected. No sensible man adopts and goes by such opinions in his daily business transactions and social intercourse. No man of learning rejects, in scientific questions, the best grounded opinions and arguments. Why should we not act in the same way in discussing and deciding moral cases? What more unreasonable than the contrary?

Laxism is to maintain that the law does not exist, even if the reasons to prove the contrary should be considerably stronger and much weightier. It is self-evident that such an opinion is very lax, as it favors liberty beyond what is reasonable. It is true, those adhering to this opinion say, that in theory they only teach that the law does not exist, when there is a solid reason for its non-existence. They forget, however, that a real solid reason is no longer such, when considerably more solid reasons are opposed to it. They only care for having a solid reason for the non existence of the law, and leave alone the more solid reasons which prove its existence. It is clear that, in discussing the question of the existence or non-existence of the law, the reasons *pro* and *con.* must be carefully weighed and compared, and if the reasons proving the existence of the law are considerably weightier than the reasons proving its non-existence, the latter are no longer solid reasons.

Such is the doctrine of St. Alphonsus. "Those," he says, "who defend and adhere to the contrary opinion are called laxists. Their lax opinion is to be rejected in practice. Auctores elapsi sæculi quasi communiter tenuere opinionem: 'Ut quis possit licite sequi opinionem etiam minus probabilem pro libertate (stantem), licet opinio pro lege sit certe probabilior.' Hanc sententiam nos dicimus esse *laxam et licite amplecti non posse.*" (In Apologia, 1769, et Homo Apost. de consc. n. 31.) In a letter, dated July 8, 1768, St. Alphonsus writes: "Librorum censor D. Delegatum adiit ipsique retulit, se opus Meum Morale legisse ejusque sententias sanas invenisse, et *quod attinet systema circa probabilem, me non sequi systema Jesuitarum, sed ipsis adversari; Jesuitæ enim admittunt minus probabilem, sed ego eam reprobo.*" And in another letter, dated May 25, 1767, St. Alphonsus writes: "Formidarem confessiones excipiendi licentiam concedere alicui ex nostris, qui sequi vellet opinionem certo cognitam ut minus probabilem."

The more ignorant or the more stupid people are, the

less doubts they have. What a happiness, never to be tormented by a doubtful conscience!

5. *The lax conscience.*

'A lax conscience is one which, for a light reason, judges to be lawful what is very unlawful, or considers a sin which is grievous only as a venial sin; in other words, a lax conscience is one which without sufficient reason favors liberty, either in order to escape the law, or to diminish the gravity of guilt. A lax conscience is generally the consequence of the neglect of prayer, of lukewarmness of the soul, of too much care and anxiety about temporal things, of familiar intercourse with the wicked, of the habit of sinning, which destroys horror of sin, of a soft, tepid life, which enervates the heart and makes it quite worldly. Such a conscience is most dangerous, for it leads the soul to the broad road to hell.

The remedies for such a conscience are: frequent recourse to prayer, spiritual exercises, pious reading and meditation, frequent confession, conversation with the pious, and avoiding the company of the wicked.

But why speak here of a lax conscience and indicate the means to correct it? Is it not very imprudent to do so? Is it not to suggest indirectly the idea that we allude to S. O. and to the Rev. Editor of the *B. U.* and *T.?* But who could even dream of such nonsense.

6. *The perplexed conscience.*

A man's conscience is said to be perplexed, when he is placed between two actions which appear bad. There is a person: She is bound to wait upon a sick neighbor on a Sunday: she thinks that it is a sin to leave that sick person, in order to go and hear Mass, and, at the same time, it appears to her that it is also a sin to stay away from Mass, in order to wait upon her sick friend. Now, if the conscience of a person is thus perplexed, he must, as far as possible, take counsel of prudent men. If he cannot consult such, and is still under necessity of acting, he must choose what appears the lesser evil, and in so doing, he will not commit sin.

Self sufficient teachers of Catholic theology never suffer from a perplexed conscience. They say:

> "I am S. O.,
> And when I open my lips, let no dog bark."

7. *The scrupulous conscience.*

"A scruple," says St. Alphonsus, "is a vain fear of sinning, which arises from false, groundless reasons." There is a person: for frivolous reasons he imagines that something is forbidden that is not forbidden, or that something is commanded which is not commanded. So he is disturbed, and runs into doubts without any just foundation and reasonable motives. He sinks into the state of a scrupulous conscience, which is a continual torment to the soul itself, and often also to her spiritual director. Any one who has read the *Queer Explanation* will be convinced that neither the most prominent priest of the U. S., nor the Rev. Editor of the *B. U.* and *T.* ever caused any annoyance and torment to his spiritual director. Would, they were the spiritual directors of all scrupulous persons! What a blessing would not this be for them; by a few words of such unscrupulous directors they would be entirely delivered from their unspeakable torment! What a blessing for all Catholic and Protestant readers of the *B. U.* and *T.* to know that the Rev. Editor has never any scruples to print articles like the *Queer Explanation.* They feel that they can read them without scruples, because they are written and printed without scruples, and are calculated to confirm Catholics as well as *Protestants in their faith !*

8. *The erroneous or false conscience.*

A conscience is erroneous or false when it represents to us an action as good which is really bad. For instance: every one knows that a wilful lie is a sin. Now, there is one who sees his neighbor in danger of death, and knows that by telling a lie he can save the life of his neighbor. He feels certain that such a lie cannot be a sin, and that he would sin against charity if he were not to tell it.

A conscience is also erroneous when it represents what is really good as something really bad. For example: what can be better and holier than the Catholic religion? And yet there may be found a non-Catholic who, from having been brought up in heresy, is fully persuaded from boyhood that we, Catholics, impugn and attack the word of God, that we are idolaters, pestilent deceivers, and, therefore, are to be shunned as pestilences.

Another instance: The conscience of S. O. represented to him his own explanation of Father Muller's explanation, which is really bad for many reasons, *as a good action*, and it represented to him Father Muller's explanation, which is really good, as something that is really bad, and so, from his *erroneous* conscience, he declared publicly that Father Muller had misrepresented Catholic Theology, and dishonored the Holy Name of God!

Now, such errors of conscience are either culpable or inculpable. They are culpable, if they spring from voluntary ignorance, and they are inculpable, if they spring from involuntary ignorance.

Ignorance is *voluntary* or *vincible*, when one in doing something has certain doubts about the moral goodness or badness of his action, and about the obligation of examining whether his action is really good or bad, and, nevertheless, does not take the necessary means to find out whether what he is about to do is right or wrong. It is, for instance, a law to profess the true religion in order to be saved. Now, suppose there is a non-Catholic. A sermon on the true religion, which he heard, or a book which he read, or a conversation which he had with a friend on this subject, or the conversion of a wealthy or learned man from Protestantism to the Catholic faith, or any other good reason whatever, makes him doubt about the truth of his religion.

Such a one is obliged in conscience to seek for light and instruction, if he can. If he cannot do so immediately, he must firmly purpose to procure information, as soon as he can, from those who can give it in a satisfactory manner, and must be determined to renounce his error, if he finds out that he is living in a false religion. Meanwhile, he must beg of God to enlighten him and enable him to do what seems best to him in the present circumstances. If he, however, neglects to seek instruction when he can and ought to do so; if he continues not to heed his religious scruples about his salvation in Protestantism; if he is even afraid of learning the truth, or, if he knows it, contradicts it against his conscience, and obscures it every day by unnatural crimes,—ah! then the signs are not hard to read! Such a Protestant sins against his conscience, against the Holy Ghost. He is a tree, black and dead in the middle of summer. He is fit only for the fire. If he is lost, he is lost through his own fault.

Ignorance is involuntary, or invincible, if one, in doing something, has not the least reasonable doubt about the goodness of the action. To illustrate: an heir enters upon an estate which formerly was acquired unjustly by his ancestors; but at the time when he took possession of it, he had not the least doubt about the just and lawful acquisition of the estate. In this he is in error, but the error is involuntary, and, therefore, not culpable. After some years, however, he discovers the flaw in his title, and still continues in the possession of the estate. From that time, his conscience becomes voluntarily and criminally erroneous, contrary to good faith and the dictates of a good conscience.

"If your error is voluntary," says St. Thomas Aquinas, "and you do not do all you can to find out the truth, you are answerable for your conduct in following a false conscience." Such was the conscience of the persecutors of the Church, of whom Jesus Christ says: "Yea, the hour cometh, that whosoever killeth you, will think that he doth a service to God." (John, xvi. 2.) When, in arguing about something, one of the premises is false, the conclusion must necessarily be false. In like manner, all the acts of a conscience, whose error is voluntary or vincible, are bad and partake in the evil result of voluntary ignorance. If you are wilfully ignorant of what you are bound in conscience to know, you are responsible for all your actions. Such is the conscience of many sinners, who wish to be ignorant of their duties in order to live without restraint. "They say to God," says Job, " depart from us, we do not desire the knowledge of thy ways." (Job, xxi. 14.) A conscience continuing thus to act in a known voluntary error, becomes quite criminal in the sight of God. This is the most lamentable and most unhappy state into which a soul can fall; for this kind of conscience drives the sinner into all kinds of crimes, disorders, and excesses, and becomes to him the source of blindness of the understanding, of hardness of heart, and finally, of eternal reprobation, if he perseveres in this state to the end of his life.

Witness the writer of the infidel Press. With him it has become fashionable to get rid of religion and conscience. A man who wishes to gratify his evil desires, without shame, without remorse, says: "There is no God; there is no hell; there is no hereafter; there is only this present life, and all in it is good." He looks upon conscience as a creation of man. He calls its dictates an imagination. He says that the notion of guiltiness, which that dictate enforces, is simply irrational.

When he advocates the rights of conscience, he, of course, in no sense means the rights of the Creator, nor the duty to him, in thought and deed, of the creature; he means only the right of thinking, speaking, writing, and eating according to his judgment or his humor, without any thought of God at all. He does not even pretend to go by any moral rule, but he demands what he thinks is an American's prerogative, to be his own master in all things, and to profess what he pleases, asking no one's leave, and accounting any one unutterably impertinent who dares to say a word against his going to perdition, if he likes it, in his own way. With such a man the right of conscience means the very right and freedom of conscience to dispense with conscience, to ignore a Law-giver and Judge, to be independent of unseen obligations ; to be free to take up any or no religion, to take up this or that, and let it go again, to boast of being above all religions, and to be an impartial critic of each of them ; in a word, conscience is, with that man, nothing else than the right of self-will. Such is the idea which the men of the infidel Press have of conscience. Their rule and measure of right and wrong is utility, or expedience, or the happiness of the greatest number, or State convenience, or fitness, order, a long-sighted selfishness, a desire to be consistent with one's self.

But all these false conceptions of conscience will be no excuse before God for not having known better. The idea that there is no law or rule over our thoughts, desires, words, and actions, and that, without sin or error, we may think, desire, say, and do what we please, especially in matters of religion, is a downright absurdity.

"When God gave to man a free will," says St. Thomas, "he intended that man should freely choose what is good and reject what is evil, in order thus to gain merit—a privilege which is denied to beasts, for they blindly follow their instincts. Who can be foolish enough to think that God, in giving man a free will, dispensed him from the observance of his laws ? God is infinite goodness, justice, wisdom, mercy, and purity, and he impressed on man the notion of goodness, justice, mercy, purity, in order that, as he himself hates all wickedness, injustice, errors, and impurity, so man also should do the same. Hence it is impossible that God can concede to man a license to commit acts utterly repugnant to the divine nature, and also repugnant to the nature of man, who is made in the likeness and image of God.

"Our use of liberty, therefore, must be consistent with reason ; it must be based upon a hatred of all that is evil, unjust, unkind, false, or impure ; and upon a strong desire to attain to all that is good, true, and perfect.

"Who, then, are the worst enemies of the liberty of man ? First, that ignorance and error which prevent him from distinguishing clearly that which is just and right from that which is evil and false. Secondly, his passions, which keep him from embracing the good which he knows and sees, and induce him to desire that which he knows to be bad. Thirdly, any powers or authorities external to man, which prevent him from doing that which he knows to be good and which he desires to do, or force him to do that which he sees to be unlawful, and which he shrinks from doing. Fourthly, all those who deny and pervert religious and moral truths. What wickedness, what impiety to sneer at what is good, in the present and in the future, for the intellect and will of man! How detestable are they who entangle men in the subtle webs of sophisms, and expel religion and morality from the hearts of men, who instil doubts and disputes about social truth, which is the only stable foundation on which nations and empires can tranquilly repose! Most execrable men, those who assume the right to insult the Lord and to destroy man."

After the devil has used these men for his own diabolical purposes, he will cast the vile wretches, like worn-out brooms, into the fire of hell.

> The privilege that bad men have in evil,
> Is that they go unpunished to the devil."

The hell of the wicked begins even in this world, and it continues throughout all eternity in the next. Hence St. Paul says: "Tribulation and anguish upon every soul of man that worketh evil." (Rom. ii. 9.) "By what things," says Holy Scripture, "a man sinneth, by the same he is also tormented." (Wisd. xi. 17.) "He who speaks (against his conscience) whatever he pleases, will hear in his heart what he does not like to hear," says Comicus.

> "He that hides a dark soul and foul thoughts,
> Benighted walks under the midday-sun,
> Himself is his own dungeon."

In order to avoid such great evils, we must rectify our conscience when it is vincibly erroneous—that is, when we are confused with doubts and suspicions about the lawfulness or unlawfulness of an action which we are about to perform; we must try, by examination, consultation, and employing the ordinary means, to find out whether we are right or wrong in what we are about to undertake.

But as long as a man's conscience is invincibly erroneous, he must follow it. "His will is then not in fault," says St. Thomas. No doubt, a person who, from an invincibly erroneous conscience, believes that charity obliges him to tell a lie, if thereby he can save the life of his neighbor, performs a meritorious act, and he would sin against charity if he did not tell the lie.

Conscience, then, is that faithful, inward monitor, that warns every man when he is about to offend God and leave the right road to heaven. Whenever we are on the point of desiring, saying, or doing something that is against God's law, conscience says to us on the part of God: "It is not lawful for thee." (Matt. xiv. 4.) No, thou art not allowed to perform that action, to speak that word, to entertain that desire, to read that book, to frequent that company, to go to that place of sin, to make that unlawful bargain.

If, in spite of these remonstrances of conscience, we still proceed, it rises up against us and cries out: "What hast thou done?" (Kings, iii. 24.) Thou hast sinned; thou hast offended God, by transgressing his law and going against his voice, which warned thee not to do so; thou art guilty in his sight, and deserving to be punished according to the law of his justice. It was his conscience that made David say: "My sin is always before me." (Ps. lxxx. 5.) It was his conscience that made Judas cry out: "I have sinned in betraying innocent blood." (Matt. xxvii. 4.)

Thus every sinner is accountable for his conduct to his conscience, which, as Menander says, is his God. It is by means of conscience that God judges man. Conscience, as the organ and instrument of God, pronounces, in his name, the sentence of condemnation; it passes, under his sovereign authority, the decree of his divine justice.

In this sense it is said that we ourselves are our first judges, and that the first tribunal to which we are cited is our own conscience, without being able to escape from its presence, or call in question its justice, or avoid its decree. Yes, this judgment is just, it is dreadful, it is without appeal. In pronouncing sentence, conscience is at the same time witness against us, and its deposition is so much the more dreadful as it is interior, clear, and personal to us.

Ah! how unfortunate is it to be condemned by ourselves, and to have nothing to oppose to the condemnation! And what, indeed, can be opposed when our own conscience is the accuser, witness, and judge? Therefore, it only remains for conscience to assume the character of executioner, and to exercise its vengeance upon us. Dreadful charge, which is more terrible than all the rest! It punishes us. God intrusts the interest of his justice and revenge in the hands of conscience; and in how many ways does it not discharge this dreadful office against the sinner after his sin?—By those racking remorses which tear him, as it were, to pieces; by the gnawing worm which eats him up; by the constant remembrance of his guilt, which follows him everywhere; by the fears, terrors, and continual alarms in which he lives. If he is visited by illness, if the least infirmity attacks him, death incessantly presents itself to his eyes. If thunders roar, if the earth quakes, if any unexpected accident happens, he believes that the hand of God is lifted up against him, fearing every instant to be swallowed up. Alas! can there be any more dreadful torturer, any more cruel executioner, any more severe minister of vengeance for the sinner than his own conscience! What more torturing for Cain than the bloody spectre of his brother Abel which presented itself continually to him? What more frightful for the impious Balthasar than the sight of the hand which appeared on the wall and wrote the sentence of condemnation upon it? What more horrifying for Antiochus than the picture of the temple of Jerusalem which he had profaned? What more alarming and terrifying for Henry VIII., King of England, than to behold, on his death-bed, the legions of monks whom he had so cruelly treated?

And why were these men thus tortured? It was because conscience, whose rights they had trampled upon, sought atonement by setting the remembrance of their crimes continually before them.

> "Thus conscience pleads her cause within the breast:
> Though long rebelled against, not yet suppressed."

No wonder that men sometimes commit suicide. They cannot bear the remorse of conscience, and so they try to find rest in death.

Now, such a remorse of conscience, though a punishment, is at the same time a grace for the sinner. It warns him to enter into himself, by sincere repentance, to ask pardon of God, and promise amendment of life, and be saved. But if a sinner does not experience such a remorse he is, no doubt, in a most lamentable condition. The want of this grace forbodes a certain reprobation for all eternity. Now, this voice of conscience, which strikes terror into the souls of the wicked, fill the just with peace and happiness.

There is a great sinner: he is very sorry for all his sins. He firmly purposes amendment of life; he makes a good confession. See him after confession. His countenance is radiant with beauty. His step has become again light. His soul reflects upon his features the holy joy with which it is inebriated. He smiles upon those whom he meets, and every one sees that he is happy. He trembles now no longer when he lifts his eyes to heaven. He hopes, he loves. A supernatural strength animates him. He feels himself burning with zeal to do good. A new sun has risen upon his life, and every thing in him puts on the freshness of youth. And why? Because his conscience has thrown off a load that bent him to the earth. It tells him that now he is once more the companion of angels; that he has again entered that ·sweet alliance with God, whom he can now justly call his Father; that he is rein-

stated in his dignity of a child of God. He is no longer
afraid of God's justice, of death, and of hell.

We must, then, always follow the voice or dictates of
conscience, for " this is the keeping of the commandments," says the Holy Scripture; but " whatever is contrary to conscience, is sinful." (Rom. xiv. 23.)

"What rule," says St. Thomas Aquinas, "can a man
follow, unless reason, which is the imperative voice of
conscience? He who does not appeal to his conscience on
all occasions can have no rule of conduct. He is always in
doubt and perplexity, wavering between vice and virtue,
not knowing to which side to turn. He is like a vessel
whose helm is lost in a violent storm."

§ 6. HAVING EXPLAINED WHAT CONSCIENCE IS, AND THE DIFFERENT KINDS OF CONSCIENCE, WE CAN NOW EASILY SHOW WHO ARE NOT GUILTY OF THE SIN OF HERESY.

Not guilty of the sin of heresy are all those who, without
any fault of theirs, were brought up in a sect of Protestantism, and who never had an opportunity of knowing
better. This class of Protestants are called invincibly or
inculpably ignorant of the true religion, or material heretics.

Now, let us see what the Rev. Alfred Young, a Paulist
Father of New York, says of material heretics, in an article
which he had published in the *Buffalo Union and Times*
on March 22, 1888. He says: "He was baptized in his
infancy, and was then a Catholic child as good as any other
Catholic child."—This is quite correct, and if he had died
before he came to the use of reason, he would have gone
straight to heaven.

But, after he had come to the years of understanding,
he was brought up in heresy; but, according to his statement, he was only a *material*, not a *formal*, heretic.

It can hardly be doubted that, amongst Protestants, many
are only material heretics. Reiffenstuel gives this as his
opinion regarding great numbers amongst the mass of
heretics. The same is the opinion of Lacroix, and several

other authors cited by him, with regard to the Protestants of Germany; and what is true of them is equally true of Protestants in other countries. "Some of them," he says, "are so simple, or so prejudiced by the teaching of their ministers, that they are persuaded of the truth of their own religion, and at the same time so sincere and conscientious, that, if they knew it to be false, they would at once embrace ours. Such as these are not formal, but only material heretics; and that there are many such is testified by numbers of confessors in Germany and authors of the greatest experience."

"What is most deplorable in their case," says Lacroix, "is that, should they fall into any other mortal sin, as may *very easily* happen to such persons, (because without special grace it is impossible to keep the commandments,) they are deprived of the grace of the principal sacraments, and are *commonly* lost, not on account of *material* heresy, but on account of other sins they have committed, and from which they are not freed by the sacrament of penance, which does not exist amongst them; nor by an act of contrition or perfect charity, which they commonly do not attend to, or think of eliciting (to say nothing of the very great difficulty such men would have in doing so), thinking they are justified by faith alone and trust in Christ; and by this accursed confidence they are miserably lost." (Lacroix, Lib. ii. n. 94.)

It is well to distinguish here between two classes of Protestants.

The first is that of those who either live among Catholics or have Catholics living in the same country with them; who know there are such persons, and often hear of them. The second regards those who have no such knowledge, and who seldom or never hear Catholics spoken of, except in a false and odious light.

We read in Holy Scripture that Almighty God, at different times, scattered the Jews among the heathen and performed great miracles in favor of his chosen people. He thus wished the Gentiles to come to the knowledge of the true God. In like manner, Almighty God has scattered the Roman Catholics, the children of his Church, among the heathens of our time and the Protestants. He has never failed to perform miracles in the Catholic Church. Who has not heard of the many great miracles performed in France, and elsewhere, by the use of the miraculous water of Lourdes? Who has not witnessed the wonderful protection of the Catholic Church? Who has not read the truths of the Catholic Church, even in Protestant newspapers? Who has not heard of the conversion of so many wealthy and learned Protestants to the Catholic Church? The Lord, who wishes that all should come to the knowledge of the true religion, makes use of these and other means to cause doubts to arise in the souls of those who are separated from his Church. Hence it is, as Bishop Hay says, next to the impossible for those Protestants who live among Catholics to be in a state of invincible ignorance.

Such doubts as to their salvation in Protestantism are, for our separated brethren, a great grace, as Almighty God, by these doubts, begins to lead them to the way of salvation, by obliging them to seek in all sincerity for light and instruction. But those who do not heed these doubts remain culpably erroneous in a matter of the greatest importance; and to die in this state is to die in the state of reprobation; it is to be lost forever through one's own fault, as we have seen above.

But let us remember here, that "it is a mistake," as Bishop Hay well says, "to suppose that a formal doubt is necessary to render one's ignorance of his duty voluntary and culpable; it is enough that there be sufficient reason for doubting, though from his unjust prejudices, obstinacy, pride, or other evil dispositions of the heart, he hinder these reasons from exciting a formal doubt in his mind. Saul had no doubt when he offered sacrifice before the prophet Samuel came; on the contrary, he was persuaded that he had the strongest reasons for doing so, yet he was condemned for that very action, and himself and his family rejected by Almighty God. The Jews believed that they were acting well when they put our Saviour to death ; nay, their high priest declared in full council that it was expedient for the good and safety of the nation that they should do so. They were grossly mistaken, indeed, and sadly ignorant of their duty; but their ignorance was culpable, and they were severely condemned for what they did, though it was done in ignorance. And, indeed, all who act from a false and erroneous conscience are highly blamable for having such a conscience, though they have never entertained any formal doubt. Nay, their not having such a doubt when they have just and solid grounds for doubting, rather renders them the more guilty, because it shows greater corruption of the heart, greater depravity of disposition. A person brought up in a false faith, which the Scripture calls *sects of perdition, doctrines of devils, perverse things, lies, and hypocrisy*—and who has heard of the true Church of Christ, which condemns all these sects, and sees their divisions and dissensions—has always before his eyes the strongest reason to doubt the safety of his own state. If he makes any examination with sincere dispositions of heart, he must be convinced that he is in the wrong; and the more he examines, the more clearly will he see it,—for this plain reason, that it is simply impossible that *false doctrine, lies,* and *hypocrisy* should ever be supported by solid arguments sufficient to satisfy a reasonable person, who sincerely seeks the truth and begs light from God to direct him in the search. Hence, if such a person never doubt, but go on, as is supposed, *bona fide*, in his own way, notwithstanding the strong grounds of doubt which he daily has before his eyes, this evidently shows either that he is supinely negligent in the concern of his soul, or that his heart is totally blinded by passion and prejudice. There were many such persons among the Jews and heathens in the time of the apostles, who, notwithstanding the splendid light of truth which these holy preachers everywhere displayed, and which was the most powerful reason for leading them to doubt of their superstitions, were so far from having such doubts, that they thought by killing the apostles they did God a service. Whence did this arise ? St. Paul himself informs us. "We renounce," says he, "the hidden things of dishonesty, not walking in craftiness, nor adulterating the Word of God, but, by manifestation of the truth, commending ourselves to every man's conscience in the sight of God." Here he describes the strange light of the truth which he preached; yet this light was hidden to great numbers, and he immediately gives the reason: "And if our Gospel be also hid, it is hid to them that are lost; in whom the God of this world hath blinded the minds of unbelievers, that the light of the Gospel of the glory of Christ, who is the image of God, should not shine upon them." (II. Cor. iv. 2.) Behold the real cause of their incredulity: they are so enslaved to the things of this world by the depravity of their heart, and the devil so blinds them, that they cannot see the light; but ignorance arising from such depraved dispositions is a guilty, a voluntary ignorance, and therefore never can excuse them.

If this kind of material heretics, then, are lost, they are not lost on account of their heresy, which for them was no sin, but on account of the grievous sins that they committed against their conscience. "For whosoever have sinned without the law," says St. Paul, "shall perish without the law." (Rom. ii. 12.) The great Apostle wishes to say: Those of the heathens who do not know anything of the Christian Law, but sin against the natural Law, their conscience, will be lost, not on account of the sin of infidelity, which was no sin for those who were invincibly ignorant of the Christian Law, but on account of the great sin which they committed against the voice of God speaking to them by their conscience. The same must be said of those Protestants who are inculpably ignorant of the Catholic religion, but sin grievously against their conscience.

"God," says St. Thomas, "enlightens every man who

comes into the world, and produces in all mankind the light of nature and of grace, as the sun does the light which imparts color and animation to all objects. But if any obstacle prevented its rays from falling on a certain object, would you attribute that defect to the sun? Or if you closed up all your windows and made your room quite dark, could you say the sun is the cause of that darkness? It is the same with the man who, by grievous sins, closes the eyes of his understanding to the light of heaven; for he is then enveloped in profound obscurity and walks in moral darkness. A scholar, who wishes to learn a more sublime science or doctrine, must have a brighter and more comprehensive conception, in order to understand clearly his master. In like manner, man, in order to be more capable of receiving divine inspirations, must have a particular disposition for them. 'The Lord God hath opened my ear, and I do not resist, neither do I withdraw from Him.' (Isai. i. 5.) Hence all vices are contrary to the gifts of the Holy Ghost, because they are in opposition to divine inspiration; and they are also contrary both to God and to reason, for reason receives its lights and inspirations from God. Therefore, he who grievously offends God, and is, on this account, not enlightened to know and believe the truths of salvation, must blame himself for his spiritual misfortune and punishment. Of these St. Paul says: In whom the God of this world hath blinded the minds of unbelievers, that the light of the Gospel of the glory of Christ, who is the image of God, should not shine unto them. (Cor. iv. 4.) 'Blind the heart of this people, and shut their ears and eyes.' (Isai. vi. 10.)"

Be it also remembered that the light of faith is withheld from those Protestants who resemble the Pharisees. "They form to themselves," says Bishop Hay, "a great idea of their good works, not observing the vast difference there is between natural good moral actions, and supernatural Christian good works, which alone will bring a man to heaven. However corrupted our nature is by sin, yet there are few or none of the seed of Adam, who have not certain good natural dispositions, some being more inclined to one virtue, some to another. Thus some are of a humane, benevolent disposition; some tender-hearted and compassionate towards others in distress; some just and upright in their dealings; some temperate and sober; some mild and patient; some also have natural feelings of devotion, and of reverence for the Supreme Being. Now, all such good natural dispositions of themselves are far from being Christian virtues, and are altogether incapable of bringing a man to heaven. They indeed make him who has them agreeable to men, and procure him esteem and regard from those with whom he lives; but they are of no avail before God with regard to eternity. To be convinced of this, we need only observe that good natural dispositions of this kind are found in Mahometans, Jews, and heathens, as well as among Christians; yet no Christian can suppose that a Mahometan, Jew, or heathen, who dies in that state, will obtain the kingdom of heaven by means of these virtues.

The Pharisees, among the people of God, were remarkable for many such virtues; they had a great veneration for the law of God; they made open profession of piety and devotion; gave large alms to the poor; fasted and prayed much; were assiduous in all the public observances of religion; were remarkable for their strict observance of the Sabbath, and had an abhorrence of all profanation of the holy name of God; yet Jesus Christ himself expressly declares: "Except your righteousness exceed that of the Scribes and Pharisees, ye shall not enter into the kingdom of heaven." (Matt. v. 20.) We are told that one of their number went up to the temple to pray, who was, in the eyes of the world, a very good man, led an innocent life, free from those grosser crimes which are so common among men, fasted twice a week, and gave tithes of all he possessed; yet Christ himself assures us that he was condemned in the sight of God. All this proves that none of the above good dispositions of nature are capable in themselves of bringing any man to heaven. And the reason is, because "there is no other name given to men under heaven by which we can be saved, but the name of Jesus only," (Acts iv. 12); therefore, no good works whatsoever, performed through the good dispositions of nature only, can ever be crowned by God with eternal happiness. To obtain this glorious reward, our good works must be sanctified by the blood of Jesus, and become Christian virtues. Now, if we search the Holy Scriptures, we find two conditions absolutely required to make our good works agreeable to God, and conducive to our salvation. *First*, that we be united to Jesus Christ by true faith, which is the root and foundation of all Christian virtues; for St. Paul expressly says, "Without faith it is impossible to please God." (Heb. xi. 6.) Observe the word *impossible;* he does not say it is difficult, but that it is *impossible*. Let, therefore, a man have ever so many good natural dispositions, and be as charitable, devout, and mortified as the Pharisees were, yet if he have not true faith in Jesus Christ, he cannot enter into the kingdom of heaven. They refused to believe in him, and therefore all their works were good for nothing as to their salvation; and unless our righteousness exceed theirs in this point, as Christ himself assures us, we shall never enter into his heavenly kingdom. But even true faith itself, however necessary, is not sufficient alone to make our good works available to salvation; for it is necessary, in the *second* place, that we be in charity with God, in his friendship and grace, without which even true faith itself will never save us. To be convinced of this, let us only give ear to St. Paul, who says, "Though I should have all faith, so as to remove mountains, though I should distribute all my goods to feed the poor, though I should give my body to be burnt, and have not charity, it profiteth me nothing." (I. Cor. xiii. 2.) So that, let a man be ever so peaceable, regular, inoffensive, and religious in his way, charitable to the poor, and what else you please, yet if he have not the true faith of Jesus Christ, and be not in charity with God, all his apparent virtues go for nothing; it is impossible for him to please God by them; and if he live and die in that state, they will profit him nothing. Hence it is manifest that those who die in a false religion, however unexceptionable may be their moral conduct in the eyes of men, yet, as they have not the true faith in Christ, and are not in charity with him, they are not in the way of salvation; for nothing can avail us in Christ but "faith that works by charity." (Gal. v. 6.)

Let us see now what the Rev. A. Young says of the other class of inculpably ignorant Protestants.

In his article "Have Protestants divine faith," published March 22, 1888, in the *Buffalo Catholic Union and Times*, the Rev. A. Young says:—

"Protestants can have divine faith. That it is possible for some Protestants to have divine faith is a fact I am as certain of as I am that I have such faith myself. I was once a Protestant, and *my faith was just as truly and theologically divine, as it is to-day*. I never had human faith, and when I explain myself I honestly believe that a great number of Protestants, could they read my words, would say—'You have stated my case exactly.'

"That we may not be misled by any fanciful ideas or notions about what is *divine faith*, I will give at once the definition of it from the mouth of one of the greatest doctors of the Church—St. Thomas. He says: '*Ipsum credere* est actus intellectus assentientis veritati divinæ ex imperio voluntatis a Deo motæ per gratiam.' (22., q. ii. art. 9.) 'To believe is an act of the intellect assenting to divine truth by command of the will moved by the grace of God.' That is an exact definition of what my belief (faith) was as a Protestant, and *in becoming a Catholic* IT UNDERWENT NO CHANGE, and *plainly could not undergo any*."

When St. Thomas says, "*Ipsum, (i.e. Deum) credere, to believe God*," etc., he speaks of Catholics who have the true faith, as is evident from all that precedes, especially from q. i., art. 10., in which he says that it belongs especially to the Pope, whom Christ made the visible head of his Church, to see to the arrangement and publication of the symbol of faith. It is, therefore, to say the least, unwise for the

Rev. A. Young to apply to himself and other material heretics what St. Thomas says only of the faith of Catholics; for he says expressly that those who have not the true faith cannot make an act of faith as it ought to be made, that is, in the manner determined by the true faith. And what St. Thomas means by "*Ipsum credere,* to believe God," he tells us in q. v., art. 3, in which he says: "The formal object of faith is the First Truth (that is, God himself) such as he is known from Holy Scripture and from the *doctrine of the Church,* which (doctrine) proceeds from the First Truth. Hence any one who does not adhere to the infallible and divine rule of faith—to the doctrine of the Church, which proceeds from the First Truth as made known in the Holy Scripture, cannot have the habit of faith; but if he holds certain truths of faith, he holds them *not by faith,* but by some other reasons. But it is clear that he who adheres to the doctrine of the Church as to the infallible rule of belief, assents to all that the Church teaches; he, however, who chooses to believe some of those truths which the Church teaches, and to reject others, instead of adhering to the doctrine of the Church as the infallible rule of faith, adheres only to his own private will or judgment.

"Those articles of faith in which a heretic does not err, he does not believe in the same manner as a Catholic believes them; for a Catholic believes them by unhesitatingly adhering to the First Truth (as made known in Holy Scripture and in the doctrine of the Church), to do which he needs the help of the habit of faith; but a heretic does not hold certain articles of faith by this infallible rule, but only by his own choice and private judgment. He whose faith is not based upon the infallible and divine rule of faith, has no true faith at all; for he who does not believe God in the way determined by the true faith, does not believe God.

"We cannot believe absolutely a divine truth proposed for our belief unless we know that such a truth is proposed for our belief by an infallible and divine authority; it is only then that both the intellect and the will are infallibly directed to believe, and to adhere to the object of faith—God and his revealed truths—as the principle end of man, on account of which he assents to divine truths. As this infallible and divine authority is found only in the Catholic Church, it is evident that true acts of faith can be made only by him who adheres to this authority. (Sum. 22 q. ii., art. ii., ad 3 ; 3, 22, q. iv., art. 5. As the Rev. A. Young, when a Protestant, did not, and could not, have this infallible and divine rule of faith, he did not, and could not, according to the doctrine of St. Thomas, make acts of divine faith. If it is true, then, what he asserts, namely, "*that his faith underwent no change when he became a Catholic,*" it must be true also that he is a peculiar kind of a Catholic.

That the Rev. A. Young, as long as he was a Protestant, could not make acts of divine faith in the manner determined by faith, is also evident from the doctrine of St. Alphonsus.

God begins the work of man's salvation, says St. Alphonsus, by working upon the soul *inwardly* and *outwardly*. God works upon the soul inwardly by inspiring it first with the thought of salvation. From the thought of salvation arises the desire of salvation. The desire of salvation prepares the soul to comply with the conditions of salvation. Now, the first condition of salvation is true, divine faith. The beginning of true faith, then, is the desire thereof, arising from the thought of salvation. The pious desire of faith, however, is not as yet formal faith ; it is but the good thought of wishing to believe, which, as St. Augustine says, precedes belief.

The desire of salvation, inspired by Almighty God, must also be accomplished by him. So he also works upon the soul outwardly. The most usual means which he employs to work upon the soul outwardly and lead it to the possession of the true faith is to give it an opportunity to learn the truths of salvation from the Catholic Church. "Faith is from hearing," says St. Paul. He then enlightens the intellect of man to see the truths of salvation ; he inclines the will to believe those truths as coming to him from God, through the divine authority of his Church, and to trust in

God's faithfulness to his promises. He believes especially that God pardons the repentant sinner and receives him into his friendship on account of the merits of Jesus Christ. But in hearing the sacred Law promulgated he perceives that he is a sinner, and therefore fears the justice of God, which is provoked by his iniquities. Having been cast down by this salutary shock, a feeling of confidence in the infinite mercy of God presents itself and raises him up. He hopes that, in consideration of Christ's merits, God will pardon him. Animated by this hope, he begins to love. This love leads him to detest his sins, to repent of them, to repair them, as far as possible; it makes him resolve to keep the commandments, and to become reconciled with God by the means given by Him, that is, Baptism for unbaptized persons, and the sacrament of Penance for those Christians who have lost the grace of God.

Faith, therefore, to be truly divine and saving, must be based upon the divine Authority of God as invested in the Roman Catholic Church.

"Without a visible, infallible Head of the Church," says St. Alphonsus, "it would be impossible to have an infallible rule of faith, whereby to know with certainty what to believe and what to do. Hence he who is separated from the Church and is not obedient to her has no infallible rule of faith; he has no longer any criterion whereby he can know what he has to believe and to do. Without this divine authority of the Church, neither the principles of divine revelation nor even those of human reason have any support, because the utterances of the one as well as those of the other will then be interpreted by every one as he pleases; and then every one can deny all the truths of faith —The Most Holy Trinity, the Incarnation of Christ, heaven and hell, and whatever else he chooses to deny. I, therefore, repeat: If the divine authority of the Church and the obedience due to her are renounced, every error will be endorsed and must be tolerated in others. This undeniable argument made a Calvinist preacher renounce his errors." (Appendix to his work, Council of Trent.)

Hence St. Thomas, speaking of faith, says: "The virtue of faith consists principally in submitting our intellect and will, with the help of God's grace, to the divine authority of the true Church charged by Jesus Christ to teach us what we must believe. He who does not follow this rule of faith, has no true faith at all." The reason of this is given above by St. Alphonsus; for how could we, without the Church, know that God has revealed anything at all? How could we know what he has revealed? How could we know the meaning of his revelations? How could we know the written Word of God? How could we know the meaning of Holy Scripture? For Holy Scripture does not consist in the words, but in the sense of the words. How could we know the extent of the divine revelations? For the extent of the divine revelations is greater than that of Holy Scripture. So, without the divine authority of the Roman Catholic Church, we can hold no revealed truth on divine authority; if we hold any Catholic truths, we believe them only on human authority; and such belief is no divine faith. Acts of divine faith, therefore, consist in believing firmly what God tells us through the divine authority of his Church. All heretics, formal as well as material, are separated from this divine authority, and therefore even the acts of faith made by material heretics are by no means acts of divine faith, in spite of their inculpable ignorance of the divine authority of the Church. Suppose such a Protestant has counterfeit money in his possession, which he innocently believes to be quite genuine, is his money, from being counterfeit, changed into genuine money by his inculpable ignorance in the matter. In like manner, the acts of faith made by a material heretic are counterfeit acts of faith, because they are not based upon the authority of God, speaking through the authority of his true Church. These acts are without a divine foundation.

In inculpable ignorance of this fundamental truth for true acts of faith there is no power whatever to change counterfeit acts of faith into divine acts of faith. All that can be said in favor of this kind of heretics is that they may have the disposition for believing what is right, and this disposition comes from God and prepares such Protestants for receiving the gift of the true faith when they come to know it.

Now let us suppose to be true what is impossible to be true, namely, that the act of faith made by a material heretic is a *divine* act of faith, as the Rev. A. Young asserts, it is very wrong for him to say that such an act of faith, as described by him, is, according to St. Thomas, *meritorious*, which means, deserving of an eternal reward in heaven. St. Thomas never said anything of the kind; he says that an act of faith is meritorious only when it proceeds from, and is united with, divine charity.—All good works, that are performed by a person without being in the state of true divine charity, are dead works.—If the Rev. Young gives the definition of faith given by St. Thomas, why has he not given us St. Thomas's explanation of his definition of faith?—A few lines after, St. Thomas says: "Charitate superveniente actus fidei fit meritorius per charitatem." When divine charity becomes joined to faith, the act of faith becomes meritorious. When St. Thomas gives the above definition of an act of faith, he speaks of a person who believes God, who speaks to him by his Church, as is evident from other passages in which he speaks of the faith of heretics. As long, then, as a material heretic, though through inculpable ignorance, adheres to an heretical sect, he is separated from Christ, because he is separated from his Body —the Catholic Church. In that state he cannot make any supernatural acts of divine faith, hope, and charity, which are necessary to obtain life everlasting, and therefore, if he dies in that state, he is pronounced infallibly lost by St. Augustine, St. Alphonsus and all the great Doctors of the Church.

But, says the Rev. A. Young: "I was baptized in infancy by a minister of the Protestant Episcopalian Church. I then received, as all baptized persons do, whether adults or infants, the infused virtues of divine faith, hope, and charity, with sanctifying grace, and was made capable, by the grace of God thus given, to make distinct meritorious acts of divine faith, hope, and charity."

One of the effects of Baptism is that, when children are validly baptized, they receive, together with the indelible character of a Christian, the habit of faith,—or a capacity, a power or faculty which enables them, when they come to the use of reason, and are instructed by the Catholic Church in revealed truths, to make acts of divine faith, this habit of faith enabling them to see clearly and believe firmly the truths of the Catholic religion. A baptized child is a child of God, and God lives in the soul of that child and is its Father. So, when God speaks through his Church to that child, it easily recognizes the voice that speaks to him as the voice of God, and firmly believes whatever that voice teaches him to believe. But this habitual divine faith is lost by the profession of heresy, material heresy not excepted. To a child that is brought up in heresy, God does not speak when it hears the voice of a heretical teacher; if it believes that teacher, it believes not God, but man, and its faith is human, which cannot lead it to God. (See St. Thomas, De Fide, Q. V., art. iii.; Cursus Compl. Theologiæ, vol. 21, Q. III., art. iii., de Suscipientibus Baptismum Instruction in Christ, Doct. chapt. ii.)

This may be more clear from the following: If a person who has come to the use of reason and professes heresy at the time of his baptism, he is indeed indelibly marked as a Christian, but he is not sanctified—the other supernatural effects of baptism being suspended for want of the proper dispositions or preparations which are required to receive not only the sacrament, but also its supernatural effects. One of the most essential requisites to receive these effects is to have the true faith, *i e*, to believe God, speaking through the Catholic Church. Now heresy, material heresy not excepted, is a want of this faith, on account of which the supernatural effects of baptism are suspended. God cannot unite himself with a soul that lives in heresy, even though it be only material heresy. As the supernatural sanctifying effects in this case are suspended, so they are, for the same reason, destroyed in him who was baptized in his infancy and became a heretic, though only a material heretic, when he came to the use of reason. This person, to be again reconciled with God, must renounce heresy, believe the Catholic Church, and receive worthily the sacrament of penance; or if this cannot be had, he must have perfect contrition or charity with the desire (at least implicit) to receive the sacrament of penance. The other person, however, will be reconciled with God and truly sanctified, as soon as he renounces heresy, believes the Catholic Church, and has at least attrition (imperfect supernatural sorrow) for his sins, because it is then that the supernatural sanctifying effects of baptism take place. It is therefore evident that, if these persons and others like them were to die in heresy, they would be lost forever. (See Theolog. Curs. Compl. De Confirmatione, Part II., Q. II., art. vi.)

"The Church," says Dr. O. A. Brownson, "teaches that the infant validly baptized, by whomsoever the baptism be administered, receives in the sacrament the infused habit of faith and sanctity, and that this habit (*habitus*) suffices for salvation till the child comes to the use of reason. Hence all baptized infants dying in infancy are saved.

"But when arrived at the use of reason, the child needs something beyond this infused habit, and it is bound to elicit the act of faith. The habit is not actual faith, and is only a supernatural facility infused by grace, of eliciting the actual virtue of faith. The habit of sanctity is lost by mortal sin, but the habit of faith, we are told, is lost by a positive act of infidelity or heresy. This is not strictly true; for the habit may be lost by the omission to elicit the act of faith, which neither is nor can be elicited out of the Catholic Church; for out of her the credibie object, which is *Deus revelans et Ecclesia proponens*, (God revealing and the Church proposing for our belief) is wanting. Consequently, outside of the Church there can be no salvation for any one, even though baptized, who has come to the use of reason. The habit given in Baptism then ceases to suffice, and the obligation to elicit the act begins.

"We may be told that it may not be through one's own fault that he omits to elicit the act, especially when born and brought up in a community hostile or alien to the Church. Who denies it? But from that it does not follow either that the habit is not lost by the omission, or that the elicitation of the act is not necessary, in the case of every adult, to salvation. Invincible ignorance excuses from sin, we admit, in that whereof one is invincibly ignorant, but it confers no virtue, and is purely negative. It excuses from sin, if you will, the omission to elicit the act, but it cannot supply the defect caused by the omission. Something more than to be excused from the sin of infidelity or heresy is necessary to salvation."

But, continues the Rev. A. Young, " as I was a baptized Christian, I did not, neither could I, lose the *capacity* to make *meritorious* acts of *divine* faith, no matter whether I made them or not; no matter what I believed or disbelieved as I grew up; no matter whether I became a Protestant, Jew, Mahomedan, or infidel. I will be a baptized Christian for all eternity, because the indelible mark of baptism cannot be taken out of my soul. In this case, I was capable of making meritorious acts of divine faith."

What stupid and most absurd assertion this! Is it possible that a priest can be so ignorant as to assert what no well-instructed Catholic child would assert! Only he who lives in the true faith and in true charity with God has the capacity of making *meritorious* acts of divine faith. And yet the Rev. A. Young, in his unpardonable ignorance, solemnly asserts that a baptized Protestant, or a baptized Jew, or a baptized Mahomedan, or a baptized infidel is as such capable of making *meritorious* acts of divine faith, because he bears in his soul the indelible mark of baptism. Who ever taught and believed such nonsense! How can a priest be so ignorant as to confound the indelible character of baptism with the supernatural graces of this sacrament, which are lost by the profession of heresy and infidelity!

"Again," continues the Rev. A. Young, " God gives his grace to all persons; that is, he moves their will, as St.

Thomas says in his definition, to compel the intellect to give assent to divine truth. Therefore God moved my will to that end."

To understand how necessary the grace of God is to believe the true religion, we quote the following from St. Thomas: "The final beatitude of man, says St. Thomas, consists in the beatific vision of God. As this end of man is far above the strength of human nature, it was necessary that God should teach him how to obtain everlasting beatitude. So God has revealed certain supernatural truths, which are above the human understanding, to lead him to the beatitude of heaven. To acquire the knowledge of these truths, he must learn them from God, through those to whom God has communicated them and whom he has commissioned to teach them infallibly, in his name. Then it is necessary that he who learns these truths from God through his infallible teacher, should give his firm assent to them. The cause which induces man to give his assent to these supernatural truths may be twofold: it may be exterior, such as a miracle which a person sees, or some one who tries by his words to persuade a person to believe. Neither of these two causes is sufficient to create faith; for of those who see one and the same miracle, and of those who hear the same sermon on faith, there are some who believe and others do not believe. Hence it is necessary to assign another interior cause which induces a person to assent to the truths of faith. The Pelagians (heretics) taught that the free-will of man is this interior cause which induces him to believe, and that on this account the beginning of faith is of man himself, in as much as he is ready to believe divine truths, but that the perfection of faith is from God, who proposes the truths which must be believed. But this is false, for by giving his assent to the truths of faith man is raised above his natural condition, and therefore the cause that raises man above his natural state must be supernatural, moving man interiorly to believe, and this interior supernatural cause is God. Hence the assent to the truths of faith, which is the principal act of faith, must be attributed to God who, by his grace, interiorly moves man to believe the truths of faith. Although the act of believing consists in the will, yet it is necessary that the will of man should be prepared by the grace of God, in order to be raised to those things which are above human nature." (22. q. ii., art. 3., and q. vi., art. 1.) It is, therefore, necessary that God should enlighten the intellect and move the will of man to believe the true religion when it is preached to him; but it would be blasphemous to say that God moves the will of man to believe heretical doctrine. And yet the Rev. A. Young asserts "that God moved his will to give his assent to divine truth" in Protestantism. And what he believed of the true divine teacher of God—the Roman Catholic Church, he candidly tells us when he says:

"I was brought up to believe that the Roman Catholic Church was the Church of Antichrist; that she was the scarlet woman of Babylon, and the Pope the man of sin; that she taught false doctrines; that she was the great enemy of all the Christian truth, morality, and love of God. I read the wandering Jew, I also read many other horrible, lying, immoral books written to defame the Roman Catholic Church; and as there was no opportunity for me to learn better I believed them to be true."

Now, who will be foolish enough to believe that God moved the will of Rev. A. Young to believe such devilish doctrines? God enlightened his intellect and moved his will when he detested those doctrines and made his profession of faith in the only true Holy Catholic Church; God moves the will towards what is good, but not towards what is bad; he cannot be the author of evil.

"As a Protestant," continues the Rev. A. Young, "I was always taught that the Christian religion was divinely true, because it was the religion of Christ, who was God incarnate. I was taught and firmly assented to all the doctrines of the Christian religion as formulated in the Apostles' and the Nicene Creed, in precisely the same words, and, to all intents and purposes, in *precisely the same sense that I now recite them as a Catholic.* Whatever the Apostles meant and whatever the Council of Nice meant to convey, whether I perfectly understood it or not, I meant to believe, and did believe; and therefore, whensoever I recited those Creeds, I made distinct acts of divine faith, most unquestionably. And it is also beyond a doubt that I implicitly included in my acts of divine faith *all* divine truth that God has ever revealed to mankind."

From the time of the Apostles there have been men who called themselves Christians, because they were baptized; but as they did not believe in Christ as made known in Holy Scripture and in the doctrine of the Church, they were called anti-Christs. ("Qui enim non credit Christum esse sub his conditionibus, quas fides determinat" says St. Thomas, "non vere Christum credit et ideo Christum credere non convenit ipsis sub ea ratione qua ponitur actus fidei.")

"Insane people," said one day a certain gentleman to me, "are also called men, but they are not the right sort of men." In like manner material heretics may call themselves Christians, and their sects Christian Churches; but they are not the right sort of Christians and their sects are not the true Church of Christ. They are not Catholic Christians, and therefore they are not the Church of Christ.

In his catalogue of heresies, St. Augustine mentions eighty-eight heresies, and then he adds: "If any one does not believe these heresies, he must not therefore think or say that he is a Catholic Christian; for there may be other heresies, or others may still arise, and he who should adhere to any one of them, can not be a Catholic Christian.

So the Rev. A. Young believed in a Christian religion, but not in the right sort of Christian religion, because it was not the Catholic Christian religion. He believed in the Christian Church, but not in the Catholic Christian Church, "which," as he candidly avows, "he, in his ignorance, hated, detested, and feared, believing her to be the Church of Antichrist, etc." That he recited the Apostles' and Nicene Creed does not change the matter. For "it may happen," says St. Augustine, "that a heretic holds all the words of the Creed, and yet does not believe rightly, because he does not believe the divine truths of the Creed, as explained by the Church; under these words heretics generally hide their venomous doctrines." (De Fide et. Symb. c. i.)

St. Cyprian says the same (Epist. 76 ad Magn.): "Should any one say that a Novatian holds the same law that the Catholic Church holds, that he baptizes in the symbol (Creed) as we do, etc., let him know first that the law of our symbol is not one and the same with that of the schismatics, nor are our questions the same with theirs: for if any one is asked, dost thou believe the remission of sins and life everlasting through the Holy Church? their answer to this question is a lie, since they have not the Church."

St. Jerome (Advers. Lucif. c. v.) says: "When we baptize, we solemnly ask, after the profession of faith in the Most Holy Trinity: 'Dost thou believe the Holy Church? Dost thou believe the forgiveness of sins? Which Church dost thou say to believe in? In that of the Arians? But they have not ours; and therefore, as he was baptized out of her he could not believe *in that one which he knew not*." Ask, in like manner, an Episcopalian: "Do you believe the Catholic Church?" he will answer, "Yes; but not the Roman Catholic Church," which he is taught to hate and detest, and to look upon the Pope as the man of sin.

"Being unfortunately brought up a Protestant," continues the Rev. A. Young, "I *was like* an ignorant Catholic in good faith who failed to learn all that the Catholic Church, the visible, authorized teacher of all divine truth, does teach."

Now it is wholly untrue that the Rev. A. Young as a Protestant "was like an ignorant Catholic who failed to learn all that the Catholic Church, the visible authorized teacher of all divine truth, does teach."

An ignorant Catholic is not a material heretic; he is a member of the Body of Christ; if he is a dead member of it, being in the state of mortal sin, he as such is able still to make acts of divine faith, though not meritorious, because he believes all that God teaches him through his infallible teacher—the Catholic Church; if he is in the state of sanctifying grace, his acts of faith will be meritorious to eternal life. Nothing of the kind is true of a material heretic, because he is out of the Church and therefore no member of Christ's body.

"As only those members," says St. Augustine, "are vivified by the soul which are united with the body, so, in like manner, only those are vivified by the Spirit of Christ, who remain members of his Body—the Church. He who is separated from Christ's Body is not a member of Christ; and if he is not a member of Christ, he cannot be vivified by Christ's Spirit. But any one who has not Christ's Spirit does not belong to Christ. Hence a Christian must fear nothing so much as separation from Christ's Body, which is the Church." (Tract. 27, in Joan.)

"So long, continues the Rev. A. Young, as one's faith is a willing oblation, or spiritual sacrifice of self authority, by referring his *reason* for believing to what he thinks (according to his lights and opportunities) to be a divinely authorized source of instruction by which he is directly taught, or through which he honestly believes God wills him to learn divine truth, that man is a Catholic in the sight of God, and he is a Catholic in the sight of the Church, no matter what he calls himself, and though such a one dies piously as an Episcopalian, Presbyterian, Methodist, Baptist, or what not, St. Peter will let him into heaven as a Catholic. And many a one rejoices to find himself so recognized after death, in spite of his earthly name and ignorance. That such a baptized Protestant is a Catholic in the sight of the Church is proved by the fact that he is treated as one when he becomes a convert and applies to be received into the Church, for he is absolved as one who has been, or, as the ritual wisely adds, 'if perchance he has been' an excommunicated Catholic, on account of professed heresy."

Was the Rev. A. Young quite honest in believing what

he has just said ? How then could he write : "They (material heretics) openly refuse to hear the divine authority of the Church, and so they are heretics *in foro externo*" (of the Church).

As the Rev. A. Young was unfortunate in explaining the doctrine of St. Thomas on faith, so, in like manner, he is again unfortunate in the explanation of the formula of absolution from heresy, which the Church has prescribed for the priest to use in absolving heretics from heresy when they are about to be received into the Church.

Before giving the true, genuine explanation of that formula of absolution, we must remark that this formula of absolution is never used by the Church when an excommunicated *Catholic* is to be absolved from the censure of excommunication, nor does the Church look upon an excommunicated heretic as an excommunicated Catholic. By what right, therefore, does the Rev. A. Young call an excommunicated heretic *an excommunicated Catholic ?*

Now what is the true explanation of the formula of absolution prescribed by the Church for absolving an excommunicated heretic ?

"It may be assumed, " says the Rev. J. O' Kane, "that amongst Protestants there are many whose heresy is only material ; and it may be added that this is most likely to be the case with those who are converted to the faith, the very fact of their conversion being, generally speaking, an evidence of the sincerity with which they previously adhered to their errors.

"Now it is *formal* heresy alone (that is, heresy to which one pertinaciously adheres, though the true doctrine and the motives of its credibility are clearly proposed to him) *which is reserved to the Pope*, and not material heresy, even when the person is guilty of grievous sin by his neglect to inquire when doubts occurred, or by his culpable ignorance ; for this, though it may be a grievous sin against faith, is not, after all, the sin of formal heresy. Hence, it may easily happen that *no special faculty* is required for the absolution of these converts. (LACROIX, lib. vi., p., ii., n. 1613.)

"Again, since there is a doubt, as we suppose, whether they have been *really* baptized, there must be a doubt whether they could incur the censures of the Church. De Lugo discusses the question, and gives it as his opinion that, when, after diligent inquiry, there remains a doubt as to the validity of the baptism of one who is guilty of heresy, he is not to be regarded as having incurred the censures of the Church attached to heresy. (De Fide, Disp. xx., n. 143.

"We look on it, then, as very probable, that the converts of whom there is question have not incurred the excommunication annexed to heresy; and since the case is reserved to the Pope, dependently on the excommunication annexed to it. (St. Alphonsus, lib. vi., n. 580), and since an ordinary confessor can absolve from reserved cases when there is a doubt either as to law or fact, (Ibid., n. 600), it would seem to follow that no special faculty is required to absolve in the cases we are discussing, so far, at least, as the papal reservation is concerned.

"The practice is, however, to deal with all converts from heretical sects, as if they had incurred the *reserved* excommunication. Kenrick observes (De Bapt., n. 243) that the Church does not acknowledge, *in foro externo*, the distinction between '*material*' and '*formal*,' which would except from the *reserved* censure any one living in a heretical communion, and cites a decree of the Holy Office, reprehending one who, relying on that distinction, had absolved a Calvinist : 'Eo quod ignarus hæresum et errorum Calvini non posset dici hæreticus formalis, sed tantum materialis.' The doubt whether a convert has incurred a *reserved* censure, may be expressed in the form of absolution, as is directed in the ritual for the use of the American clergy, by inserting the word *forsan* : ' . . . . a vinculo excommunicationis quam *forsan* incurristi,' etc.

"Although bishops cannot, by their ordinary power, absolve from heresy, they can do so in virtue of special faculties, which they usually have from the Holy See, and they can delegate a priest to absolve from the excommunication." (Rev. J. O' Kane on Rubrics, n. 467, 468.)

The word "*forsan*" (perchance), then, instead of proving that material heretics belong to the Catholic Church and are considered by her as belonging to her, proves clearly the very reverse. The Church considers all Protestants (*formal as* well as *material*) as separated Christians, but material and doubtful heretics are not excommunicated with that kind of excommunication the absolution from which is reserved to the Pope. Hence St. Alphonsus says: " Heretics though baptized, are separated from the Church." (First Command, n. 4.) The fact that the Church receives converts into her communion clearly proves that she considers them as persons who did not belong to it. And be it also remembered that the Catholic Church would never bury a deceased material heretic, nor allow a priest to announce to his congregation that the holy sacrifice of the Mass will be offered up for him, for the simple reason that she considers him as separated from her Communion or Christ's Body.

Alas! how could the Church look upon a material heretic as one of her members, so long as he adheres to doctrines quite opposite to hers; so long as he has not renounced the errors of his sect, has not made profession of her faith, and is not received into her communion. To become a citizen of the United States, you have to renounce allegiance to all foreign potentates, etc.; in like manner, to become a member of the Church, a citizen of the Kingdom of God on earth, you have to renounce all allegiance to every doctrine contrary to that of the Church.

"I, moreover," continues the Rev. A. Young, "naturally (providentially, I must say, since it was not my fault) mistook my own Episcopalian Church to be what the Roman Catholic Church is. Therefore it cannot be questioned that, when I recited the Creed, and said, ' I believe in the Holy Catholic Church, ' and believed at the same time that the Episcopal Church was that Catholic Church, I certainly made acts of divine faith."

In answer to this, we say with Dr. A. O. Brownson, who asks: "But may not those who are baptized in heretical societies through ignorance, believing them to be the

Church of Christ, be regarded as in the way of salvation? Not they who are born and educated in Protestant Churches have separated themselves from the unity of the Catholic Church, but their ancestors, Calvin, Luther, Henry VIII., etc. Let St. Augustine reply: 'But those who *through ignorance* are baptized there (with heretics), judging the sect to be the Church of Christ, sin less than these (who know it to be heretical); *nevertheless they are wounded by the sacrilege of schism*, and therefore sin not lightly, because others sin more gravely. For when it is said to certain persons, it shall be more tolerable for Sodom in the day of judgment than for you, it is not therefore said because the Sodomites will not be punished, but because the others will be more grievously punished.'

And again, St. Augustine says: "It is true, Donatists who baptize heathens heal them of the wound of idolatry or infidelity; but they inflict on them *a more serious wound instead, the wound of schism*. Those of the people of God in the Old Law, who fell into idolatory, were destroyed by the sword, but under the feet of the authors of schism the earth opened and swallowed them up, (Ps. cv. 17.) and the rest of their followers were consumed by a flame of fire from heaven. (Ecclus. xlv. 24.) Who, therefore, can doubt that those who were more severely punished had also sinned more grievously?" (De Bapt. contr. Donatist., lib. i, c. 8.) Those idolaters who were baptized by the Donatists, and believed in Christ, were healed of their wound of infidelity; they never lived in the unity of the Catholic Church. They never wilfully left her in their ancestors, as Rev. A. Young and other heretics did; and yet St. Augustine tells us that the wound of schism which they received by adhering to the sect of the Donatists was more fatal for them than that which they had received before by the crime of idolatry. Now the wound inflicted by heresy, though material, is still more fatal than that of schism. Hence those who are separated from the Church cannot be innocent. (St. Augustine, lib. i. contr. Epist. Parm., c. 3) "Where there is no unity in faith, there can be no divine charity. Therefore divine charity can be kept *only in the unity of the Church.*" (St. Augustine, contr. lit. Petil. lib. ii., c. 77.)

As a person who has, in his ignorance, taken very poisonous food, becomes very sick from it and may even die, if the effects of it cannot be controlled in due time by medicine, so, in like manner, he who has taken, though ignorantly, the very poisonous food of heretical doctrines, becomes most fatally wounded by it in his soul, and unless this poison is expelled from the soul before death, by a sincere renunciation of heresy and by profession of the true faith in the Church, the soul will be lost for ever.

Our Blessed Saviour, in one short sentence, clearly shows the miserable fate of all those who follow false teachers, when he says: " They are blind teachers of the blind ; and if the blind lead the blind, both shall fall into the pit." (Matt. xv. 14.) This evidently shows that the lot of both shall be the same, and that all the dreadful curses pronounced in Holy Scripture upon the teachers of false religions will also fall upon those who follow them blindly.

"If any one without the true faith," says St. Thomas, " receives baptism out of the Church, he does not receive it unto his salvation. Hence St. Augustine says (De Bapt. contr. Donatist , lib. iv., in princip.) 'The Church likened to paradise signifies to us that people may, it is true, receive her baptism, out of her, but *no one can, out of her, receive or* KEEP *everlasting happiness,*' that is, KEEP sanctifying grace in his soul. (Sum. Pars. iii. q. 68, art. 8.)

"There is no salvation out of the Church," says St. Augustine. Who denies this truth ? And therefore whatever is held out of her communion, is of no avail out of the Church. Those who are out of her unity, do not gather with Christ, but scatter. (Matt. xii. 30.) (Contra Donatist.) " Out of the Church," says St. Fulgentius, " Baptism avails nothing unto salvation, nor can any one out of her receive the forgiveness of his sins, nor obtain eternal life in spite of all alms he may give." (Lib. 1, de Remiss. Peccat. cap. 22, and Lib. de Fide ad Petrum.)

How absurd, then, is it not for the Rev. A. Young to assert that, if such a material heretic dies, he will be admitted as a Catholic into heaven.

"Another excuse," says Brownson, "which is alleged for these (schismatics) is: They say that they have been baptized, that they believe in Christ, apply themselves to good works, and therefore may hope for salvation, although they adhere to the party divided from the Church.

"St. Augustine replies: 'We are accustomed from these words of the Apostle "If I speak with the tongues of angels, etc.," (I. Cor. xiii. 1–8.) to show men that it avails them nothing to have either the sacraments or the faith, if they have not charity, in order that, when you come to Catholic unity, you may understand what is conferred on you, and how great is that in which you were before deficient. *For Christian charity cannot be kept out of the unity of the Church;* and thus you may see that without it you are nothing, even though you have baptism and faith, and by your faith were able even to remove mountains. If this is also your opinion, let us not detest and scorn either the sacraments which we acknowledge in you, or the faith itself, but let us maintain charity, without which we are nothing, even with the sacraments and the faith. But we maintain charity, if we embrace unity; and we embrace unity when our knowledge is in unity through the words of Christ, not when through our own words we form a partial sketch.'

"Another excuse," says Brownson, "for such people is: Some say that God is to be believed according to the measure of grace received from him; Catholics, indeed, believe many things which Protestants do not, but the former have received the five talents, the latter the two or three. They do not condemn Catholics, but they hope to be saved in the small measure which they have themselves received.

"But here may avail what we have just adduced from St. Augustine; for if even baptism and faith profit nothing without indispensable charity, much less will profit a mere portion which is held in division and schism. (De controversiis Tract. General, IX. de unit. Eccl. et Schism, cap. 15; Vide etiam Lib. 1. de Bapt. contr. Donat. cap. v. ; lib. 1 contr. litt. Petil. cap. 23, et lib. 2. cap. 8; et de Unit. Eccl. cap. 2. S. Optat. Milevit. 1 et 2.)"

This is high authority and express to the purpose. It cuts off every possible excuse which our countrymen can allege, or which can be alleged for them. They who are brought up in the Church, instructed in her faith, and admitted to her sacraments, if they break away from her, can be saved only by returning and doing penance; and all who knowingly resist her authority, or adhere to heretical and schismatical societies, knowing them to be such, are in the same category, and have no possible means of salvation without being reconciled to the Church, and loosened by her from the bonds with which she has bound them. Thus far all is clear and undeniable. But even they who are in societies separated from the Church through ignorance, believing them to be the Church of Christ, according to the authorities adduced, are wounded by sacrilege, a most grievous sin, are destitute of charity. which cannot be kept *out of the unity of the Church*, and without which they are nothing, and therefore, whatever may be the comparative degree of their sinfulness, are in the road to perdition, as well as the others, and no more than the others can be saved without being reconciled to the Church. But these several classes include all of our countrymen not in the Church, and therefore, as every one of these is exposed to the wrath and condemnation of God, we have the right, and are in duty bound, to preach to them all, without exception, that, unless they come into the Church, and humbly submit to her laws, and persevere in their love and obedience, they will inevitably be lost. "Out of the Church there is positively no salvation for any one." (Fourth Lat. Council.)

"Unquestionably, all must enter into the Church," some will say; "but not necessarily into the visible Church. We must distinguish between the Body or exterior communion of the Church, and the soul, or interior communion.

The dogma of faith simply says: out of the Church there is no salvation, and you have no right to go further and add the word *visible* or *exterior*."

"We add the word *exterior* or *visible*," says Dr. O. A. Brownson, "to distinguish the Church out of which there is no salvation from the invisible Church contended for by Protestants, and which no Catholic does or can admit. Without it, the dogma of faith contains no meaning. Unquestionably, as our Lord in his humanity had two parts, his body and his soul, so we may regard the Church, his Spouse, as having two parts, the one exterior and visible, the other interior and invisible, or visible only by the exterior, as the soul of man is visible by his face; but to contend that the two parts are separable, or that the interior exists disconnected from the exterior and is sufficient independently of it, is to assert, in so many words, the prevailing doctrine of Protestants, and so far as relates to the indispensable conditions of salvation, to yield them, at least in their understanding, the whole question. In the present state of controversy with Protestants, we cannot save the integrity of the faith, unless we add the epithet, visible or external. But it is not true that by so doing we add to the dogma of faith. The sense of the epithet is necessarily contained in the simple word *Church* itself, and the only necessity there is of adding it at all is in the fact that heretics have mutilated the meaning of the word *Church*, so that to them it no longer has its full and proper meaning. Whenever the word *Church* is used generally, without any specific qualification, expressed or necessarily implied, it means, by its own force, the visible as well as the invisible Church, the Body no less than the Soul; for the Body, the visible or external communion, is not a mere accident, but is essential to the Church. The Church, by her very definition, is the congregation of men called by God through the evangelical doctrine, and professing the true Christian faith under their infallible Pastor and Head —the Pope. This definition takes in nothing not essential to the very idea of the Church. The Church, then, is always essentially visible as well as invisible, exterior as well as interior; and to exclude from our conception of it the conception of visibility would be as objectionable as to exclude the conception of body from the conception of man. Man is essentially body and soul; and whosoever speaks of him—as *living* man—must, by all the laws of language, logic, and morals, be understood to speak of him in that sense in which he includes both. So, in speaking of the Church, if the analogy is admissible at all. Consequently, when faith teaches us that out of the Church there is no salvation, and adds herself no qualification, we are bound to understand the Church in her integrity, as Body no less than as Soul, visible no less than invisible, external no less than internal. Indeed, if either were to be included rather than the other, it would be the Body; for the Body, the congregation or society, is what the word primarily and properly designates; and it designates the soul only for the reason that the living Body necessarily connotes the soul by which it is a living Body, not a corpse. We have then, the right, nay, are bound by the force of the word itself, to understand by the Church, out of which there is no salvation, the visible or external as well as the invisible or internal communion.

"What Bellarnime, Billuart, Perrone, and others say of persons pertaining to the soul and yet not to the Body of the Church makes nothing against this conclusion. They, indeed, teach that there is a class of persons that may be saved, who cannot be said to be *actually* and *properly* in the Church. Bellarmine and Billuart instance catechumens and excommunicated persons, in case they have faith, hope, and charity; Perrone, so far as we have seen, instances catechumens only; and it is evident from the whole scope of their reasoning that all they say on this point must be restricted to catechumens, and such as are substantially in the same category with them; for they instance no others, and we are bound to construe every exception to the rule strictly, so as to make it as little of an exception as possible. If, then, our conclusion holds true, notwithstanding the apparent exception in the case of catechumens and those substantially in the same category, nothing these authors say can prevent it from holding true universally.

"Catechumens are persons who have not yet received the visible sacrament of baptism *in re* (in reality), and therefore are not *actually* and *properly* in the Church, since it is only by baptism that we are made members of Christ and incorporated into his Body. 'With regard to these there is no difficulty,' says Bellarmine, 'because they are of the *Faithful*, and if they die in that state may be saved; and yet no one can be saved out of the Church, as no one was saved out of the ark, according to the decision of the fourth Council of Lateran, C. 1: "Una est fidelium Universalis Ecclesia, extra quam nullus omnino salvatur." Still, it is no less certain that catechumens are in the Church, not actually and properly, but only potentially, as a man conceived, but not yet formed and born, is called man only potentially. For we read (Acts, ii. 41.) "they therefore that received his word were baptized; and there were added to them that day about three thousand souls." Thus the Council of Florence, in its instructions for the Armenians, teaches that men are made members of Christ and of the Body of the Church when they are baptized; and so all the Fathers teach . . . Catechumens are not actually and properly in the Church. How can you say they are saved, if they are out of the Church?"

"It is clear that this difficulty, which Bellarmine states, arises from understanding that to be in the Church means to be in the visible Church, and that, when faith declares, out of the Church no one can be saved, it means out of the visible communion. Otherwise it might be answered, since they are assumed to have faith, hope, and charity, they belong to the soul of the Church, and that is all that faith requires. But, Bellarmine does not so answer, and since he does not, but proceeds to show that they do in a certain sense belong to the body, it is certain that he understands the article of faith as we do, and holds that men are not in the Church unless they, in some sense, belong to the body.

"But," Bellarmine continues, "The author of the book 'De Ecclesiasticis Dogmatibus,' replies, that they are not saved. But this appears too severe; certain it is that St. Ambrose, in his oration on the death of Valentinian, expressly affirms that catechumens can be saved, of which number was Valentinian when he departed this life. Another solution is therefore to be sought. Melchior Cano says that catechumens may be saved, because, if not in the Church properly called Christian, they are yet in the Church which comprehends all the faithful, from Abel to the consummation of the world. But this is not satisfactory; for, since the coming of Christ, there is no true Church but that which is properly called Christian, and therefore, if catechumens are not members of this, they are members of none. I reply therefore, that the assertion, 'out of the Church no one can be saved,' is to be understood of those who are of the Church neither actually nor in desire, as theologians generally say when treating of baptism." (De. Eccl. Milit. lib. 3, cap. 3.)

"I have said," says Billuart, "that catechumens are not *actually* and *properly* in the Church, because, when they request admission into the Church, and when they already have faith and charity, they may be said to be in the Church proximately and in desire, as one may be said to be in the house because he is in the vestibule for the purpose of immediately entering. And in this sense must be taken what I have elsewhere said of their pertaining to the Church, that is, that they pertain to her inchoately, as aspirants who voluntarily subject themselves to her laws; and they may be saved, notwithstanding there is no salvation out of the Church; for this is to be understood of one who is in the Church neither actually nor virtually—*nec re nec in voto.* In the same sense St. Augustine, (Tract. 4 in Joan. n. 13.) is to be understood when he says, 'Futuri erant aliqui in Ecclesia excelsioris gratiae catechumeni,' that is, in will and proximate disposition, 'in voto et proxima dispositione.' (Theolog. de Reg. Fid. Dissert. 3, art. 3.)

"It is evident, both from Bellarmine and Billuart, that no

one can be saved unless he belongs to the visible Communion of the Church, either actually or virtually, and also that the salvation of catechumens can be asserted only because they do so belong; that is, because they are in the vestibule, for the purpose of entering, have already entered in their will and proximate disposition. St. Thomas teaches with regard to these, in case they have faith working by charity, that all they lack is the reception of the visible sacrament *in reality*; but, if they are prevented by death from receiving it *in reality* before the Church is ready to administer it, that God supplies the defect, accepts the will for the deed, and reputes them to be baptized. If the defect is supplied, and God reputes them to be baptized, they are so in effect, have in effect received the visible sacrament, are truly members of the external communion of the Church, and therefore are saved in it, not out of it. (Summa, 3, q. 68, a. 2, corp. ad 2. et ad 3.

"The case of the catechumens disposes of all who are substantially in the same category. The only persons, not catechumens, who can be in the same category, are persons who have been validly baptized, and stand in the same relation to the sacrament of Reconciliation that catechumens do to the sacrament of Faith. Infants, validly baptized, by whomsoever baptized, are made members of the Body of our Lord, and, if dying before coming to the age of reason, go immediately to heaven. But persons having come to the age of reason, baptized in an heretical society, or persons baptized in such society in infancy, and adhering to it after having come to the years of understanding—for there can be no difference between the two classes—whether through ignorance or not, are, as we have seen, out of unity, and therefore out of charity, without which they are nothing. Their faith, if they have any, does not avail them; their sacraments are sacrilegious. The wound of sacrilege is mortal, and the only possible way of being healed is through the sacrament of Reconciliation or Penance. But for these to stand in the same relation to this sacrament that catechumens do to the sacrament of Faith, they must cease to adhere to their heretical societies, must come out from among them, seek and find the Church, recognize her as the Church, believe what she teaches, voluntarily subject themselves to her laws, knock at the door, will to enter, standing waiting to enter as soon as she opens and says, Come in. If they do all this, they are substantially in the same category with catechumens; and if, prevented by death from receiving the visible sacrament in reality, they may be saved, yet not as simply joined to the soul of the Church, but as in effect joined or restored to her external Communion. By their voluntary renunciation of their heretical or schismatic society, by their explicit recognition of the Church, by their actual return to her door, by their dispositions and will to enter, they are effectually, if not in form, members of the Body as well as the soul. Persons excommunicated stand on the same footing as these. They are excluded from the Church, unless they repent. If they repent and receive the visible sacrament of Reconciliation, either in reality or in desire, they may be saved, because the Church, in excommunicating them, has willed their amendment, not their exclusion from the people of God; but we have no authority to affirm their salvation on any other condition.

"The apparent exception alleged turns out, therefore, to be no real exception at all; for the persons excepted are still members of the Body of the Church in effect, as the authorities referred to labor to prove. They are persons who renounced their infidel and heretical societies, and have found and explicitly recognized the Church. Their approach to the Church is *explicit*, not *constructive*, to be inferred only from a certain vague and indefinite longing for the truth and unity in general, predicable in fact, we should suppose, of nearly all men; for no man ever clings to falsehood and division, believing them to be such. Their desire for truth and unity is explicit. Their faith is the Catholic faith; the unity they will is Catholic unity; the Church at whose door they knock is the Catholic Church; the sacrament they solicit, they solicit from the hands of her legitimate priest. They are in effect Catholics, and though not actually and properly in the Church, nobody ever dreams of so understanding the article, 'out of the Church no one can be saved,' as to exclude them from salvation.*

"The Church is always and everywhere, at once and indissolubly, as the living Church, interior and exterior, consisting, like man himself, of soul and body. She is not a disembodied spirit, nor a corpse. The separation of the soul and body of the Church is as much her death as the separation of the soul and body of man is his. She is the Church, the living Church, only by the mutual commerce of soul and body. There may be grave sinners in her body who have no communion with her soul; these are indeed members, but not living members and are *in* the Body rather than *of* it, as vicious humors may be in the blood without being of it, for they must have communion with the soul in order to be living members.

"The life of the Church, as all theologians teach, is in the mutual commerce of the exterior and interior, the body and soul; and therefore no individual not joined to her body can live her life. Indeed, to suppose that communion with the Body alone will suffice, is to fall into mere formalism, to mistake the corpse for the living man; and, on 'the other hand, to suppose that communion with the soul out of the body and independent of it is practicable, is to fall into pure spiritualism, simple Quakerism, which tapers off into Transcendentalism or sentimentalism. Either extreme is the death of the Church, which is, as we have said, to be regarded as always, at once and indissolubly, soul and body. (See Perrone, de Loc. Theolog. p. 1, cap. 2, art. 3, et cap. 4, art. 1. ad 1.)

"To assume that real or virtual communion with the body is not necessary, or that we may be joined to the spirit without being joined to the body is to make the body only occasionally or accidently necessary to sal-

---

* (Wherever we have spoken in any of our works of the soul and body of the Church, we wish to be understood in no other manner than has just been explained.)

vation; and, in fact, some modern speculations imply, perhaps expressly teach, that it is necessary only in the case of those who recognize it to be necessary, as if its necessity depended on the state of the human intellect, and not on the appointment of God, or as if a man's belief could excuse or make up for his want of faith, —a doctrine not to be extracted from the Holy Scripture, taught by no Father or Mediæval Doctor, and from which, we should suppose, every Catholic would instinctively turn with loathing and disgust.

"The Church is the living Temple of God, into which believers must be builded as so many living stones. It is his Body, and his Body is no more to be dispensed with than his Soul; otherwise we could not call her always visible, for to some she would be visible, to others only invisible, and then there would be no visible *Catholic* Church."

Hence we were surprised to find the following erroneous opinion in a little work, *Catholic Belief*, page 230, § 7:—

"Catholics do *not* believe that Protestants who are baptized, who lead a good life, love God and their neighbor, and are *blamelessly* ignorant of the just claims of the Catholic religion to be the only one true Religion (which is called *being in good faith*), are excluded from Heaven, provided they believe that there is one God in three Divine Persons; that God will duly reward the good and punish the wicked; that Jesus Christ is the son of God made man, who redeemed us, and in whom we must trust for our salvation; and provided they thoroughly repent of having ever, by their sins, offended God.

"Catholics hold that Protestants who have these dispositions, and who have no suspicion of their religion being false, and no means to discover, or fail in their honest endeavors to discover, the true religion, and who are so disposed in their heart that they would *at any cost* embrace the Roman Catholic Religion if they knew it to be the true one, *are Catholics in spirit* and in some sense within the Catholic Church, without themselves knowing it. She holds that these Christians belong to, and are united to the "*soul*," as it is called, of the Catholic Church, although they are not united to the visible *body* of the Church by external communion with her, and by the outward profession of her faith."

How deceptively is not this opinion put? It is a well-known fact that many Protestants are baptized only when they are grown up. If validly baptized, they were, it is true, indelibly marked with the character of the sacrament of Baptism, but they did not receive the supernatural effects of Baptism—they were not justified—for want of the proper dispositions. The Council of Trent teaches that the very first condition to receive the grace of justification in Baptism is true Catholic faith. When this faith is wanting in a person, the supernatural effects of Baptism remain suspended until such a baptized person becomes a true member of the Catholic Church. If such baptized Protestants die in that state they will be lost forever.

Those Protestants who were baptized in their infancy, and were brought up in heresy after they had come to the use of reason, became separated from the Church, and could not preserve, as St. Augustine says, divine charity out of the unity of the Church, and without such charity it is impossible to be saved.

Besides, those four great truths of salvation must be believed, as Cornelius a Lapide remarks, with divine faith, to be of any avail towards salvation. But how could those persons have this divine faith and true repentance for sins without the special mercy of God, who grants these gifts only to true converts to the Church. "Remission of sin" says St. Fulgentius, "cannot be obtained anywhere except in the Church."

And how could such persons even think of joining the Church, unless they are made to understand that they can find their salvation only in the Church. And then they would need a special grace to come up to their duty. And how could they be Catholics in spirit without having the true faith and divine charity? And how could they belong to the Soul of the Church, since that soul is not in them—that is, true faith and divine charity, which, we repeat, can be had only in the unity of the Church?

"The Catholic," says Dr. O. A. Brownson, "who holds implicitly the Catholic faith, but errs through invincible ignorance with regard to some of its *consectaria* and even dogmas, may be saved; but how can a man be said to hold implicitly the Catholic faith, who holds nothing, or rejects every principle that implies it? It is not safe to apply to Protestants, who really deny everything Catholic, a rule that is very just when applied to sincere but ignorant Catholics, or Catholics that err through inculpable ignorance. Protestantism does not stand on the footing of ordinary heterodoxy; it is no more Christian than was Greek and Roman paganism.

"It is worthy of special notice," says Brownson, "that those recent theologians who seem unwilling to assent to this doctrine cite no authority from a single Father or Mediaeval doctor of the Church, not strictly compatible with it.

"Unquestionably, authorities in any number may be cited to prove—what nobody disputes—that pertinacity in rejecting the authority of the Church is essential to formal or culpable heresy, that persons may be in heretical societies without being culpable heretics, and therefore, that we cannot say of all who live and die in such societies that they are damned precisely for the sin of heresy. Father Perrone cites passages in abundance to this effect, which, as Suares says, is the uniform doctrine of all the theologians of the Church; but he and others cite not a single authority of an earlier date than the seventeenth century, which ever hints anything more than this. But this by no means militates against St. Augustine, St. Fulgentius and others; because it by no means follows from the fact that one who is not a formal heretic is, so long as he is in a society alien to the Church, in the way of salvation.

"A man may, indeed, not be damned for his erroneous faith, and yet be damned for sins not remissible without the true faith, and for the want of virtues impracticable out of the communion of the Church. Father Perrone very properly distinguishes *material* heretics from *formal* heretics; but when treating the question *ex-professo*, he by no means pronounces the former in the way of salvation; he simply remits them to the judgment of God, who, he assures us, —what nobody questions—will consign no man to endless tortures, unless for a sin of which he is voluntarily guilty. (Tract. de Vera Relig. adv. Heterodox., prop. ix.)

"Moreover, Father Perrone, when refuting those who contend that salvation would be attainable if the visible Church should fail, that is, by internal means, by being joined in spirit to the true Church, maintains that in such case there would be no *ordinary* means of salvation; that, when Christ founded his Church, he intended to offer men an ordinary means, or rather a collection of means, which all indiscriminately, and at all times, should use for procuring salvation; that, if God had been willing to operate our salvation by the assistance of internal means, there would have been no reason for instituting the Church; that, what is said of being joined to the Church through the spirit, and of invincible ignorance, or of *material* heretics, could be admitted only on the hypothesis that God should provide no other means; that, since it is certain that God has willed to save men by other means, namely, by the institution of the Church visible and external, and which is at all times easily distinguished from every sect, it is evident that the subterfuge imagined by non-Catholics is altogether unavailable." (De Loc. Theologic., p. 1, cap. 4, art. 1.)

The Rev. A. Young seems not to become tired of repeating, though in other words, the same erroneous opinion of the faith of Protestants. So he says again: "If we Catholics could be, shall I say, *fearless enough* to acknowledge that the common actual faith of Protestants, who are in good faith, is *identical with ours in its essential quality* and saving their great pitiable ignorance, I am convinced that it would open the way for the conversion of many of them."

Let us therefore repeat again a most essential quality of our faith as given by St. Thomas. He says:—

"The formal object of faith is the *First Truth* (that is, God himself) such as he is made known in Holy Scripture and *in the doctrine of the Church,* which (doctrine) comes from the First Truth. Hence, whosoever does not adhere to the *infallible* and *divine* rule (of faith)—to the doctrine of the Church, which proceeds from the First Truth (God) as made known in Holy Scripture, *such a one has not the habit of faith*; but those truths of faith which he holds, he holds them not by faith, but in some other way. But it is evident that he who adheres to the doctrine of the Church as the infallible rule (of faith), gives his assent to all that the Church teaches; but he who holds of the truths of faith which the Church teaches such as he chooses, and rejects such as he chooses, does not adhere to the doctrine of the Church as infallible rule of faith; he adheres to his own private judgment as rule of his faith.

Faith adheres to all the articles of faith on account of one medium, namely, on account of the First Truth (God) as proposed for our faith in Holy Scripture according to the doctrine of the Church; (that is, as Sylvius explains, the Church, proposing or declaring what is of faith, is the ordinary medium established by God, in order that we may know for certain what he has revealed and what he obliges the faithful to believe). "And therefore," continues St. Thomas, "he who has not this medium, (that is, he who has not the Church for his teacher in all matters of faith) *has no faith whatever.*" *

Such is the doctrine of St. Thomas, of St. Alphonsus, and of all the Fathers and Doctors of the Church concerning those who have divine faith, and those who have none what-

---

* "Formale objectum fidei," says St. Thomas, "est veritas prima (*i. e.* Deus ipse) secundum quod manifestatur in Scripturis sacris et *in doctrina Ecclesiæ,* quæ procedit ex veritate prima. Unde *quicunque* non inhærit sicut infallibili et divinæ regulæ, doctrinæ Ecclesiæ, quæ procedit ex veritate prima in Scripturis sacris manifestata, ille non habet habitum fidei; sed ea, quæ sunt dei, alio modo tenet quam per fidem. Manifestum est autem, quod ille, qui inhæret doctrinæ Ecclesiæ tanquam infallibili regulæ, omnibus assentit quæ Ecclesia docet. alioquin,

ever. Our faith is divine and infallible, because it comes to us from God through the divine and infallible medium of the Church. But "material Protestants," as the Rev. A. Young candidly says, "*openly refuse to hear the divine authority of the Church, and so they are heretics in foro externo*" of the Church. They, therefore, have no infallible and divine rule of faith, and consequently cannot have divine faith. Their faith is human, ours is divine.

Another essential *quality* of our faith is that it is always *one* and *unchangeable*; Protestant faith is as *changeable* as the wind; hence we see so many different sects of Protestants.

Again, a very *essential quality* of our faith is that it is holy, because it comes from Jesus Christ. We believe absolutely in Jesus Christ and all that he teaches us through his Church. Protestants, material Protestants not excepted, have no absolute faith in Christ, first, because they do not believe him to be such as he is made known in Holy Scripture and in the infallible doctrine of his Church; secondly, because they do not believe all that Christ commanded his Church to teach all nations, obliging all to believe her doctrine under pain of eternal damnation.

Moreover, the Church is *holy*, because she has the *sacraments* instituted by Jesus Christ as a means by which his grace is conferred upon those who are members of his body —the Catholic Church. Protestants have rejected most of these means of holiness, and therefore even material heretics are deprived of them. If they receive baptism, it is not unto their salvation, as St. Thomas, St. Augustine, and other Fathers of the Church say (Only those Protestant children are saved who, if baptized, die before they come to

si de his quæ Ecclesia docet, quæ vult tenet, et quæ non vult non tenet, jam non inhæret Ecclesiæ doctrinæ, sicut infallibili regulæ, sed propriæ voluntati

Omnibus articulis fidei inhæret fides propter unum medium, scilicet *propter veritatem primam propositam* nobis in Scripturis *secundum doctrinam, Ecclesiæ intelligentis sane;* (i. e , ut explicat Sylvius : Ecclesiæ propositio vel declaratio, medium est ordinarium a Deo institutum, ut certo sciamus, quænam ipse revelaverit et a fidelibus credenda voluerit). "Et ideo, qui ab hoc medio decidit, TOTALITER *fide caret.* "

the years of understanding); but those who grow up in heresy forfeit the supernatural graces of baptism, and are most fatally wounded by heresy. But in our faith the forgiveness of sins is obtained, and we become holy by living up to it. All this is impossible in Protestant faith. Their faith is derived from the enemies of Christ.

Our faith teaches us a holy worship, established by Jesus Christ—the holy sacrifice of the Mass, in which Jesus Christ offers himself, through the hands of his priest, to his heavenly Father in an unbloody manner, as he did in a bloody manner on the cross; it is by this holy, unbloody sacrifice that he applies to our souls the merits of his bloody sacrifice, and that we, by offering it up to the heavenly Father, honor him with that infinite honor by which Jesus Christ has honored him on earth, especially by his death on the cross, and continues to honor him for us, to thank him for us, to pacify him for us, and to obtain immense blessings for the members of his Church Militant and Suffering; so that he stands with his heavenly Father for every faithful Catholic who is united to his Body—the Church, and that every faithful Catholic presents himself to the heavenly Father, in Christ and with Christ, with whom he is united through his Body—the Church, from which Christ will never be separated.

Alas! Protestant belief rejected Christ when it rejected the holy sacrifice of the Mass. With the rejection of this unbloody sacrifice it rejected the most holy worship of God. If the sin of the sons of Heli was very great in the sight of the Lord, because they prevented the people from offering the imperfect sacrifices of the Jewish Law, which were only figures of the unbloody perfect sacrifice of the New Law— and which were abolished by Christ, and replaced by his unbloody sacrifice,—how great must not be the sin of those who prevent Protestants from becoming Catholics, from serving and honoring God in the manner which Jesus Christ has prescribed under pain of eternal damnation! Protestant belief cuts off all its followers from this inexhaustible source of temporal and spiritual blessings; it makes them worship God with a false worship, which is so severely condemned by God in the first commandment. From the beginning of the world God himself prescribed the sacrifices and the manner in which his people should worship him; in the New Law also Christ instituted a new and perfect worship of God—for the divine worship which God wishes to receive from his own people is a most essential part of the true religion. Hence good Catholics are so anxious on Sundays and holy-days of obligation to be in due time present at the holy sacrifice of the Mass, to give to God, by this sacrifice of infinite value, that divine honor which he has prescribed, and to obtain by it all possible blessings for soul and body.

By the Catholic faith the world has been Christianized and civilized; but by the principles of Protestant belief the world has been filled with millions of infidels, because the essential quality of Protestant belief is that it rests upon negation; if Protestants, even material ones, hold some Catholic truths, they hold them from Catholics, and these truths are so many proofs to convince them that they should also believe the other truths of the Catholic Church, and be Catholics; that they are separated from the Church, which is Christ's Body, and consequently separated from Christ himself; and whatever Catholic truths they seem to hold, they cannot hold them by faith, but by some other way, as St. Thomas says; and these truths are not theirs, but ours, says Brownson; what is all theirs, is their denial of the other truths of the Catholic Church.

Another *essential quality* of our faith is that it is *Apostolic*, that is, it has come to us from the Apostles through their lawful successors who have, through Holy Orders, all the powers which Christ conferred upon his Apostles; but Protestant belief comes from apostate Catholics, who left the Church from the passion of lust, or pride, or avarice, and therefore their preachers and bishops have no more power from Christ, than a man in the moon has from the United States Government to declare war against the English Government.

Another *essential quality* of our faith is that it is *Catholic*, binding in conscience all men who come to know it to embrace it under pain of eternal damnation; but Protestant belief, as it does not come from Christ, has no power to bind persons in conscience.

Our faith will last to the end of the world all the same and unchanged; that of Protestants, like so many other heresies, will gradually disappear in the vapor of infidelity.

Our faith has been confirmed by thousands of miracles; but all the authors of heresies have died a most melancholy death, and frighful punishments have been inflicted by God upon all the persecutors of the Catholic faith, as is well known from history.

Now all this shows that the difference between the essential qualities of our faith and those of Protestant belief is greater than the distance between heaven and earth.

What a shame, therefore, for the Rev. A. Young to proclaim, through the *Catholic Union and Times* of Buffalo, " If we Catholics could be *fearless enough* to acknowledge that the common actual faith of material Protestants is *identical with ours in its essential quality.*" What an outrage and insult to Catholic faith! Such a fearless heretical acknowledgment has never been made and will never be made by any true, well-instructed Catholic.

By telling us, " If we Catholics could be *fearless enough* to acknowledge that the common, actual faith of material Protestants is *identical with ours* in its essential quality," the Rev. A. Young gives Catholics sufficient reason to believe that what he says of himself is really true, namely, that " *in becoming a Catholic, his faith underwent no change!* "

What a great difference is there not between his manner of speaking of Catholic and Protestant belief and that of Cardinals Manning and Newman, of Bishop Hay, of Dr. O. A. Brownson, Marshall, and many other celebrated converts. They speak like men of great faith; but the Rev. A. Young speaks like one whose faith is not much enlightened.

Let Father Young never forget what St. Augustine says of schismatics: " We are accustomed from the words of the Apostle ('If I speak with the tongues of angels, etc., I. Cor. xiii. 1–8) to show men that it avails them nothing to have either the sacraments or the faith, if they have not charity, *in order that, when you come to Catholic unity, you may understand what is conferred on you, and how great is that in which you were before deficient. For Christian charity cannot be kept out of the unity of the Church,* and thus you may see that without it you are nothing, even though you have Baptism and faith, and by your faith were able even to remove mountains."

§ 7. INVINCIBLE OR INCULPABLE IGNORANCE NEITHER SAVES NOR DAMNS A PERSON.

"But, suppose," some one will say, "a person, in his inculpable ignorance, believes that he is on the right road to heaven, though he is not a Catholic; he tries his best to live up to the dictates of his conscience. Now, should he die in that state of belief, he would, it seems, be condemned without his fault. We can understand that God is not bound to give heaven to anybody, but, as he is just, he certainly cannot condemn anybody without his fault."

Whatever question may be made still in regard to the great truth in question is sufficiently answered in the explanation already given of this great truth. For the sake of greater clearness, however, we will answer a few more questions. In the answers to these questions we shall be obliged to repeat what has already been said.

Now, as to the question just proposed, we answer with St. Thomas and St. Augustine: "There are many things which a man is obliged to do, but which he cannot do without the help of divine grace: as, for instance, to love God and his neighbor, and to believe the articles of faith; but he can do all this with the help of grace; and '*to whomsoever God gives his grace he gives it out of divine mercy*: and *to whomsoever he does not give it, he refuses it out of divine justice,* in punishment of sin committed, or at least in punishment of original sin, as St. Augustine says. (Lib. de corrcptione et gratia, c. 5 et 6 ; Sum. 22. q. ii. art. v.) "And the ignorance of those things of salvation, the knowledge of which men did not care to have, is, without doubt, a sin for them ; but for those who were not able to acquire such knowledge, the want of it is a punishment for their sins," says St. Augustine ; hence both are justly condemned, and neither the one nor the other has a just excuse for being lost." (Epist. ad Sixtum, Edit. Maur. 194, cap. vi., n. 27.)

Moreover, a person who wants to go East, but, by an innocent mistake, gets on a train going West, will, as soon as he finds out his mistake, get off at the next station, and take a train that goes East. In like manner, a person who walked on a road that he, in his inculpable ignorance, believed was the true road to heaven, must leave that road, as soon as he finds out his mistake, and inquire for the true road to heaven. God, in his infinite mercy, will not fail to make him find out, in due time, the true road to heaven, if he corresponds to his grace. Hence we asked the following question in our *Familiar Explanation*:

"What are we to think of the salvation of those who are out of the pale of the Church without any fault of theirs, and who never had any opportunity to know better?

To this question we give the following answer: "Their inculpable (invincible) ignorance will not save them ; but if they fear God and live up to their conscience, God, in his infinite mercy, will furnish them with the necessary means of salvation, even so as to send, if needed, an angel to instruct them in the Catholic faith, rather than let them perish through inculpable ignorance." (St. Thomas Aquinas.)

S. O. remarks about this answer, "that the author is not theologically correct, for no one will ever be punished *through*, *by*, or *because* of inculpable ignorance." In these words, S. O. impudently imputes to us what we never have asserted, namely, *that a man will be damned on account of his inculpable ignorance*. From the fact that a person tries to live up to the dictates of his conscience, and cannot sin against the true religion on account of being invincibly ignorant of it, many have drawn the false conclusion that such a person is saved, or, in other words, is in the state of sanctifying grace, making thus invincible ignorance a means of salvation. This conclusion is contra "latius hos quam præmissæ." To give an example. The Rev. Nicholas Russo, S. J., professor of philosophy in Boston College, says in his book, *The true Religion and its dogmas:*—

"This good faith being supposed, we say that such a Christian (he means a baptized Protestant) is in a way a member of the Catholic Church. Ignorance alone is the cause of his not acknowledging the authority of his true mother. The Catholic Church does not look upon him as wholly a stranger; she calls him her child; she presses him to her maternal heart; through other hands she prepares him to shine in the kingdom of heaven. Yes, the profession of a creed different from the true one will not, of itself, bar the gates of heaven before this Christian; invincible ignorance will, before the tribunal of the just God, ensure the pardon of his errors against faith; and, *if nothing else be wanting,* heaven will be his home for eternity." We have already sufficiently refuted these false assertions, and we have quoted them, not for the purpose of refuting them, but for the purpose of denying emphatically what follows after these false assertions, namely: "*This* is the *doctrine* held by almost all theologians, and *has received the sanction of our late Pope Pius IX*. In his Allocution of December 9, 1854, we read the following words: "It is indeed of faith that no one can be saved outside the Apostolic Roman Church; that this Church is the one ark of salvation; that he who has not entered it will perish in the deluge. But, on the other hand, it is equally certain that, were a man to be invincibly ignorant of the true religion, he would not be held guilty in the sight of God for not professing it."

Now, *in which* of these words of Pope Pius IX. is any of the above false assertions of the Rev. N. Russo, S. J., sanctioned? In which words does Pius IX. say that a Protestant in good faith is in a way a member of the Catholic Church? Does not Pius IX. teach quite the contrary in the following words, which the Rev. N. Russo, S. J., quotes pp. 163-166?

"Now, whoever will carefully examine and reflect upon the condition of the various religious societies, divided among themselves, and separated from the Catholic Church—which, from the days of Our Lord Jesus Christ and his Apostles, has ever exercised, by its lawful pastors, and still does exercise, the divine power committed to it by this same Lord —will easily satisfy himself that none of these socities, singly nor all together, are in any way or form that one Catholic Church which our Lord founded and built, and which he chose should be; and that he cannot by any means say that these societies are *members* or *parts* of that Church, *since they are visibly separated from Catholic unity*........

"Let all those, then, who do not profess the unity and truth of the Catholic Church, avail themselves of the opportunity of this (Vatican) Council, in which the Catholic Church, to which their forefathers belonged, affords a new proof of her close unity and her invincible vitality, and let them satisfy the longings of their hearts, and *liberate themselves from that state in which they cannot have any assurance of their own salvation.* Let them unceasingly offer fervent prayers to the God of Mercy, that he will throw down *the wall of separation,* that he will scatter the darkness of error, and that he will lead them back to the Holy Mother Church, in whose bosom their fathers found the salutary pastures of life, in whom alone the whole doctrine of Jesus Christ is preserved and handed down, and the mysteries of heavenly grace dispensed."

Now does not Pius IX. say in these words, very plainly and distinctly, that the *members* of all other religious societies are *visibly separated from Catholic unity;* that in this state of separation they cannot have salvation; that, by fervent prayer, they should beseech God to throw down *the wall of* separation, to scatter the darkness of error, and lead them to the Mother Church, in which alone salvation is found." And in his Allocution to the Cardinals, held Dec. 17, 1847, Pius IX. says: "*Let those,* therefore, *who wish to be saved*, come to the pillar and the ground of faith, which is the Church; let them come to the true Church of Christ, which, in her Bishops, and in the Roman Pontiff, the Chief Head of all, has the succession of apostolical Authority, which has never been interrupted, which has never counted anything of greater importance than to preach, and by all means to keep and defend the doctrine proclaimed by the Apostles at Christ's command. . . . . . We shall never at any time abstain from any cares or labors that, by the grace of Christ himself, we may bring those *who are ignorant, and who are going astray*, to THIS ONLY ROAD OF TRUTH and SALVATION." Now does not Pius IX. teach most clearly in these words that the ignorant cannot be saved by their ignorance, but that, in order to be saved, they must come to *the only road of truth and salvation*, which is the Roman Catholic Church?

Again, does not Pius IX. most emphatically declare, in the words quoted above by the Rev. N. Russo, S. J., that " It is indeed of faith, that NO ONE *can be saved out of the Apostolic Roman Church?* How, then, we ask, can the Rev. N. Russo, S. J. say in truth, that a Protestant in good faith, such as he described, is in a way a member of the Catholic Church? that the Catholic Church does not look upon him as wholly a stranger? that she calls him her child, presses him to her maternal heart, prepares him, through other hands, to shine in the kingdom of God? that the profession of a creed different from the true one will not, of itself, bar the gates of heaven before this Christian, etc.? How can this professor of philosophy at the Boston College assert all this, whilst Pius IX. teaches the very contrary? And mark especially the scandalous assertion of the Rev. N. Russo, S. J., namely: *" This our opinion is the doctrine which has received the sanction of our late Pope Pius IX."* To prove his scandalous assertion, he quotes the following words of Pius IX: " It is equally certain that, were a man to be *invincibly* ignorant of the true religion, he would not be held guilty in the sight of God for not professing it." If, in these words, Pius IX. says what no one calls in

216 Out of the Catholic Church there is No Salvation.

question, that invincible ignorance of the true religion excuses a Protestant from the sin of heresy, does Pius IX. thereby teach that such invincible ignorance saves such a Protestant? Does he teach that invincible ignorance supplies all that is necessary for salvation—all that you can have only in the true faith? How could the Professor of philosophy at the Jesuit College in Boston draw such a false and scandalous conclusion from premises in which it is not contained? Pius IX. has, on many occasions, condemned such liberal opinions. Read his Allocution to the Cardinals, held Dec. 17, 1847, in which he expresses his indignation against all those who had said that he had sanctioned such perverse opinions. "In our times," says he, "many of the enemies of the Catholic Faith direct their efforts towards placing every monstrous opinion on the same level with the doctrine of Christ, or confounding it therewith; and so they try more and more to propagate that impious system of the indifference of religions. But quite recently —we shudder to say it, *certain men* have not hesitated to slander us by saying that we share in their folly, favor that most wicked system, and think so benevolently of every class of mankind as to suppose that not only the sons of the Church, but that the *rest also*, however *alienated from Catholic unity they may remain*, are alike in the way of salvation, and may arrive at everlasting life. We are at a loss, from horror, to find words to express our detestation of this new and atrocious injustice that is done to us."

Mark well, Pius IX. uttered these solemn words against "*certain men*," whom he calls the enemies of the Catholic Faith,—he means liberal minded Catholics and priests, as is evident from other Allocutions, in which he says that he has condemned not less than forty times their perverse opinions about religion. Is it not, for instance, a perverse and monstrous opinion, when the Rev. N. Russo, S. J., says: "The spiritual element (of the Church) comprises all the graces and virtues that are the foundation of the spiritual life; it includes the gifts of the Holy Ghost; in other words, it is what theologians call the soul of the Church. (Now follows the monstrous opinion) This mysterious soul is not limited by the bounds of the exterior organization (of the Church); it can go far beyond; exist even in the midst of schism and heresy unconsciously professed, and bind to our Lord hearts that are connected by no exterior ties with the visible Body of the Church. This union with the soul of the Church is essential to salvation; so essential that without it none can be saved. But the necessity of belonging likewise to the Body of the Church, though a real one, may in certain cases offer no obstacle to salvation. This happens whenever *invincible ignorance* so shrouds a man's intellectual vision, that he ceases to be responsible before God for the light which he does not see"? The refutation of this monstrous opinion is sufficiently given in all we have said before. The very Allocution of Pius IX., from which the Rev. N. Russo quotes, is a direct condemnation of such monstrous opinions. (See Preface.)

Now these modern would-be theologians are not ashamed to assure us most solemnly that their opinions are the doctrine held by almost all theologians, and yet they cannot quote one proof from Holy Scripture, or from the writings of the Fathers and Doctors of the Church, to give the least support to their opinions.

The Rev. N. Russo and S. O. seem not to see the difference between saying: Inculpable ignorance will not save a man, and inculpable ignorance will not damn a man. Each assertion is correct, and yet there is a great difference between the two. It will be an act of charity to enlighten them on the point in question.

Inculpable or invincible ignorance has never been and will never be a means of salvation. To be saved, it is necessary to be justified, or to be in the state of sanctifying grace. In order to obtain sanctifying grace, it is necessary to have the proper dispositions for justification; that is, true divine faith in at least the necessary truths of salvation, confident hope in the divine Saviour, sincere sorrow for sin, together with the firm purpose of doing all that God has commanded, etc. Now, these supernatural acts of faith, hope, charity, contrition, etc., which prepare the soul for receiving sanctifying grace, can never be supplied by invincible ignorance; and if invincible ignorance cannot supply the preparation for receiving sanctifying grace, much less can it bestow sanctifying grace itself. "Invincible ignorance," says St. Thomas Aquinas, "is a punishment for sin." (De Infid. q. x., art. 1.) It is, then, a curse, but not a blessing or a means of salvation.

But if we say that inculpable ignorance cannot save a man, we thereby do not say that invincible ignorance damns a man. Far from it. To say, invincible ignorance is no means of salvation, is one thing; and to say, invincible ignorance is the cause of damnation, is another. To maintain the latter, would be wrong, for inculpable ignorance of the fundamental principles of faith excuses a heathen from the sin of infidelity, and a Protestant from the sin of heresy; because such invincible ignorance, being only a simple involuntary privation, is no sin.

Hence Pius IX. said "that, were a man to be invincibly ignorant of the true religion, such invincible ignorance would not be sinful before God; that, if such a person should observe the precepts of the Natural Law and do the will of God to the best of his knowledge, God, in his infinite mercy, may enlighten him so as to obtain eternal life; for, the Lord, who knows the heart and thoughts of man, will, in his infinite goodness, not suffer any one to be lost forever without his own fault."

§ 8. How Almighty God leads to salvation those who are inculpably ignorant of the truths of salvation.

Almighty God, who is just and condemns no one without his fault, puts, therefore, such souls as are in invincible ignorance of the truths of salvation, in the way of salvation, either by natural or supernatural means.

There is a Protestant. He lived in a part of Germany where he always remained invincibly ignorant of the true religion, but lived up to the dictates of his conscience. At last he resolved to emigrate to this country, with a view of benefiting himself temporally. But Almighty God had other designs in regard to him. He wished to put him in the way of salvation. This Protestant goes into a Protestant church in this country. He sees at once a vast difference between the Protestants in America and those in Europe. He is perplexed at this difference, and begins to doubt about the truth of Protestantism. To make sure whether he is right or wrong in his religion, he communicates his doubts to a well-instructed Catholic friend, who explains to him what true religion is, and where it is found. Accordingly, as he is upright before God, and wishes to save his soul, he makes up his mind to become a Catholic. Thus the emigration of this Protestant to this country was, in the hands of God, the natural means of putting him in the way of salvation.

Not long ago, a friend of mine told me that a lady who was on board a steamer dropped a Catholic book into the water. The captain of the boat saved the book, and read it before returning it, and at last became a Catholic. Humanly speaking, the falling of the book into the water was quite accidental; but Almighty God made use of this circumstance to put in the way of salvation one who had been invincibly ignorant, and who had not acted against his conscience.

There is a young lady. Her parents profess no religion. They never go to church. They never speak of religion at home, but take care that their daughter may not become acquainted with wicked companions. So she remains naturally good and innocent. To give her a good education, they place her in a Catholic institution. There she becomes acquainted with Catholic companions, with Catholic devotions, ceremonies, with the service of the Church, etc. She is inquisitive, and wishes to know the meaning of everything that she sees and hears about Catholicity. She is pleased with the Catholic Church, and exclaims: "I never heard anything of the kind before." At last she becomes a Catholic. Here, education is the means which God uses to place on the road to heaven one who had been invincibly ignorant of the means of salvation, and had remained naturally good and innocent.

Many similar instances could be quoted to show that Almighty God, in his goodness, uses natural ways and means to place invincibly ignorant souls, that live up to their conscience, in the way of salvation. This is the ordinary way of his divine Providence, viz., to lead men, by natural ways and means, to what is supernatural.

But there may be exceptional cases, in which Almighty God uses supernatural means to save a man inculpably ignorant and living up to his conscience. Suppose such a one is living in a country in which, naturally speaking, during his lifetime he can hear nothing of the Catholic religion. In this case, or, as has been expressed above, "*if needed,*" Almighty God will, in his infinite mercy, make use of a supernatural means to lead that person to salvation, rather than let him perish through inculpable ignorance. He can supernaturally enlighten him, so that he may know what he must believe in order to be saved. "Many of the Gentiles," says St. Thomas, "received divine revelation concerning Christ, as is evident from what they have foretold. Job says: 'I know that my Redeemer liveth; and in the last day I shall rise out of the earth.'" (Job, xix. 25.) The Sibyls also have foretold certain things of Christ, as St. Augustine says (Cont. Faust. lib. xiii., c. 15.). At the time of Constantine Augustus and his mother Irene a certain grave was found in which a body was lying that had a plate on its chest, on which were found the words: "Christ will be born of a Virgin, and I believe in him. O Sun, at the time of Irene and Constantine you shall see me again." (Baron. ad ann. Christi, 780.) This is in harmony with what Job says: "Who teacheth us more than the beasts of the earth." (Job, xxxv. 11.) (De Fide, q. ii., art vii.) Indeed, Almighty God, in his infinite mercy, can dispose a soul, in a moment, for receiving sanctifying grace, and infuse, at the same time, this grace into the soul. The light of true faith, the voluntary inclination of free-will to conform to the will and grace of God, the determination of free-will to abstain from sin, the remission of sins, and the infusion of grace, take place by a simultaneous movement; for justification is instantaneous, and has no successive gradation. It is acquired by grace and by the operation of the Holy Ghost, who takes possession of the soul at once: "And suddenly there came a sound from heaven, as of a mighty wind, and it filled the whole house." (Acts, ii. 2.) Resistance and mental deliberation may be long and slow on the part of the sinner, but victory and triumph are quick and sudden on the part of God, by the infusion of his grace into a repentant soul.

There are, indeed, remarkable instances of sudden conversions of souls in times past and present, which prove that such powerful effects can be and are operated by the grace of God. Such a marvelous prodigy, such a sudden spiritual renovation of the soul of a man, is a most extraordinary grace, which Almighty God can grant, even to a great sinner in his last hour. "As God is good," says St. Augustine, "he may save a person without any merits on his part."

Almighty God can also, by a miracle, carry a priest to a person invincibly ignorant and living up to the dictates of his conscience; or he can carry such a person to a priest— or make use of an angel or a saint to lead him to the way of salvation.

Among the holy souls of past centuries who have been loaded with signal favors and privileges by Almighty God, we must place, in the first rank, Mary of Jesus, often styled of Agreda, from the name of the place in Spain where she passed her life. The celebrated J. Goerres, in his grand work, "Mysticism," does not hesitate to cite as an example the life of Mary of Agreda, in a chapter entitled, "The Culminating Point of Christian Mysticism." Indeed, there could not be found a more perfect model of the highest mystic ways.

This holy virgin burned with a most ardent love for God

and for the salvation of souls. One day, she beheld in a vision all the nations of the world. She saw how the greater part of men were deprived of God's grace, and running headlong to everlasting perdition. She saw how the Indians of Mexico put fewer obstacles to the grace of conversion than any other nation who were out of the Catholic Church, and how God, on this account, was ready to show mercy to them. Hence she redoubled her prayers and penances to obtain for them the grace of conversion. God heard her prayers. He commanded her to teach the Catholic religion to those Mexican Indians. From that time, she appeared, by way of bilocation, to the savages, not less than five hundred times, instructing them in all the truths of our holy religion, and performing miracles in confirmation of these truths. When all were converted to the faith, she told them that religious priests would be sent by God to receive them into the Church by baptism. As she had told, so it happened. God, in his mercy, sent to these good Indians several Franciscan fathers, who were greatly astonished when they found those savages fully instructed in the Catholic doctrine. When they asked the Indians who had instructed them, they were told that a holy virgin appeared among them many times, and taught them the Catholic religion and confirmed it by miracles. (Life of the Venerable Mary of Jesus of Agreda, § xii.) Thus those good Indians were brought miraculously to the knowledge of the true religion in the Catholic Church, because they followed their conscience in observing the natural law.

Something similar is related in the life of Father J. Anchieta, S. J. (chap. vi.). One day, this great man of God entered the woods of Itannia, in Brazil, without any assignable motive, and, in fact, as if he were guided by another. At a little distance he perceived an old man seated on the ground and leaning against a tree. "Hasten your steps," cried the old man when he saw the father, "for I have been expecting you for some time." The saintly missionary asked him who he was, and from what country he had come. "My country," said the old man, "is beyond the sea." He added other things, which led the father to infer that he had come from a distant province, near Rio de la Plata, and that he had either been conveyed by supernatural means from his own country to the place where he then was, or that, by the direction and guidance of heaven, he had been led thither with great labor and fatigue, and had placed himself where the father found him, in full expectation of the accomplishment of the divine promise. Father Anchieta then asked him why he had come to that place. "I have come hither," he answered, "in order that I might be taught the right path." This is the expression which the Brazilians use when they speak of the laws of God and of the way to heaven. Father Anchieta felt convinced, from the answers of the old man, that he had never had more than one wife, had never taken up arms except in his own just defence, and that he had never grievously transgressed the law of nature. He perceived, moreover, from the arguments of the old man, that he knew many truths relative to the Author of nature, to the soul, and to virtue and vice. When Father Anchieta had explained to him several of the mysteries of our holy religion, he said: "It is thus that I have hitherto understood them, but I knew not how to define them." After having sufficiently instructed the old man, Father Anchieta collected some rain-water from the leaves of the wild thistles, baptized him, and named him Adam. The new disciple of Christ immediately experienced in his soul the holy effects of baptism. He raised his eyes and hands to heaven, and thanked Almighty God for the mercy which he had bestowed upon him. Soon after, he expired in the arms of Father Anchieta, who buried him according to the ceremonies of the Church.

About these miraculous conversions Dr. O. A. Brownson well remarks:—

"That there may be persons in heretical and schismatical societies, invincibly ignorant of the Church, who so perfectly correspond to the graces they receive, that Almighty God will, by extraordinary means, bring them to

the Church, is believable and perfectly compatible with the
known order of his grace, as is evinced by two beautiful
examples recorded in Holy Scripture. The one is that of
the eunuch of Candace, Queen of Ethiopia: he, following
the lights that God gave him, though living at a great
distance from Jerusalem, became acquainted with the
worship of the true God, and was accustomed to go from
time to time to Jerusalem to adore him. When, however,
the Gospel began to be published, the Jewish religion
could no longer save him; but being well disposed, by
fidelity to the graces he had hitherto received, he was not
forsaken by Almighty God; for when he was returning to
his own country from Jerusalem, the Lord sent a message
by an angel to St. Philip to meet and instruct him in the
faith of Christ, and baptize him (Acts, viii. 26). The
other example is that of Cornelius, who was an officer of
the Roman army of the Italic band, and brought up in
idolatry. In the course of events, his regiment coming to
Judea, he saw there a religion different from his own,—the
worship of one only God. Grace moving his heart, he
believed in this God, and following the further notions of
divine grace, he gave much alms to the poor, and prayed
earnestly to this God to direct him what to do. Did God
abandon him? By no means; he sent an angel from
heaven to tell him to whom to apply in order to be fully
instructed in the knowledge and faith of Jesus Christ, and
to be received into his Church by baptism. Now, what
God did in these two cases he is no less able to do in all
others, and has a thousand ways in his wisdom to conduct
souls who are truly in earnest to the knowledge of the truth,
and to salvation. And though such a soul were in the
remotest wilds of the world, God could send a Philip, or an
angel from heaven, to instruct him, or, by the superabundance of his internal grace, or by numberless other ways
unknown to us, could infuse into his soul the knowledge of
the truth. The great affair is, that we carefully do our part
in complying with what he gives us; for of this we are
certain, that, if we be not wanting to him, he will never be

wanting to us, but, as he begins the good work in us, will also perfect it, if we be careful to correspond and to put no hindrance to his designs.

"However, in all the instances of extraordinary or miraculous intervention of Almighty God, whether in the order of nature, or in the order of grace known to us, he has intervened *ad Ecclesiam*, and there is not a shadow of authority for supposing that he ever has miraculously intervened or ever will intervene otherwise. To assume that he will, under any circumstances, intervene to save men without the *medium ordinarium*, (the Church) is perfectly gratuitous, to say the least. To bring men in an extraordinary manner to the Church is easily admissible, because it does not dispense with the revealed economy of salvation, nor imply its inadequacy: but to intervene to save them without it appears to us to dispense with it, and to imply that it is not adequate to the salvation of all whom God's goodness leads him to save. That those in societies alien to the Church, invincibly ignorant of the Church, if they correspond to the graces they receive, and persevere, will be saved, we do not doubt, but not where they are, or without being brought to the Church. They are sheep in the prescience of God, Catholics, but sheep not yet gathered into the fold. "Other sheep I have," says our Blessed Lord, "that are not of this fold; them also I must bring; they shall hear my voice; and there shall be made one fold and one shepherd." This is conclusive, and that these must be brought, and enter the fold, which is the Church, in this life, as St. Augustine expressly teaches."

But is no one brought to the Faith and Church of Christ but those who correspond as they ought with the graces received before?

"God forbid," says Bishop Hay: "for, though it be certain that God will never fail to bring all those to the Faith and Church of Christ who faithfully correspond with the graces he bestows upon them, yet he has nowhere bound himself to bestow that singular mercy on no other. Were this the case, how few, indeed, would receive it! But God, to show the infinite riches of his goodness and mercy, bestows it on many of the most undeserving; he bestowed it even upon many of the hardened Jews who crucified Jesus Christ, and of the priests who persecuted him to death, even though they had obstinately opposed all the means he had previously used by his doctrine and miracles to convert them. In this he acts as Lord and Master, and as a free disposer of his own gifts; he gives to all the helps necessary and sufficient for their present state; to those who co-operate with these helps he never fails to give more abundantly; and in order to show the riches of his mercy on numbers of the most undeserving, he bestows his most singular favors for their conversion. Hence none have cause to complain; all ought to be solicitous to co-operate with what they have; none ought to despair on account of their past ingratitude, but be assured that God, who is rich in mercy, will yet have mercy on them, if they return to him. Those only ought to fear and tremble who remain obstinate in their evil ways, who continue to resist the calls of his mercy, and put off their conversion from day to day. For though his infinite mercy knows no bounds in pardoning sins, however numerous and grievous, if we repent, yet the offers of his mercy are limited, and if we exceed these limits by our obstinacy, there will be no more mercy for us. The time of mercy is fixed for every one, and if we fail to embrace its offers within that time, the gates of mercy will be closed against us. When the bridegroom has once entered into the marriage-chamber the doors are shut, and the foolish virgins who were unprepared are for ever excluded, with this dreadful reproach from Jesus Christ,—*I know ye not, depart from me, ye workers of iniquity.* Seeing, therefore, that no man knows how long the time of mercy will last for him, he ought not to delay a moment; if he neglect the present offer, it may be the last. That hour will come like a thief in the night, when we least expect it, as Christ himself assures us, and therefore he commands us to be always ready."

Let us mark well: *To assert that acts of divine faith,*

hope, and charity are possible out of the Catholic Church is a direct denial of the article of faith: There is positively no salvation out of the Catholic Church; for, on account of these acts, God unites himself with the soul in time and in eternity. If these acts, then, were possible out of the Catholic Church, there would be salvation out of the Catholic Church, to say which is a direct denial of the above article of faith, and therefore the assertion is heretical.

"A theologian," says St. Augustine, "who is humble, will never teach anything as true Catholic doctrine, unless he is perfectly sure of the truth which he asserts. If he is corrected in anything in which he erred, he thanks for the correction, because his only desire is to know the truth." (Epist. ad S. Hier. 73 n. 1)

He hates novelties—*Animus ab omni novitate alienus et antiquitatis amans.* What he tries to assert and to defend is the pure doctrine of faith contained in Holy Scripture and Tradition. True Catholic doctrine, says Tertullian, is easily distinguished from false doctrine by the following rule : " *Manifestetur id esse dominicum et verum, quod sit prius traditum ; id autem extraneum et falsum, quod sit posterius immissum.*" (Lib. de Praescrip. cap. 31. Ed. Rig. 1675, p. 213.) A doctrine which has been taught and believed from the beginning is true Catholic doctrine; but any other doctrine is false.

Hence St. Paul admonishes St. Timothy, "O Timothy, keep that which is committed to thy trust, avoid the profane novelties of words and oppositions of knowledge falsely so called." (Chapt. vi. 20.)

" *Vocum, id est, dogmatum, rerum, sententiarum novitates, quæ sunt vetustati et antiquitati contrariæ, quæ si recipiantur, necesse est ut fides beatorum Patrum, aut tota, aut certe magna ex parte violetur.* (Vincentius Lirinensis, Commonit., cap. 24.)

What has been believed by *all* the faithful at *all times* and *everywhere,* is truly Catholic doctrine. Any doctrines that are either wholly or at least very much opposed to the faith of the holy Fathers of the Church, are novel teachings, which are to be avoided. The article of faith reads not, "Out of the soul of the Church there is no salvation;" it reads, "Out of the Church (consisting of Body and Soul) there is positively no salvation for any one."

Hence rest assured that, as no one will let you have a precious article for counterfeit money, neither will Almighty God let you have heaven for serving him in a counterfeit religion by which he is greatly insulted and which he has most strictly forbidden, and which St. Paul and the Church have most solemnly accursed.

Such is, and such has always been the faith of the Church. It would be endless to collect all the testimonies of the Fathers of the Church on this subject. Let a few suffice, as a sample of the whole. St. Ignatius, bishop of Antioch, and disciple of the Apostles, in his Epistle to the Philadelphians, says: "Those who make a separation shall not inherit the kingdom of God." St. Irenæus, bishop of Lyons, and martyr in the second age, says: "The Church is the gate of life, but all the others are thieves and robbers, and therefore to be avoided." (*De Hær.*, lib. i. c. 3.) St. Cyprian, bishop of Carthage, and martyr about the middle of the third age, says: "The house of God is but one, and no one can have salvation but in the Church." (*Epist.* 62, *alias* 4.) And in his book on the unity of the Church, he says: "He cannot have God for his father who has not the Church for his mother. If any one could escape who was out of the ark of Noe, then he who is out of the Church may also escape." So much for these most primitive fathers.

In the fourth century, St. Chrysostom speaks thus: "We know that salvation belongs to the Church ALONE, and that no one can partake of Christ, nor be saved, out of the Catholic Church and the Catholic faith." (*Hom.* i. *in Pasch.*)

St. Augustine, in the same age, says: "The Catholic Church alone is the body of Christ; the Holy Ghost gives life to no one who is out of this body." (*Epist.* 185, § 50, *Edit. Bened.*) And in another place, "Salvation no one can have but in the Catholic Church. Out of the Catholic Church he may have anything but salvation. He may have honor, he may have baptism, he may have the Gospel, he may both believe and preach in the name of the Father, and of the Son, and of the Holy Ghost; but he can find salvation nowhere but in the Catholic Church." (*Serm. ad. Cæsariens. de Emerit.* Again, "In the Catholic Church," says he, "there are both good and bad. But those that are separated from her, as long as their opinions are opposite to hers, cannot be good. For though the conversation of some of them appears commendable, yet their very separation from the Church makes them bad, according to that of our Saviour (Luke, xi. 23), 'He that is not with me is against me; and he that gathers not with me scattereth.'"—(*Epist.* 209, *ad Feliciam.*)

"Let a heretic," says St. Augustine, "confess Christ before men and shed his blood for his confession, it avails nothing to his salvation; for, though he confessed Christ, he was put to death out of the Church." This is very true; any one who is put to death out of the Church could not have divine charity, for St. Paul says: "If I should deliver my body to be burned, and have not charity, it profiteth me nothing.'" (I. Cor. xiii. 3.)

"Out of the Church there is no salvation;" Who can deny it? And therefore, whatever truths of the Church are held, out of the Church they avail nothing unto salvation. Those who are separated from the unity of the Church are not with Christ, but are against him, and he that gathereth not with him, scattereth. (Matt. xii. 30.) (Contra Donatistas.)

Lactantius, another great light of the fourth age, says: "It is the Catholic Church only which retains the true worship. This Church is the fountain of truth, it is the house of faith, it is the temple of God. If any one either comes not into this Church, or departs from it, his eternal salvation is desperate. No one must flatter himself obstinately, for his soul and salvation are at stake."—(*Divin. Instit.*, lib. iv., c. 30.)

St. Fulgentius, in the sixth century, speaks thus: "Hold most firmly, and without the least doubt, that neither any heretic or schismatic whosoever, who is baptized out of the Catholic Church, can partake at all of eternal life if, before the end of this life, he be not restored to the Catholic Church and incorporated therein." (*Lib. de Fid.*, c. 37.) According to the first Canon of the Fourth Council of Carthage, the last of the articles which a Bishop-Elect is to be asked before his ordination is: " Credatne quod extra Ecclesiam nullus salvetur." Whether he believes that no one can be saved out of the Church.

We repeat the words of St. Alphonsus :—

" How grateful, then," he says " ought we to be to God for the gift of the true faith. How great is not the number of infidels, heretics, and schismatics. The world is full of them, and, if they die out of the Church, they will all be condemned, except infants who die after baptism." (Catech. first command., No. 10 and 19) Because, as St. Augustine says, where there is no divine faith, there can be no divine charity, and where there is no divine charity, there can be no justifying or sanctifying grace, and to die without being in sanctifying grace is to be lost forever. (Lib. I. Serm. Dom. in monte, cap. v.)

All the Fathers of the Church have never hesitated to pronounce all those forever lost who die out of the Roman Catholic Church. " He who has not the Church for his mother," says St. Cyprian, " cannot have God for his Father ; " and with him the Fathers in general say that, " as all who were not in the ark of Noe perished in the waters of the Deluge, so shall all perish who are out of the true Church." St. Augustine and the other bishops of Africa, at the Council of Zirta, A. D. 412, say : " Whosoever is separated from the Catholic Church, however commendable in his own opinion his life may be, he shall, for the very reason that he is separated from the union of Christ, not see life, but the wrath of God abideth on him." Therefore, says St. Augustine, " a Christian ought to fear nothing so much as to be separated from the body of Christ (the Church). For, if he be separated from the body of Christ, he is not a member of Christ ; if not a member of Christ, he is not quickened by his Spirit." (Tract. xxvii. in Joan., n. 6, col. 1992, tom. iii.)

"To an enlightened Catholic," says Brownson, "there is something very shocking in the supposition that the article of faith, 'out of-the Church positively no one can be saved,' should be only *generally* true, and therefore not an article of faith. All Catholic dogmas, if Catholic, are not only generally, but universally true, and admit no exception or restriction whatever. If men could come to Christ and be saved without the Church, or union with Christ in the Church, she would not be Catholic, and it would be false to call her the 'One, Holy, Catholic Church,' as in the Creed."

"The Church is called Catholic," says the Catechism of the Council of Trent, "because all who desire eternal salvation must embrace and cling to her, like those who entered the ark, to escape perishing in the flood."

Hence any one who explains away the dogma of exclusive salvation, denies, in principle, the Catholicity of the Church and the faith she holds and teaches.

Of every dogma of the Church is true what Pope Pius IX. has declared of the dogma of the Immaculate Conception of the Blessed Virgin Mary, namely: "wherefore, if any persons—which God forbid—shall presume to think in their hearts otherwise than we have defined, let them know that they are condemned by their own judgment, that they have suffered shipwreck in faith, and have fallen away from the unity of the Church." And in the definition of the dogma of the Infallibity of the Roman Pontiff it is said: "But if any one—which God may avert!—presume to contradict this our definition, let him be anathema."

We must believe the truths of faith, not on account of human reasons, which are given in support and corroboration of any article of faith, but on account of the divine authority, which has revealed the articles of faith and proposes them for our belief by the Church. Any one who believes these articles only on account of human reasons, says St. Gregory, has no merit of his faith. (Homil. 26 in Evang.) The truths of the Gospel have been revealed by God, not to be understood, but to be believed. So, when we know that our Lord Jesus Christ has taught something and proposes it for our belief by his Church, we have to believe it most firmly and without the least doubt.

There are, says St. Thomas, three kinds of infidelity: there is the infidelity of the heathen or the gentiles, the infidelity of the Jews, and the infidelity of heretics. The errors of the Gentiles concerning God are, it is true, more numerous than those of the Jews, and the errors of the Jews regarding the true faith are more numerous than those of heretics, yet the sin of infidelity of the Jews is greater than that of the infidelity of the heathen, and the sin of infidelity of heretics is greater than the sin of infidelity of the Jews and Gentiles. The reason is: The Gentiles never received the faith of the Gospel, but the Jews received it in its figure in the Old Testament, which they perversely interpret and corrupt, and therefore their sin of infidelity is greater than that of the Gentiles. The sin of infidelity of the heretics is greater than that of the Jews, because they profess the faith of the Gospel, but oppose this faith by corrupting it, and therefore they sin more grievously than the Jews. Hence St Peter says: "For it had been been better for them not to have known the way of justice, than, after they have known it, to turn back from that holy commandment which was delivered to them. (II. Pet. ii. 21.) The Gentiles never knew the way of justice, but heretics and the Jews knew it to a certain degree and yet have left it, and therefore their sin is greater.

"Here some one might say: "If the errors of the Gentiles concerning faith are more numerous than those of the Jews, does it not follow that the Gentiles are more guilty than the Jews? And if the Jews are in more points more remote from the true faith than heretics, does it not follow that the Jews are more guilty before God than heretics?

"By no means; for the greatness of the guilt of the sin of infidelity does not arise from the number of errors about the things that belong to the faith, but from the knowledge of the faith which one has received. Hence he who sins against the faith which he has received, by perversely interpreting and corrupting it, sins more grievously than he who has never received the faith, just as one sins more grievously who does not keep what he has promised, than another who does not do what he never promised. As the Gentiles never received the faith, they sin against it less grievously than the Jews, who received it at least in figure, believing, as they do, the Old Testament, in which the New Testament, the Law of Grace, was prefigured; and the Jews sin less grievously against the true faith of the Gospel, which they never received, than heretics do, who make profession of faith in the Gospel, which they receive but perversely interpret and corrupt." (Pars 2a 2æ quaest. x., art. v. et vi.)

"Hence," says Cornelius a Lapide, "it is never lawful to be glad to see heresy preached and, propagated, even among the heathens; for, though they announce Christ, yet, at the same time, they also announce many heresies concerning Christ or his Church and sacraments, and these heresies are more pernicious than paganism itself; so that it is far better for the heathens not to receive any truth or doctrine from heretics, than to receive it mixed with so many perverse errors and heresies." (Comment. in Epist. ad Philip., c. i., v. 18.) St. Augustine, as we have seen, says the same.

Alas! how shocking, therefore, for Catholics were those articles in the *Buffalo Catholic Union and Times*, in which so many things were falsely asserted in favor of Protestant belief, and altogether contrary to Catholic faith.

"If it then be true," says O. A. Brownson,—and as sure as God exists and can neither be deceived nor deceive, it is true,—that there is no salvation out of the Church, what a fearful responsibility should we not incur, were we to forbear to proclaim it, or by our mistimed or misplaced qualifications to encourage the unbelieving, the heretical, or the indifferent to hope the contrary! And how much more fearful still, if we should go farther, and attempt in our publications to prove that he who firmly insists on it is harsh, unjust, uncharitable, running in his rash zeal to an unauthorized extreme!"

"Those who have learned theology well," says St. Basil,

"will not allow even one iota of Catholic dogmas to be betrayed. They will, if necessary, willingly undergo any kind of death in their defence." (Apud. Theod., lib. 4, Hist. Eccl., c. xvii.)

"Not to oppose erroneous doctrine," says Pope Innocent III. (Dist. 85.), "is to approve of it; and not to defend true doctrine is to suppress it."

Let us always remember the words of Leo XIII., quoted at the end of chapter I., namely: "That method of teaching which rests on the authority and judgment of individual professors has a changeable basis, and hence arise different and conflicting opinions, which foster dissensions and controversies which have agitated Catholic schools for a long time and *not without great detriment to Christian science*. To gather and to scatter opinions according to our own will and pleasure is to be reputed the vilest license, lying, and false science, a disgrace and slavery of the mind."

"A true, genuine Catholic," says Vincent of Lerins, "is he who loves the truths of God, the Church, the Body of Christ; who values nothing more highly than our divine religion, our holy Catholic faith; who does not suffer himself to be led into any kind of religious error by the authority, learning, eloquence, philosophy of any person. He despises this human greatness; he remains firm and unshaken in his faith, and is determined to believe only what the Catholic Church has everywhere and always taught and believed from the beginning; he rejects, as novel doctrine, whatever is taught against the doctrine of the Fathers of the Church, and looks upon modern opinions in religion as snares of the devil in which the ignorant and unwise are caught, " for there must also be heresies," says St. Paul (I. Cor. xi. 19.) by which the faith of good and firm Catholics becomes better known and more remarkable. Let, therefore, all those who have not learned sound Catholic theology, unlearn well what they have not learned well; let them try to understand each dogma of the Church as far as possible, but let them firmly believe whatever they cannot understand." (Commonit.)

In the history of the foundation of the Society of Jesus, in the Kingdom of Naples, is related the following story of a noble youth of Scotland, named William Ephinstone. He was a relative of the Scottish King. Born a heretic, he followed the false sect to which he belonged; but enlightened by divine grace, which showed him his errors, he went to France, where, with the assistance of a good Jesuit Father, who was also a Scotchman, he at length saw the truth, abjured heresy, and became a Catholic. He went afterward to Rome and joined the Society of Jesus, in which he died a happy death. When at Rome, a friend of his found him one day very much afflicted, and weeping. He asked him the cause, and the young man answered that in the night his mother had appeared to him, and said: "My son, it is well for thee that thou hast entered the true Church; I am already lost, because I died in heresy." (St. Liguori, *Glories of Mary*.)

We read, in the Life of St. Rose of Viterbo, that she was inflamed with great zeal for the salvation of souls. She felt a most tender compassion for those who were living in heresy. In order to convince a certain lady, who was a heretic, that she could not be saved in her sect, and that it was necessary for salvation to die a true member of the Catholic Church, she made a large fire, threw herself into it, and remained in it for three hours, without being hurt. This lady, together with many others, on witnessing the miracle, abjured their heresy, and became Catholics.

When the Emperor Valens ordered that St. Basil the Great should go into banishment, God, in the high court of heaven, passed, at the same time, sentence against the emperor's only son, named Valentinian Galatus, a child then about six years old. That very night the royal infant was seized with a violent fever, from which the physicians were unable to give him the least relief; and the Empress Dominica told the emperor that this calamity was a just punishment of heaven for his banishing the bishop, on which account she had been disquieted by terrible dreams. Thereupon Valens sent for the saint, who was about to go into exile. No sooner had the holy bishop entered the palace, than the fever of the child began to abate. St. Basil assured the parents of the absolute recovery of their son, on condition that they would order him to be instructed in the Catholic faith. The emperor accepted the condition, St. Basil prayed, and the young prince was cured. But Valens, unfaithful to his promise, afterwards allowed an Arian bishop to baptize the child. The young prince immediately relapsed and died. (Butler's *Lives of the Saints*, June 14th.) By this miraculous cure of the child, God made manifest the truths of our religion; and by the sudden death of the child, which followed upon the heretical baptism, God showed in what abomination he holds heresy.

§ 9. THOSE WHO SINCERELY SEEK THE TRUE RELIGION.

If no one, then, can be saved except in the Roman Catholic Church, all those who are out of it are bound to become members of the Church. This is what commonsense tells every non-Catholic. In worldly affairs, Protestants never presume to act without good advice. They never compromise their pecuniary interests or their lives, by becoming their own private interpreters and practitioners of law or medicine. Both the legal and the medical books are before them, written by modern authors, in clear and explicit language, but they have too much practical common-sense to attempt their interpretation. They prefer always to employ expert lawyers and physicians, and accept their interpretations, and act according to their advice. Now, every non-Catholic believes that every practical member of the Catholic Church will be saved. Hence, when there is question about eternal salvation and eternal damnation, a sensible man will take the surest way to heaven. It was this that decided Henry IV. of France to abjure his errors. A historian relates that this king, having called before him a conference of the doctors of either Church, and seeing that the Protestant ministers agreed, with one accord, that salvation was attainable in the Catholic religion, immediately addressed a Protestant minister in the following manner: "Now, sir, is it true that people can be saved in the Catholic religion?" "Most assuredly it is, sire, provided they live up to it." "If that be so," said the monarch, "prudence demands that I should be of the Catholic religion, not of yours, seeing that in the Catholic Church I may be saved, as even you admit; whereas, if I remain in yours, Catholics maintain that I cannot be saved. Both prudence and good sense tell me that I should follow the surest way, and so I propose doing." Some days after, the king made his abjuration at St. Denis. (Guillois, ii. 67.)

Christ assures us that the way to everlasting life is narrow, and trodden by few. The Catholic religion is that narrow road to heaven. Protestantism, on the contrary, is that broad way to perdition trodden by so many. He who is content to follow the crowd, condemns himself by taking the broad way. A man says: "I would like to believe, but I cannot." You say you "cannot believe." But what have you done, what means have you employed, in order to acquire the gift of faith? If you have neglected the means, you show clearly that you do not desire the end.

God bestowed great praise upon his servant Job. He said of him that "he was a simple and upright man, fearing God and avoiding evil." (Job, i. 8.) There is nothing that renders a soul more acceptable to God than simplicity and sincerity of heart in seeking him. There is, on the other hand, nothing more detestable to him than a double-minded man, who does not walk sincerely with his God: "Woe to them that are of a double heart, . . . and to the sinner that goeth on the earth two ways." (Ecclus. ii. 14.) Such a man should not expect that the Lord will enlighten and direct him. Our Saviour assures us that his heavenly Father makes himself known to the little ones, that is, to those who have recourse to him with a simple and sincere heart.

This sincerity and uprightness of heart with God are especially necessary for him who is in search of the true religion. We see around us numberless jarring sects, con-

tradicting one another; we see the one condemning what
the other approves, and approving what others condemn;
we see some embracing certain divine truths, and others
rejecting those truths with horror, as the doctrine of devils.
Now common-sense tells every one that both parties cannot
be right; that the true religion cannot be on either side.
Among such confusion of opinions, the mind is naturally at
a loss how to discover that one true Church in whose bosom
the truth is to be found.

In the search after truth, one must find immense difficulties. There is prejudice. It is the effect of early training,
of life-long teaching, of reading, and of living in the world.
It is the result of almost imperceptible impressions, and yet
its force, as an obstacle, is such as in many cases to defy
human efforts to remove it It is like the snow which
begins to fall, as the darkness sets in, on roof and road, in
little flakes that come down silently all the night, and in the
morning the branches bend, and the doors are blocked, and
the traffic on road and rail is brought to a standstill.

There, again, is the favor of friends, the fear of what the
world will say, worldly interest, and the like. All these
will be set to work by the enemy of the souls to blind the
understanding, that it may not see the truth, and to avert
the will from embracing it. Nothing but a particular
grace from heaven can enlighten the mind to perceive the
light of truth through such clouds of darkness, and to
strengthen the will with courage to embrace it, in spite of
all these difficulties. It is, without doubt, the will of God,
that "all men should be saved, and come to the knowledge
of the truth" (I. Tim. ii. 4.) ; but it is also the will of God
that, in order to come to this knowledge, men must seek it
with a sincere and upright heart, and this sincerity of heart
must show itself in their earnest desire to know the truth:
"Blessed are they that hunger and thirst after justice, for
they shall be filled." Hence they must labor diligently to
find out the truth, using every means in their power for
that purpose. Negligence of inquiry, and the evidences of
our faith, are great, and therefore the ignorance of many

must needs be highly sinful. Man's understanding was given to him, to enable him to embrace holy and salutary truths. Negligence in this is worthy of damnation; and as everything tends easily to its natural end, so our natural, intellectual virtue is nearer finding God than it is finding his contrary, for God is always ready to aid those who seek him with a good and honest heart; and thus we find that to Cornelius, a Pagan, yet living religiously, and fearing God, St. Peter was sent to convert him and all his family. God, says St. Thomas Aquinas, will send an angel to a man ignorant of the Christian law but living up to his conscience, to instruct him in the Christian religion, rather than let him perish through inculpable ignorance.

In reference to this matter, Mr. Pelisson, a celebrated convert to our holy religion, says: "Will you expostulate with Almighty God, like Job? He will confound you; you will imagine that many things are in your favor with God. You say, you have done what was in your power. The Lord will make you see that you have not done the hundreth part of what you should and could have done. Is there nothing that you liked better than the desire to please God? Is there nothing that you loved more ardently than God? Is there nothing that you like better to know than the truths he has revealed? Has your want of the spirit of penance, or your spirit of vanity, or your hardness of heart, not put an obstacle to the heavenly lights which God wished to shed upon your mind. Say what you please, as to myself, who have been led by his infinite mercy to his Church, I know that I have not done one thousandth part of what I could have done to obtain this great grace of his infinite mercy." (See Cursus Completus Theologiae, vol. iv., p. 293.)

There are laws to regulate man's will and affections, and so there are also laws to fix limits to his understanding—to determine what he should believe and what he should not believe; and therefore ignorance is damnable, for man ought carefully to inquire what he must believe; and what laws he must observe; whereas the multitude run, with all their strength, to sin and death as their end, and it is not strange that they should find it.

The first and great cause of all these errors is negligence of inquiry; and the second is aversion to believe what ought to be believed of God, and a hatred for the things that would enlighten and convert the soul. If men will not heed either holy words or miracles, it is not strange that they remain in error. They must study religion, with a sincere desire to find out the truth. If they wish to find out the truth they must not appeal to the enemies of truth. They must consult those who are well instructed in their religion, and who practise it. They must consult the priest. He will explain to them the true doctrine of the Catholic Church.

In the Memoir of Bishop Hay it is stated that he became a convert to our Church in 1749. As a Protestant he never showed any Catholic tendencies, as is sufficiently evident from the fact that in the fervor of his youth he had bound himself by a double vow to read a portion of the Bible daily, and to do his utmost to extirpate Popery from his native country. One day he went from Edinburgh, where he had made his studies for the medical profession, to London, where he heard the doctrines of the Catholic Church explained by an English gentleman, in a manner which excited his surprise. From London he went to Ayrshire, where he found a well-known little work, "*A Papist represented and misrepresented, or a twofold character of Popery.*" Doubts were excited in his mind; but Mr. Hay was not of a character to set aside doubts upon an important subject without due investigation.

As the surest means to obtain correct information regarding the Catholic faith, he resolved to apply to a Catholic priest, and accordingly obtained an introduction to Sir Alexander Seaton, the Jesuit missionary, then resident in Edinburgh. From him he received the information desired, and after a lenghtened course of instruction he was received into the Church, 21st Dec., 1749.

Moreover, sincerity of heart must show itself in a firm resolution to embrace the truth whenever it shall be found, and whatever it may cost the seeker. He must prefer it before every worldly consideration, and be ready to forfeit everything in this life: the affections of his friends, a comfortable home, temporal goods, and prospect in business, rather than deprive his soul of so great a treasure.

The New York *Freeman's Journal*, Sept. 2d, 1854, contains the following notice on the late General Thomas F. Carpenter. The words of this notice are written by ex-Governor Laurence. The general, when about to become a Catholic, made known his intention to a friend. The friend, of course, was surprised. He instanced the fearful results consequent upon a proceeding so unpopular, the loss of professional practice, the alienation of friends, the scoffs of the crowd, etc. "All such blessings," replied General Carpenter, "I can dispense with, all such insults I can despise, but I cannot afford to lose my immortal soul." The general spoke thus, because he knew and firmly believed what Jesus Christ has solemnly declared, to wit: "He who loveth father or mother more than me, is not worthy of me; and he that loveth son or daughter more than me is not worthy of me"(Matt. x. 37.); and as to the loss of temporal gain, he has answered: "What will it profit a man if he gain the whole world, and suffer the loss of his soul?" (Mark, viii. 36.)

But would it not be enough for such a one to be a Catholic in heart only, without professing his religion publicly? No; for Jesus Christ has solemnly declared that "he who shall be ashamed of me and of my words, of him the Son of man shall be ashamed when he shall come in his majesty, and that of his Father, and of the holy angels." (Luke, ix. 26.)

But might not such a one safely put off being received into the Church till the hour of death?

This would be to abuse the mercy of God, and, in punishment for this sin, to lose the light and grace of faith, and die a reprobate. In order to obtain heaven, we must be ready to sacrifice all, even our lives. "Fear ye not them," says Christ, "that kill the body, and are not able to kill the soul; but rather fear ye him that can destroy both soul and body into hell" (Matt. x. 28)

How often do we meet with men who tell us that they would gladly become Catholics, but it is too hard to live up to the laws and maxims of the Church! They know very well that, if they become Catholics, they must lead honest and sober lives, they must be pure, they must respect the holy sacrament of marriage, they must check their sinful passions; and this they are unwilling to do. "Men love darkness rather than light," says Jesus Christ, "because their deeds are evil." Remember the well-known proverb: "There are none so deaf as those that will not hear."

They are kept back from embracing the faith, because they know that the truths of our religion are at war with their sinful inclinations. It is not surprising that these inclinations should revolt against immolation. The prudence of the flesh understands and feels that it loses all, if the truths of faith are listened to and taken for the rule of conduct; that it must renounce the unlawful enjoyments of life, must die to the world and to itself, and bear the mortification of Jesus Christ in its body.

At the mere thought of this crucifixion of the flesh and its concupiscence, imposed on every one who would belong to the Saviour, the whole animal man is troubled. Self-love suggests a thousand reasons to delay at least the sacrifices that affright them. The prudence of the flesh, having the ascendancy, obscures the most simple truths, attracts and flatters the powers of the soul; and when, afterward, faith endeavors to interpose its authority, it finds the understanding prejudiced, the will overcome or weakened, the heart all earthly-minded; and hard, indeed, is it for faith to reduce the soul to its dominion. Those who listen to the prudence of the flesh will never become Catholics.

Finally, those who seek the truth must show their sincerity of heart in fervently and frequently praying to God that they may find the truth, and the right way that leads to it. Faith is not a mere natural gift; it is not an acquired virtue or habit; it is something altogether supernatural. The right use of the natural faculties can, indeed, prepare one to receive faith; but true faith,—that is, to believe, with an unwavering conviction, in the existence of all those things which God has made known,—is a supernatural gift, —a gift which no one can have of himself; it is the free gift of God: "For by grace you are saved, through faith, and that not of yourselves, for it is the gift of God." (Eph. ii. 8.) God is so great a good, that we cannot merit and possess this good by anything we may do. Now, it is by the gift of faith that we have in some measure a glimpse of all that God is, and that consequently we attach ourselves to this supreme good; and behold! we are saved. We can say with David, in the truest sense, that in enlightening us the Lord saves us: "The Lord is my light, and my salvation." (Ps. xxvi. 1.) Hence it is evident that this gift is a free gift of God, without the least merit on our part. When this light or grace shines upon the understanding, it enlightens the understanding, so as to render it most certain of the truths which are proposed to it. But this mere knowledge of the truth is not as yet the full gift of faith. St. Paul says (Rom. i. 2) that the heathens knew God, but they would not obey him, and consequently their knowledge did not save them. You may convince a man that the Catholic Church is the true Church, but he will not, on that account, become a Catholic. Our Saviour himself was known by many, and yet he was followed only by few. Faith, then, is something more than knowledge. Knowledge is the submission of the understanding to truth; but faith implies also the submission of the will to the truth. It is for this reason that the light or grace of faith must also move the will, because a good will always belongs to faith, since no one can believe unless he is willing to believe. It is for this reason that faith is also rewarded by God, and infidelity punished: "He that believeth and is baptized shall be saved, but he that believeth not shall be condemned." (Mark, xvi. 16.) No man has the natural ability to come into the Church, any more than he has the natural ability to save himself after he has come in. All before and all after is the work of God. We can do nothing of ourselves alone—make not even the first motion without his grace inciting and assisting us. Of no use would have been his Church—it would have been a mere mockery, or a splendid failure—if he had not provided for our entrance as well as for our salvation afterwards.

But he *has* provided for our entrance. He gives sufficient grace to all men. The grace of prayer is given freely, gratuitously, unto every one. All receive the ability to ask; all, then, can ask; and if they do ask, as sure as God cannot lie, they shall receive the grace to seek; and if they seek, the same divine veracity is pledged that they shall find; and if they find, they may knock; and if they knock, it shall be opened to them. God has said it: Christ is in the Church; he is out of it. In it and out of it he is one and the same, and operates ever *ad unitatem* (towards unity). He is out of the Church to draw all men into the Church; all have, then, if they will, the assistance of the Infinite God to come in, and if they do not come in, it is their own fault. God withholds nothing necessary. He gives to all, by his grace, everything requisite, and in superabundance. Indeed, God will never refuse to bestow this gift of faith upon those who seek the truth with a sincere heart, use their best endeavors to find it, and sincerely pray for it with confidence and perseverance. Witness Clovis, the heathen king of the Franks. When he, together with his whole army, was in the greatest danger of being defeated by the Alemanni, he prayed as follows:—

"Jesus Christ, thou of whom Clotilde (the king's Christian wife) has often told me that thou art the Son of the living God, and that thou givest aid to the hard-pressed, and victory to those who trust in thee! I humbly crave thy powerful assistance. If thou grantest me the victory over my enemies I will believe in thee, and be baptized in thy name; for I have called upon my gods in vain. They must be impotent, as they cannot help those who serve them. Now I invoke thee, desiring to believe in thee; do, then, deliver me from the hands of my adversaries!"

No sooner had he uttered this prayer than the Alemanni were panic-stricken, took to flight, and soon after, seeing their king slain, sued for peace. Thereupon Clovis blended both nations, the Franks and the Alemanni, together, returned home, and became a Christian.

Witness F. Thayer, an Anglican minister. When as yet in great doubt and uncertainty about the truth of his religion, he began to pray as follows:—

"God of all goodness, almighty and eternal Father of mercies, and Saviour of mankind! I implore thee, by thy sovereign goodness, to enlighten my mind, and to touch my heart, that, by means of true faith, hope, and charity, I may live and die in the true religion of Jesus Christ. I confidently believe that, as there is but one God, there can be but one faith, one religion, one only path to salvation; and that every other path opposed thereto can lead but to perdition. This path, O my God! I anxiously seek after, that I may follow it, and be saved. Therefore I protest, before thy divine majesty, and I swear by all thy divine attributes, that I will follow the religion which thou shalt reveal to me as the true one, and will abandon, at whatever cost, that wherein I shall have discovered errors and falsehood. I confess that I do not deserve this favor for the greatness of my sins, for which I am truly penitent, seeing they offend a God who is so good, so holy, and so worthy of love; but what I deserve not, I hope to obtain from thine infinite mercy; and I beseech thee to grant it unto me through the merits of that precious blood which was shed for us sinners by thine only Son, Jesus Christ our Lord, who liveth and reigneth, etc. Amen."

God was not slow to hear so sincere and fervent a prayer, and Thayer became a Catholic. Let any one who is as yet groping in the darkness of infidelity and error pray in the same manner, and the God of all light and truth will bestow upon him the gift of faith in a high degree. It is human to fall into error, devilish to remain in it, and angelical to rise from it, by embracing the truth which leads to God, by whom it has been revealed and is preserved in his Church.

All may have the Church for their mother, if they choose. Christ is in the Church, but he is also out of the Church. In the Church he is operating by his grace to save those who enter; out of her he operates also by his grace, or is ready to operate, in the hearts of all men, to supply the will and the ability to come in. If we come not at his call, on our own heads lies the blame. We have no excuse, not the least shadow of an excuse. The reason why we come not can be only that we do not choose to come, that we resist his grace, and scorn his invitations, and will not yield to his inspirations. No nice theological distinctions, no scholastic subtlety, no latitudinarian ingenuity, can relieve us of the blame, or make it not true that we could have come, had we been so disposed. If, then we stay away, and are lost, it is we who have destroyed ourselves.

Sectarian systems are the dark and shifting vapors that obscure the surface of the heavens; and their ever-varying masses are drifted into numberless fantastic forms by every passing gale, "by every wind of doctrine," as St. Paul expresses it. Cloud of heresy after cloud of heresy has fallen in rain, or disappeared in the boundless fields of ether,—*they were and are not,*—whilst other vapors occupy their place, as fleeting and as unsubstantial. But, like the vast and universal arch of heaven, the Church over-canopies alike all Christian climes and ages; and, like that arch, she is one, unbroken, wheresoever she appears. *The arch stills stands,* for the sacred Word of Christ, her Founder, is pledged for its perpetual stability.

Yes, the Church still stands. She speeds on, on her heaven-sent mission, conquering and to conquer.

Only in the Catholic Church there are certainty and security against errors in religion. Around this Rock we behold nothing but raging tempests, nothing but disastrous shipwrecks, indifference to religion, negation of all true worship, the abomination of atheism and immorality, derision of sacred things, a fanatic pietism, a delirious religiousness, rationalism, or the denial of all revelation and of everything supernatural. Every non-Catholic who earnestly seeks to learn what he is to believe, every one who yearns to obtain certainty in religious matters, must sooner or later turn to the Church as the only source of certainty, the only guardian of the true religion, the only fountain of true peace and happiness in this life and in the next.

Here are the great mass of our countrymen aliens from the Church of God. Why do they not come and ask to be received as children and heirs? Is it lack of opportunity? It is false. There is no lack of opportunity. God does not deny them, not one of them, the needed grace. The Church is here; through her noble and faithful pastors, her voice sounds out from Main to Florida, from the Atlantic to the Pacific. How can they hear without a preacher? But they have heard; verily the voice of the preacher is gone out into all the earth. They have no need to say, who shall ascend into heaven to bring Christ down? The Word is nigh them. It sounds in every ear; it speaks in every heart. We all know they might come, if they would. From all sections, and from all ranks and conditions, some have come, and by coming proved that it is possible for all to come. Witness the late Most Rev. James Roosevelt Bailey, D. D., Archbishop of Baltimore; Most Rev. James Frederick Wood, D. D., Archbishop of Philadelphia; Right Rev. William Tyler, late Bishop of Hartford, Conn.; Right Rev. John Young, D. D., late Bishop of Erie, Pa.; Right Rev. Sylvester Horton Rosecrans, D. D., late Bishop of Columbus, O.; Right Rev. Monsignor George H. Doane, V. G., of Newark, N. J., son of the Protestant Bishop of that name and a brother of Bishop Doane (Protestant Episcopal,) of Albany, N. Y.; Very Rev. Thomas S. Preston, V. G., of the Archdiocese of New York; Rev. J. Clark, S. J., formerly a professor of mathematics at West Point, late commissioned a brigadier-general in the United States Army and president of Gonzaga College, Washington; Rev. Francis M. Craft, S. J., of Loyola College,

Baltimore, Md. ; Rev. James Kent Stone, C. P., Father Fidelis of the Cross, formerly president of Hobert and Kenyon College, Ohio; Rev. E. D. Hudson, C. S. C., editor of the Ave Maria ; Rev. Isaac T. Hecker, C. S. P., Rev. Xavier Donald Macleod, D. D., author of " Devotion to the B. V. M. in North America," etc., etc. ; the late Rev. George Foxcroft Haskins, founder of the House of the Angel Guardian; Rev. Levi Silliman Ives, L L. D., formerly a Protestant Bishop of North Carolina ; Rev. George Goodwin, the second pastor of St. Mary's Church, Charleston, Mass. ; Hon. Thomas Ewing, Senator from Ohio, and for sometime Secretary of the United States Treasury ; Dr. Joshua Huntington, the well-known author of "Rosemary," "Gropings after Truth," etc. ; James McMaster, Esq., editor of the New York *Freeman's Journal*; Rev. Orestes A. Brownson, L L. D., the distinguished reviewer, whom Lord Brougham is said to have styled "the master mind of America"; Dr. Albert Myers, sub-editor of the Boston Pilot; Howard Haine Caldwell, of Newbery, S. C., and son of Chancellor Caldwell ; Gen. Jones of Columbia, S. C. ; Rev. Clarence A. Walworth, author of " The Gentle Skeptic," etc. ; Miss Mary Agnes Tincker, author of " Grapes and Thorns," " House of Yorke," and " Signor Monaldini's Niece"; Mother Seton, founder of the Sisters of Charity in America; Mrs. Judge Tenny, born Sarah M. Brownson ; Miss Francis C. Fisher ; Christian Reid, author of " A Question of Honor," " Hearts and Hands," etc. etc. ; Miss Mary Longfellow, cousin of the deceased poet Longfellow; the widow of ex-president Tyler, and so many others who have sacrificed everything rather than die out of the Catholic Church and be lost forever.

Mrs. Moore, a very intelligent lady of Edinton, North Carolina, and a convert to our holy faith, said to her Protestant children, when on her death-bed : "O my children ! there is such hope, such comfort in our holy religion ! When I was so near death and believed I should never see you again, my soul was filled with anguish. When I thought I was so soon to meet my God, I feared; but after I had made my confession to his own commissioned minister, and received absolution in the name of the Most Holy Trinity, death was divested of every sting. Each day I thank God more and more that he has given me grace to break the ties that kept me from the Church. I have never looked back, and, in fact, I wonder why I could ever have been anything but a Catholic."

In joining the Catholic Church, these and many other converts have rendered invalid the plea of ignorance or inability. Those who have not come can as well come as those who have come; and their guilt in not coming is aggravated by their knowledge of the fact that some of their own number have come; for they are no longer in ignorance. (St. Aug., lib. 1. de Bapt. contr. Donat. cap. v.; St. John Chrys. in Epist. ad Rom. xxvi.) The fault is their own. They stay away because they do not will to come. "Ye will not come to me that you may have life, because your deeds are evil." They disregard divine grace, they disdain the Church, they despise her pastors, they scorn her sacraments. For what Catholic can doubt, if they were to seek, *with anxious care*, as St. Augustine says they must, even to excuse them from formal heresy or infidelity, that they would find, and finding and knocking, that they would be admitted?

No; let us love our countrymen too much to be ingenious in inventing excuses for them, to strain the faith in their behalf till it is nearly ready to snap. Let us, from a deep and tender charity, which, when need is, has the nerve to be terribly severe, thunder, or, if we are no Boanerges, breathe in soft but thrilling accents, in their ears, in their souls, in their consciences, those awful truths which they will know too late at the day of judgment. We must labor to convict them of sin, to show them their folly and madness, to convince them that they are dead in trespasses and sins, and condemned already, and that they can be restored to life, and freed from condemnation only by the the grace of our Lord Jesus Christ, which is dispensed through the Church, and the Church only.

250 *Out of the Catholic Church there is No Salvation.*

§ 10. *S. O. on Confession.*

He continues to quote from our Explanation of Christian Doctrine, dishonestly suppressing five questions and answers that are in immediate connection with those he quotes, namely:

"*Q.* Are Protestants willing to confess their sins to a bishop or priest, who alone has from Christ power to forgive sins? 'Whose sins you shall forgive they are forgiven them.' *Ans.* No, for they generally have an utter aversion to confession, and *therefore* their sins will not be forgiven them throughout all eternity. *Q.* What follows from this? *Ans.* That they die in their sins and are damned."

"To which I, S. O., say that, as long as Protestants honestly believe, (and we have no right to question their honesty in the matter,) that God has not appointed priestly absolution as the outward and visible sacramental sign and instrument of His forgiveness to the truly penitent sinner, it is not at all strange that they are unwilling to confess their sins to a priest or seek his absolution. When they are instructed to know, and by God's grace led to believe, that the Catholic religion is the true religion of Christ, they will be just as willing to go to confession as we Catholics are, and will have no more aversion to it than we have."

You see, S. O. never states clearly and precisely any point in question. He speaks here of those Protestants who *honestly* believe that they have not to go to confession to obtain forgiveness. We suppose he means those who live in inculpable ignorance of the divine law of confession. But such inculpable ignorance, as we have clearly proved, is no means to obtain the forgiveness of their sins. "And we have no right," he says, " to question their honesty." Alas! Tell Protestants that they can be good Catholics without confessing their sins, and there will be thousands and thousands of them whose honesty we need not question.

But have we no right, no duty to instruct those honest Protestants and heathens and show them the true road to heaven? Why, then, did St. Francis de Sales and so many other holy priests expose their lives so often to reclaim honest Protestants from their heresy and bring them back to the true Church?

As to those Protestants who have been instructed in our religion and are willing to confess their sins, they no longer belong to the number of those who are in question.

He continues his answer. "But who told this explainer of Christian doctrine (the Rev. M. Muller) that no sinner will be forgiven throughout all eternity, or that he will die in his sins and be damned, if he has not confessed those sins to a priest and received his absolution? That is not Catholic Christian doctrine, and he had no right to say it is, or to write in such a manner as to be so understood."

Here, you see, S. O. wants to know where we learned the divine law of confession. Well, we learned it from the infallible teaching of the Catholic Church, from Holy Scripture, from the Fathers and Doctors of the Church. Strange, that S. O. does not know what every Catholic school-boy knows. He must have learned a bad catechism. But, in the name of common sense, where did S. O. learn that every sinner, especially every Protestant sinner, will be forgiven throughout all eternity, or that he will not die in his sins, though he is not willing to confess his sins to a Catholic priest? He says that "to assert that no baptized sinner will be forgiven unless he is willing to go to confession, is no Catholic Christian doctrine; that we had no right to say it is, or to write in such a manner as to be so understood." Now this assertion of Sir Oracle is quite heretical, because it is an article of faith, declared by the Council of Trent, that the sacrament of penance is as necessary for the salvation of those who have fallen into mortal sin after baptism, as baptism is for those who have not received spiritual regeneration. Sir Oracle's assertion, therefore, is directly opposed to the divine law of confession, which must be complied with in *reality, if possible*, or at least in *true implicit desire*, if confession is impossible.

S. O. is rather incorrect in stating all the conditions of

forgiveness which God has made for those who, after baptism, have committed grievous sins. "These conditions," he says, "are the three following: A sincere sorrow for our sins, a firm purpose of sinning no more, and, under ordinary circumstances, an honest, humble confession to God's appointed ministers."

This is not a full statement of the conditions of forgiveness. We will give them, as every school-boy knows them who has learned a good catechism:—

I. *Contrition*, or sorrow, which is good only:
1. When it is interior, or sorrow from the heart or will;
2. When it is sovereign, or sorrow above all other sorrows;
3. When it is universal, or sorrow at least for all our mortal sins;
4. When it is supernatural, or sorrow for having offended God, joined with the hope of pardon.

There are three kinds of contrition:—
1. Perfect contrition, or sorrow for sin on account of the injury offered to God's goodness;
2. Imperfect contrition, or sorrow for sin on account of the injury done to our souls, which, by offending God, lose heaven, and deserve hell;
3. Natural contrition, or sorrow for sin on account of the injury done to our temporal welfare.

The effects of sorrow are:—
1. Perfect contrition, as an act of perfect love of God, joined with the desire of confessing our sins, cancels them before confession;
2. Imperfect contrition disposes us to receive the grace of God in the sarament of Penance;
3. Natural contrition cannot dispose us to receive the grace of God by absolution, because it is a sorrow, not for offending God, but only for temporal injury.

II. *Purpose of amendment* is a firm resolution, by the grace of God:—
1. To avoid all mortal sins, and the proximate occasions of sin;

2. To make use of the necessary means of amendment;
3. To make due satisfaction for our sins;
4. To repair whatever injury we may have done to our neighbor.

III. *Confession*, which is good only:—
1. When it is entire, or a confession of at least all our mortal sins, with the necessary circumstances;
2. When it is sincere, or a confession of sins without concealing or excusing them.

He who is in danger of death and cannot make his confession, *must earnestly wish to confess his sins to the priest*, and try to be very sorry for having offended so good a God.

This last point S. O. has omitted, and yet the sincere (at least implicit) desire to confess his sins is as necessary for him who is not able to confess them, as real confession is for him who is able to make it, in order to obtain forgiveness.

"But to say or imply," continues S. O., "that every Catholic who dies without having been able to confess his sins to a priest is *therefore* damned for all eternity, is nonsense." Did S. O. dream that we or any Catholic ever said such nonsense? Why then does he mention such nonsense?

§ 11. S. O. POINTS OUT THE ROAD TO HEAVEN FOR HEATHENS AND PROTESTANTS OF EVERY DENOMINATION.

"What he (the Catholic) does, and *what surely obtains God's forgiveness*," says S. O., "is just what in point of fact every sincere, God-fearing Protestant,—and I go further and say, every God-fearing heathen who never heard of Church, Bible or Christ—may do, and what, in the charity of Christ, who died for *all* sinners, I hope and pray they do: he lifts up his heart to God his Creator, he acknowledges his sins and offences against God with true contrition of heart and asks forgiveness, and the Protestant, like the Catholic, always adds 'trusting in the merits of Jesus Christ, my Saviour,' or, 'for the love of my Redeemer, who died on the cross for me.' "

Here you have an oracle of the greatest wisdom that

ever was uttered by S. O. You see, he declares that a dying sinful heathen, or a dying Protestant sinner, is in the same condition as a dying Catholic sinner, and if he, like the Catholic sinner, makes an act of contrition, asks forgiveness, and trusts in the merits of Christ, he (the dying Protestant sinner) *surely obtains forgiveness.*

As S. O. sees no difference between divine and human faith, so, in like manner, he does not see any difference between the condition of a dying Catholic sinner and that of a dying Protestant sinner, though the difference is greater than the distance between heaven and earth.

The sinful Catholic has divine faith. In the light of this faith he knows well how far he is wrong in the sight of God. His hope in the merits of Christ is based on his divine faith, and therefore it is divine hope—two absolutely necessary requisites to obtain sanctifying grace. Hence it is that the Church, in her prayer for a dying Catholic, says: "O Lord, though he has sinned, yet he has not denied the Father, the Son, and the Holy Ghost; he has preserved the faith, and has faithfully worshipped God." All that God has to grant to the dying sinful Catholic, if he cannot receive the absolution of the priest, is the grace of perfect sorrow, which is often granted on account of the prayers and sacrifice of the Church, from which he is not excluded by grievous sins. Besides, to obtain this grace of true sorrow, the Catholic sinner prays, at least in his heart, to God and to the Blessed Mother of God. He knows her great power of intercession with Jesus Christ; he knows how merciful she is towards even the most abandoned sinners, if they invoke her prayers for a happy death. If he is happy enough to have with him a priest to assist him, though confession may be impossible for him for certain reasons, yet, having the true desire to confess, and at least imperfect sorrow (attrition) for his sins, the priest can give him absolution, by which the defect of his sorrow is supplied, and the eternal punishment forgiven. The priest gives him Extreme Unction, which wonderfully helps him to die a happy death.

But how different is the case of a dying Protestant! Suppose some Protestants and some Catholics have met with an accident. They are in a dying condition. A priest is called. He can give absolution to the dying Catholics, but he is not allowed to give absolution to Protestants, not even conditionally, for, as St. Alphonsus says, they generally have a great aversion to the Sacrament of Penance.

Moreover, the faith of the Protestant is not divine; it is all *human*. But where there is no divine faith, there can be no such hope as God requires before he can bestow upon the soul the grace of sanctifying grace. To save, therefore, such a Protestant, God would have to grant him the most extraordinary gratuitous gift of divine faith, and all the other dispositions necessary to obtain forgiveness and the grace of justification. The condition of a dying Protestant is, then, very different from that of a dying Catholic.

Let S. O. here remember well that forgiveness of sins can be obtained only in the Catholic Church. "He who has not the true faith," says St Fulgentius, "cannot receive the forgiveness of his sins. We therefore must believe that nowhere else than in the bosom of the Church, our Mother, converts can obtain the forgiveness of sins. Out of this Church, there may be Baptism, but it is not availing to salvation. Hence all those who are out of the Church receive forgiveness only after they have entered this same Church with true faith and humility. Let them join her in due time, if they wish to be saved. (Lib. I. de Remissione Peccat., cap. 5 et 6.) "We must know" says St. Gregory the Great, "that the forgiveness of sins can be granted only in the Catholic Church, as long as we live in this world and are truly sorry for them." (Lib. xviii., Moral., cap. 14.)

To console dying Protestants, Sir Oracle goes on to say:—

"And many a bitter cry for forgiveness goes up to God from many a Protestant, as the angel of death hovers over him because, knowing so much of the truth of the Catholic religion as he does, he failed to have the courage of his convictions and embrace it. It is a grievous sin to reject the known truth, but grievous as it is, even *that and any other sin will be forgiven to him, no matter what his religion may be*, who makes an act of perfect contrition and has the will to comply with every other condition which a merciful God imposes as a condition of forgiveness, though he may not know explicitly what those conditions are. And to such, this *Explanation of Christian Doctrine* notwithstanding, there is no condemnation."

Unfortunately S. O. has forgotten to tell dying Protestants where to get his soothing, sin-cancelling plaster for their souls. "To rise from the state of mortal sin," says St. Thomas, "is to repair the threefold spiritual losses which it has brought on the soul : first, the loss of the splendor of divine grace by the enormity of sin. The splendor and ornament of the soul were the brilliant rays of divine light shining on it, and can never be replenished but by the light and grace of God. Secondly, to rise from the state of mortal sin, is to repair also the contamination of human nature by a corrupt, depraved will. The will, by its depravity being alienated from God, can never be united to Him again unless by the power and efficacy of grace. Thirdly, to rise from the state of mortal sin is to repair the debt of punishment which is eternal damnation. Pardon and remission cannot be obtained but from Him who was outrageously offended by mortal sin. It is therefore as impossible for man to rise by his own natural means from the state of sin, as it is for a dead body to rise of itself from the grave. Hence St. Augustine says that, when God converts, by his grace, a sinner, he performs a greater work than he performed by creating heaven and earth. But does God perform this most extraordinary miracle for every sinner in his last hour, *no matter what his religion may be*, if he says S. O.'s act of contrition ? To say this act of contrition, is indeed in the power of man ; but to have true, perfect contrition is a miracle of the power and mercy of God alone ; it is one of the greatest gifts of God, and God cannot give this gift without bestowing before the knowledge of the necessary truths of salvation and *divine* faith, confident hope based upon divine faith, and all the other supernatural dispositions of the soul for receiving the grace of justification. If a heathen or a Protestant receives such an extraordinary grace of conversion, and dies in it, he is saved, not as a heathen or as a Protestant, but as a Catholic. This we say distinctly in our Explanation; but our would-be theologian dishonestly asserts that we say the contrary; for he says: "*And to such*, this *Explanation of Christian Doctrine* notwithstanding, *there is no condemnation.*" Strange, a little after he is constrained to avow his dishonesty.

The right of seeing God, the infinite Being in himself, belongs to God alone; and no creature or finite being, as such, can have any claim to that infinite bliss, nor, consequently, to any of the means which lead thereto. As eternal happiness, the possession of God, or anything leading to it, does not belong to the nature of man, God is under no greater obligation to raise him to a state in which he is rendered capable of seeing and enjoying his Creator, than he is to raise a stone to the nature of an animal.

By his own natural strength man, as we have seen, can acquire much knowledge about God; he can recognize God as the author and preserver of his being, and love him as such. But he can never know and love him so as to deserve to see him face to face. For this, there is needed a life superior to that of man,—a life flowing from God to man, by which a relationship is established between God and man,—a relationship by which God adopts man as his child. "To see the divine Essence," says St. Thomas Aquinas, "is something far above the faculties of the human soul; nay, it is something even far above the natural faculties of an angel. The soul, therefore, must be prepared for the contemplation of the Divinity."

"If we wish that a thing should produce an effect which is above its nature, we must carefully prepare it for the production of such an effect. If, for instance, we wish to set the air on fire, we must gradually raise its temperature.

In like manner, God must prepare the soul to make his Essence accessible to its intelligence. This he does by bestowing upon it here below the inestimable gift of true divine faith, hope, and charity. Faith unites us to God, because he inspires us with the knowledge of supernatural truths; hope unites us to God, because he is the Author of all our happiness; and charity unites us to God, because it puts us in direct communication with the Author of all gifts and graces. 'The charity of God is infused into our hearts by the Holy Ghost, who has been given to us.' (Rom. v. 5.) The grace of God is life eternal. Charity is a reciprocal communication and love between God and man; they exist in this life by grace, and in the other by glory. 'God is charity; and he that abideth in charity, abideth in God, and God in him! (I. John, iv. 16.)

"Natural gifts, however precious, cannot put us into this supernatural state of grace; for an effect can never surpass its cause. It is produced in us by the Holy Ghost, who is the Love of the Father and of the Son, and makes us participate even of the Divine Substance.

"Those, therefore, who leave the world and are endowed with these divine virtues are prepared to see God in a created light, called *the light of glory*. But to die without these supernatural virtues is to remain banished forever from the face of the Lord." (De Virtutibus.)

True charity forbids us to despise those who are in error; on the contrary, it teaches us to pity and to love them. But there is a great difference between loving those in error, and loving the error itself; there is a vast difference between loving the sinner and loving his sins.

It is not our business to say whether this or that one who was not received into the Church before his death is damned. What we condemn is the Protestant. and the heathen system of religion, because they are utterly false; but we do not condemn any person—God alone is the judge of all. It is quite certain, however, that, if any of those who are not received into the Church before their death, enter heaven,—a lot which we earnestly desire and beg

God to grant them,—they can only do so after undergoing a radical and fundamental change before death launches them into eternity. This is quite certain, for the reason, among others, that they are not *one ;* and nothing is more indisputably certain than this, that there can be no division in heaven : " God is not the God of dissension," says St. Paul, " but of peace." He has never suffered the least interruption of union, even in the Church Militant on earth ; most assuredly he will not tolerate it in the Church Triumphant. God most certainly will remain what he is. Non-Catholics, therefore, in order to enter heaven, must cease to be what they are, and become something which now they are not.

With regard to Catholics, the case is quite different. No change need come upon *them*, except that which is implied in passing from the state of grace to the state of glory.

They will be *one* there, as they have been one here. For *them* the miracle of supernatural unity is already worked. That mark of God's hand is already upon them. That sign of God's election is already graven upon their foreheads. Faith, indeed, will be replaced by sight, but this will be no real change, because what they *see* in the next world will be what they have *believed* in this. The same sacramental King (to borrow an expression of Father Faber), whom here they have worshipped upon the altar, will there be their everlasting portion. The same gracious Madonna who has so often consoled them in the trials of this life, will introduce her own children to the glories of the next. They will not, in that hour, have to " buy oil " for *their* lamps, for they are already kindled at the lamp of the sanctuary. No wedding-robe will have to be provided for *them*, for they received it long ago at the baptismal font, and have washed away its stains in the tribunal of penance. The faces of the saints and angels will not be strange to *them*, for have they not been familiar with them from infancy as friends, companions, and benefactors ? And being thus, even in this world, of the household of faith, and the family of God, not only no shadow of change need pass upon *them*, but to vary in one iota from what they now believe and practise, would simply cut them off from the Communion of Saints, and be the most overwhelming disaster which could befall them.

No doubt, God, in his infinite power and mercy, may enlighten even at the hour of death one who is not yet a Catholic, so that he may know and believe the necessary truths of salvation, be truly sorry for his sins, and die in such disposition of soul as is necessary to be saved. Such a one, by an extraordinary grace of God, ceases to be what he was; he dies united to the Church, and is saved, not as a Protestant, but as a Catholic. But is it wise for a Protestant to expect to be saved by a most extraordinary miracle of the infinite power and mercy of God?

The fact that it is in the power of the infinite mercy of God to convert a heathen or a Protestant to the true faith, even in his last hour, must never serve as an encouragement for some rash heathen or Protestant to continue to live in infidelity or in heresy, in the hope that God will not send him to hell, even if he continues to the end of his life to live in heathenism or Protestantism; for, as it would be a great folly to throw one's self into a deep well, in the hope that God would save him from death, because he is too good to let him perish, so, in like manner, it would be a greater folly for a Protestant to run the risk of dying in Protestantism, on the presumption that the infinite mercy of God would save him from hell by making of him a Catholic even in his last hour.

Let us, then, always bear in mind, what the Angelic Doctor St. Thomas Aquinas says: "There is a certain principle and doctrine which we must never lose sight of when there is question of salvation. This principle is that no salvation is possible for any one who is not united to Jesus Christ crucified by means of divine faith and charity, '*which*," as St. Augustine says "*cannot be kept out of the unity of the Church.*'

Since the death of Jesus Christ, sanctifying grace is

given to the souls of unbaptized persons by means of baptism, and to the souls of Christians who have grievously sinned, by the sacrament of Penance. If a person cannot receive Baptism or Penance in reality, and is aware of the obligation of receiving it, he must have the explicit desire to receive it; but, if he is not aware of this obligation, he must have at least the implicit desire to receive it, and this desire must be joined to divine faith in the Redeemer and to an act of perfect charity or contrition, which includes the sincere desire of the soul to comply with all that God requires of it in order to be saved. This act of perfect charity is a gratuitous gift and an extraordinary grace of God, which we cannot have of ourselves; it is a great miracle of grace, that God alone can perform; a miracle that changes a person from being a heathen or a heretic into a Catholic. Any one, therefore, who dies without this miraculous change of his soul will be lost forever.

Bishop Hay asks the question, "Is there any reason to believe that God Almighty often bestows the light of faith, or the grace of repentance, at the hour of death, upon those who have lived all their lives in heresy, or in sin?"

"That God," he answers, "can in an instant convert the most obdurate heart, either to the true faith, or to repentance, is manifest from the examples of St. Paul, Zacheus the publican, St. Matthew the apostle, and many others; and, in particular, of St. Peter, to whom in an instant he revealed the divinity of Jesus Christ, who said to him on that account, 'Blessed art thou, Simon Barjona, for flesh and blood hath not revealed this to thee, but my Father who is in heaven.' (Matt. xvi. 17.) That he can do this at the hour of death as easily as at any time in life, cannot be doubted, as we see in the good thief upon the cross; he is the same all-powerful God at all times. But it must be owned that there is very little reason to think that this is frequently the case. There certainly are not the smallest grounds from revelation to think so. Nay, the Scripture threatens the contrary. All that can be said is, that as God is able, he can do it; and as he is merciful, he may do it; and the possibility of this is sufficient to hinder us from passing judgment upon the state of any soul who has left this world ; but it would certainly be the height of madness, and a manifest tempting of God, for a person to go on in an evil way in hopes of finding such mercy at his last.

§ 12. S. O. GIVES US CREDIT FOR OUR CORRECT DOCTRINE BY QUOTING FROM OUR FAMILIAR EXPLANATION THE FOLLOWING QUESTIONS AND ANSWERS :—

" *Q.* Is it right, then, for us to say that one who was not received in the Catholic Church before his death, is damned ? *Ans* No.

"*Q.* Why not ? *Ans.* Because we cannot know for certain what takes place between God and the soul at the awful moment of death.

"*Q.* What do you mean by this ? *Ans.* I mean that God, in his infinite mercy, may enlighten, at the hour of death, one who is not yet a Catholic, so that he may see the truth of the Catholic faith, be truly sorry for his sins, and sincerely desire to die a good death.

"*Q.* What do we say of those who receive such an extraordinary grace and die in this manner ? *Ans.* We say of them that they are united to the soul of the Catholic Church and are saved."

S. O. gave us this credit very reluctantly, as is evident from what he adds immediately after, namely :

" All this," he says, "has the true sound of Catholic doctrine, but it contradicts, both in spirit and letter, the quotations made in the beginning of this article. But it is better to contradict oneself than to persist in error."

S. O. seems to take a delight in uttering false oracles. First, he has falsified our answer, the end of which does not read, " sincerely desire to die a good *death ;* it reads " sincerely desire to die a *good Catholic.* The biggest scoundrel may naturally desire to die a good death ; but no Protestant will, in his last moments, desire to die a *good Catholic*, unless he has received, in the hour of death, that most extraordinary grace of which we speak in our answer.

One day a Protestant gentleman came to see us. He was a perfect stranger to us. He began at once to speak about religion. We put to him about six questions, which he answered well. After his last answer he said: "I understand that I must become a Catholic, in order to be saved. But I like better to go as a Protestant to hell than as a Catholic to heaven."

Is it not, then, very dishonest for S. O. to falsify our answer?

Secondly, in the first part of our treatise we have clearly proved that the Church plainly teaches that there is no salvation for those who die without being united to her. Now S. O. emphatically asserts that, in the above words of ours, we contradict what we have clearly shown to be a revealed truth taught by the Church, and he says that it was better for us to do so than to persist in error. He therefore evidently asserts that there is salvation out of the Church, and thus proves himself to be a heretic.

Thirdly, in order to make it appear that, by the above answers, we contradicted what we have said in the first part of our treatise, S. O. most dishonesty suppressed the continuation of, or conclusion to, the above answers.—The conclusion reads as follows:—

"Q. What, then, awaits all those who are out of the Catholic Church and die without having received such an extraordinary grace at the hour of death? Ans. 'Eternal damnation, as sure as there is a God.'"—Is it not most clear from this answer that we have, neither in letter nor in spirit, contradicted anything we have said, but have, on the contrary, in letter and in spirit, confirmed all the reasons we have given for the great truth that no salvation is possible out of the Roman Catholic Church?

Alas! is it possible that S. O. should have made himself guilty of such a vile dishonesty on the Feast of the Holy Name!

§ 13. S. O. as Catechist.

"Our holy and true religion," he says, "will never suffer from telling the truth with simplicity, charity, and above all *with theological accuracy*. Neither will there be the least danger to our children from telling them the honest truth about Protestant doctrines, when it is necessary to mention them at all. Nor is it in keeping with the spirit of Catholic charity to inspire our youth with hatred and contempt of their Protestant neighbors."

A short time ago an archbishop of the U. S. said, in presence of several priests: "Is it not strange that so many of our Catholic young men, who were educated at certain Catholic colleges, are or become down right infidels soon after leaving them?" A certain lady told me one day, she could mention at least twenty-four young men of the best families of her city, who were downright infidels when they left the Catholic college where they received their education. This is a very sad fact. How is it to be accounted for? It could be easily accounted for, if S. O. were the teacher of the catechism in those colleges. He would teach the Protestant catechism admirably well, at least much better than the Catholic catechism. You may be sure, he would not teach that "there is no salvation out of the Catholic Church." He might get out a small catechism of his own, in which you would look in vain for a true explanation of the ninth article of the Creed, for the Sacrament of Penance, for the doctrine on the necessity of grace to be saved, etc., etc. However, he would tell the truth 1. *with simplicity*, that is, for instance, that Protestants believe about Christ precisely what the Catholic believes; 2. *with charity*, by suppressing such truths as might wound the feelings of honest Protestant pupils; 3. with *theological accuracy*, by making all his pupils believe that Protestants believe all the facts of Christ's life just as well as Catholics. He would not mention the difference that exists between divine and human faith, between truth and error, between true and false Christianity, etc., for the reason that the explanation of this difference would not be in keeping with the spirit of Catholic charity, which forbids him to inspire youth with hatred and contempt of their Protestant neighbors, by which, of course, he means to say that it is wrong to inspire youth with hatred and contempt of the principles of Protestantism. What he would insist upon especially is that every pupil of his should know well by heart his wonderful act of contrition, by which every one, no matter what his religion may be, and no matter what his sins may be, will obtain forgiveness and be saved. Let us now hear a better authority on the subject of Christian doctrine. Dr. O. A. Brownson, the celebrated convert and famous American Reviewer, one day said to us:—

"I feel surprised at the fact that so many of the young men educated at certain Catholic colleges have become infidels. I cannot account for this otherwise than by presuming that the religious training there is not solid enough; that the heathen world is too much read and studied; that principles somewhat too lax are in vogue; that the truths of our religion are taught too superficially; that the principles which underlie the dogmas are not sufficiently explained, inculcated, and impressed upon the minds of the young men, and that their educators fail in giving them a correct idea of the spirit and essence of our religion, which is based on divine revelation, and invested in a body divinely commissioned to teach all men, authoritatively and infallibly, in all its sacred and immutable truths—truths which we are consequently bound in conscience to receive without hesitation.

"Now what I have said of certain colleges applies also, unhappily, to many of our female academies; they are by no means what they should be, according to the spirit of the Church; they conform too much to the spirit of the world; they have too many human considerations; they make too many allowances for Protestant pupils, at the expense of the Catholic spirit and training of our young Catholic women; they yield too much to the spirit of the age; in a word, they attend more to the intellectual than to the spiritual culture of their pupils.

"But what is even more surprising than all this is, that some of our Catholic clergy, and among them some even of those who should be first and foremost in fighting for sound religious principles, and see that our youth are carefully brought up in them, are too much inclined to yield to the godless spirit of the age,—to the so-called liberal views on Catholic education, which have been clearly and solemnly condemned by the Holy See. They tell us poor people in the world, that, if we are careless in bringing up our children as good Catholics, we are worse than heathens, and have denied our faith! that, if our children are lost through our neglect, we also shall be lost! I would like to know whether God will show himself more merciful to those of our clergy who take so little interest in the religious instruction of our youth; who make little or no exertions to establish Catholic schools where we could have our children properly educated; who, when they condescend to instruct them, do so in bombastic language, in scholastic terms, which the poor children cannot understand, taking no pains to give their instructions in plain words and in a manner attractive for children?

"As the pastor is, so is the flock. We enjoy full religious liberty in our country. All we need is good courageous pastors,—standard-bearers in the cause of God and the people. We would be only too happy to follow them, and to support and encourage them by every means in our power. What an immense amount of good could thus be achieved in a short time! Our religion never loses anything of its efficacy upon the minds and hearts of men; it can lose only so far as it is not brought to bear upon them. What is most wanted is not argument, but instruction and explanation.

"I can hardly account for this want of zeal for true Catholic education in so many of our clergy, who are otherwise models of every virtue, than by supposing the fact that their ecclesiastical training must have been deficient in many respects, or that they must have spent their youth in our godless public schools, where they were never thoroughly imbued with the true spirit of the Catholic Church —the spirit of God."

Ah! This great Catholic philosopher has given, in very plain words, the reason why so many young Catholic men have become infidels at the very Catholic colleges at which they received their education Their education was not Catholic enough. To make education more Catholic, it is necessary to have catechisms and catechists that are more Catholic and more practical, that explain in a lucid manner the constitution and authority of the Church and the great mysteries of our holy religion, and clearly show that salvation is impossible out of the Roman Catholic Church.*

In this country, where reading, speaking, writing has no rule or limit, Catholics will be in daily temptation. They cannot close their eyes; and if they could, they cannot close their ears. What they refuse to read they cannot fail to hear. It is the trial permitted for the purity and confirmation of their faith. The trial is severe for many. In order that they may stand well so severe a trial, they must be prepared for it by thorough instruction in the Christian doctrine, especially in the fundamental truths of our holy religion.

§ 14. LIBERALISM.

From the manner in which the article *Queer Explanation* is written, it is evident that S. O. is in favor of Liberalism, and the Rev. Father Cronin, Editor of the *Buffalo Union and Times* strongly advocates Liberalism and preaches against *the small meanness of intolerance* in his article *Narrow-Mindedness*. (*B. U.* and *T.*, March 1, 1888.) Now what is Liberalism?

From the time of the Apostles the true followers of Christ

---

* See what we have said on this subject in our second edition of "Familiar Explanation of Christian Doctrine," published by Benziger Brothers

have been called Catholics. The meaning of this appellation has always been that they belonged to the One, Holy Catholic, Apostolic, and Roman Church. The term *Catholic* has always distinguished them from every heretical sect. They were known by this term in every part of the world.

Within the few last years, however, certain persons have arisen who are not satisfied with the name of Catholic. Hence they call themselves *Liberal Catholics*.

Liberal Catholics falsely assert, " that it is a mistake to protect and foster religion, because religion, " they say, " will flourish much better if left alone ; that the world has entered a new phase, and has begun to run a new course, and consequently the Church should accommodate herself to the spirit of the age ; that religion has nothing to do with politics ; that it has to do only with the private lives of men ; that religion must keep inside the Church—that it is meant for Sundays alone ; that we must be generous in our religious feelings toward non-Catholics ; that is, we must not tell them that there is no salvation out of the Catholic Church ; we must not explain to them the reason why salvation is impossible out of the fold of Christ ; we must not show to them the difference between divine and human faith ; for, if we do all this, we are narrow-minded and an intolerant people ; we are bigots, who visit condign reprobation on the liberal Catholic." A liberal man is never intolerant, says the Rev. Editor of the *B. U.* and *T.* In a word, a liberal Catholic is a compound of true and false principles. He has two consciences : one for his public, and another for his private life. He is Catholic with the Pope, if possible, but liberal in religious views with all those who differ from him in faith. " He is a believer, " says the Rev. Father Cronin, " in broad-minded views, and has a wide charity for the feelings of others who differ from him in faith." " Liberal Catholics, " says O. A. Brownson, " would let more people into heaven by the exception than by the rule."

" We have Catholics, or men," says Brownson, " that call themselves Catholics, who, without knowing it, defend in politics pure secularism, only another name for political atheism, and—not always the same individuals indeed—who defend in theology what, to our understanding, is a most destructive latitudinarianism. It is seldom we meet a Catholic, man or woman, priest or layman, who will permit us to say that out of the Church no one can be saved, without requiring us to qualify the assertion, or so to explain it as to make it meaningless to plain people who are ignorant of the subtleties, nice distinctions, and refinements of theologians. How many of our Catholics, though holding Protestantism to be an error against faith and antagonistic to the Church, hold that the mass of Protestants are out of the way of salvation, and can never see God in the beatific vision, unless before they die they become Catholics, united to Christ in the Church which is his Body? If we assert the contrary, are we not met with theological distinctions, logical refinements, subtle explanations and qualifications, which place us all in the wrong?" "It is only of late," says Bishop Hay, "that this loose way of thinking and speaking about the necessity of true faith and of being in communion with Christ in his Church has appeared among the members of the Church. Such language was never heard among Catholics in all former ages. And this is one of the greatest grounds of its condemnation. It is a novelty, it is a new doctrine; it was unheard of from the beginning; nay, it is directly opposite to the uniform doctrine of all the great lights of the Church in all former ages. These great and holy men, the most unexceptionable witnesses of the Christian faith in their days, knew no other language on this subject but what they saw spoken before them by Christ and his apostles; they knew their divine Master had declared, 'He that believeth not shall be condemned;' they heard his Apostle proclaiming a dreadful anathema against any one, though an angel from heaven, who should dare to alter the Gospel he had preached; (Gal. i. 8.) they heard him affirming in express terms, that 'without faith it is impossible to please God;' and they constantly held the same language. And as they saw not the smallest ground in Scripture for thinking that those who were out of the Church could be saved by invincible ignorance, that deceptive evasion is not so much as once to be met with in all their writings, or in the writings of any solid Catholic theologian, as we have shown. How, then, does it happen that some, nowadays, who profess themselves members of the Church of Christ, seem to call this truth in question by continually pleading in favor of those who are not of their communion, proposing excuses for them, and using all their endeavors to prove a possibility of salvation for those who live and die in a false religion?

"This is one of those devices which the enemy of souls makes use of in these unhappy times to promote his own cause, and which there are grounds to fear has, from various reasons, found its way even among those who belong to the fold of Christ; for, (1.) As they live among those who are of false religions, and often have the most intimate connections with them, they naturally and most laudably contract a love and affection for them. This makes them at first unwilling to think their friends should be out of the way of salvation. Then they proceed to wish and hope they may not be so. Hence they come to call in question their being so; and from this the step is easy to grasp at every pretext to persuade themselves they are not so. (2.) Latitudinarian principles are to be found everywhere in these our days; an uncovenanted mercy, forsooth, is found to be in God for Mahometans, Jews, and infidels, which had never been heard of among Christians. This is gilded over with the specious character of a liberal way of thinking and generous sentiments; and it is become the fashion to think and speak in this manner. Now fashion is a most powerful persuasive, against which even good people are not always proof; and when one hears those sentiments every day resounding in his ears, and anything that seems contrary to them ridiculed and condemned, he naturally yields to the delusion, and turns away his mind from so much as wishing to examine the strength of these sentiments, from fear of finding out their falsehood. When, from fear of being despised, we wish anything to be true, the translation is very easy to believe it to be true, and without further examination every sophistical show of reason in its favor is adopted as conclusive. (3.) Worldly interest also very often concurs with its overbearing influence to produce the same end. A member of the Church of Christ sees his separated friend in power and credit in the world, and capable of being of great service to him, and knows, should he embrace the true faith, he would lose all his influence, and become unable to serve him. This makes him cool in wishing his conversion; but the thought that his friend is not in the way of salvation pains him; he therefore begins to wish he *could* be saved as he is in his own religion. Hence he comes to hope but that *he may*, and gladly adopts any show of proof to make him think that *he will*. It is true, indeed, all these reasons would have little influence with a sincere member of the Church of Christ, who understands his religion, and has a just sense of what it teaches him on this head. But the great misfortune of many who adopt these loose ways of thinking and speaking is, (4.) that they are ignorant of the grounds of their religion; they do not examine the matter thoroughly, and if once they be infected by the spirit of the day, they are unwilling to examine; they even take it amiss if any zealous friend should attempt to undeceive them, and grasping at those miserable sophisms which are alleged in favor of their loose way of thinking, refuse to open their eyes to the truth, or even to look at the reasons which support it."

"They do not sufficiently," says Brownson, "understand the relation of the Church to the Incarnation, the order of grace, the office of the Church in the economy of salvation, the end of religion, the disposition of the world to mistake liberality for charity. They do not see that the Church grows, so to speak, out of the Incarnation, of which she is, in some sort, the visible continuation on earth, and from which she is inseparable."

The regeneration of the world was prefigured in its first creation. After five days of waiting, of preparation, of preliminary creations, God made the first man "from the slime of the earth, earthly." In him he joined, in one human person, two different substances, the one properly belonging to angels, the other to animals: mind and body. He then appointed him master and lord of all the creatures that people the air, the earth, and the waters. After he had finished this creation of the head of human nature, he completed it by the formation of Eve, drawn from the side of Adam; and by this addition the human race was created so as to live and perpetuate itself. In the same manner, after a series of five thousand years (according to the Septuagint), after these five long days devoted to the announcement, the figures, the preparations, and the preliminaries of his arrival, the new Adam appeared, "come down from heaven and heavenly." In him also two natures, the divine and the human, are joined together, in the one person of God the Son. He is appointed King of angels and of men. Afterwards his Incarnation, in a certain sense, is finished, carried out in its fulness, by the formation of the Church, his spouse, who is drawn from his side, opened for us on the cross; and by the incorporation of the faithful into Jesus Christ in the bosom of the Church, Christianity is complete—it lives, it grows, it gives life to the earth, and peoples heaven.

"God," says St. Paul, "hath subjected all things to him (Christ), and made him Head over all the Church, which is his Body, and the fulness of him, who is filled all in all." (Eph. i. 22, 23.) Of all the parts of the body, the head is the principal organ. Hence the beginning of a thing is called the head. As the human nature of Jesus Christ is hypostatically united to the Divinity, He possesses the fulness of grace and communicates it to all the members of his mystic Body. Hence the Apostle says, "He that raised up Jesus Christ from the dead, shall also vivify your mortal bodies on account of the Spirit that dwelleth in you." (Rom. viii. 1.)

The Church is Christ's mystical Body, and his complement or perfection, the head being incomplete without the body; but when the head has all the members of the body, so that none is wanting, then it is entirely complete, says St. Chrysostom.

Although Christ is most perfect himself, yet he considers himself incomplete, and, so to speak, a mutilated head to members, without having the Church as body joined to him.

Hence St. Paul says: "For as the body is one and hath many members, and all the members of the body, though they are many, yet are one body: so also is Christ." (I. Cor. xii. 12.) On these words St. Augustine comments thus: "St Paul says not: so also is the body or the members of Christ; but, *so also is Christ.* He says head and body is one Christ. And this should not appear incredible to us; for, if Christ's divine nature, which infinitely differs from and is incomparably more sublime than his human nature, was so united with it as to be only one person, how much more credible is it that the faithful and holy Christians are one Christ with the Man Christ! The whole Christ is head and body. The head and members are one Christ. The head was in heaven and said: 'Paul, why dost thou persecute me?' We are with him in heaven by hope, and he is with us on earth by charity." (Lib. I. de Peccat. Merit, c. 31.)

Hence Christ is sometimes called the whole Church. (I. Cor. xii. 12.) Hence also it is often said, that we are in Christ, that we grow, work, and suffer in him; hence also the Apostle says that Christ lives in him and he in Christ. Hence all our hope, all our consolation.

The community on earth of those Christians who are united under one common Head, the Pope, as the successor of St. Peter, and who profess the same faith and partake of the same sacraments, are called Christ's Body. "This Body," says Cornelius a Lapide, "derives its spiritual life from Christ, its Head. This life is called the soul of the Church. This life (soul of) the Church is either *general* and *imperfect,* or it is *special* and *perfect.* The *general* and *imperfect* life is the *true faith,* and the *special* and *perfect* life of the Body of the Church is divine charity. Those of the

274 Out of the Catholic Church there is No Salvation.

faithful who are animated with *true divine faith and charity*, which is poured out into their hearts by the Holy Ghost, are, thereby, united to Christ, their Head, and form *his perfect Body*. Those of the faithful who are animated only with the *general* and *imperfect* life, by faith alone, are, it is true, members of the Body of the Church, but they are *imperfect* members; and were they to die in that state, they would be lost forever. But as they are members of Christ's Body, though dead members thereof, they may become perfect members by divine charity, if they profit by the graces that flow from Christ upon all the members of his body. Hence, as the member of a body which is not united to the other members and the whole body, cannot receive any nourishment and life through its body, so, also, a Christian cannot live by the perfect life of the Church, if he is not united by divine charity with all the rest of the faithful and the whole Body of the Church." (Comment. in Epist. ad Ephes., c. iv., v. 16, and in Epist. ad Tim., c. ii., v. 20.)

"If any one," says Christ, "remaineth not in me, he shall be cast forth as a branch, and shall wither, and they shall gather him up, and cast him into the fire; and he burneth." (St. John, xv. 6.)

After being united in baptism to the Body of Christ, his Church, we can remain united to Christ, her Head, only by true divine faith and charity. But true charity cannot be kept out of the unity of the Church, says St. Augustine. As all heretics without exception are separated from Christ's Body, the Church, they are branches cut off from the vine, Christ, and therefore the sap of divine faith and charity cannot flow upon them, as long as they are not united to Christ's Body, the Church. He who thinks he can do good of himself, is not united to the vine; and he who is not united to the vine, is not united to Christ; and he who is not united to Christ is no Christian. (St. Aug. Tract. 21.)

"The Church, therefore," says O. A. Brownson, "lives in Christ, and he lives in her; his life is her life, and individuals are joined to him and live his life by being joined to her and living his life in her. To be separated from her is to be separated from him, is to be separated from the Incarnate Word himself, the one Mediator of God and men, and from our end, as well as the medium of its attainment.

All that Divine Providence has produced in the course of ages existed, as St. Augustine says, at the beginning of creation, in the so-called seminal, radical, fundamental causes, such as vegetation of every kind, animals, and material bodies. So that all things in creation attain their perfection in virtue of this imperishable seed, which exists in their nature since the beginning of the world.

Now, as man is destined for supernatural happiness, it is necessary that the imperishable seed of divine grace should be in him. St. John alludes to this divine seed when he says, "Whoever is born of God, committeth not sin, for his (God's) seed (divine grace) abideth in him, and he cannot sin because he is born of God. (chapt. iii., 9.) A rational being can obtain an object only by some act which it makes, and that act cannot have the power of putting him in possession of an object which is of a supernatural order. Now eternal beatitude is a good of a supernatural order. God alone has always enjoyed that perfect glory and happiness. No matter how great the natural perfection of a man may be, he cannot, by an act of his own natural perfection, put himself in possession of an object of supernatural perfection. It is only by divine grace that he can merit and obtain it; and this grace is granted only in the Church.

"There is" says Brownson, "no name under heaven among men but the name of Jesus Christ by which we can be saved. There is salvation in none other; and what Catholic needs to be told that Christ, as the Saviour, is in the Church, which is his Body, and that it is in the Church, and nowhere else, that he does or will save? True, though in the Church, he is also out of her, operating on the hearts of those not yet within; but he operates ad Ecclesiam, to bring them within, that he may save them there, not that he may save them without. He loves his Church; she is his *Chosen*, his *Beloved*, his *Spouse*, and he gave his life for her. In her, so to speak, centre all his affections, his graces, and his providences; and all creatures and events are ordered in reference to her. Without her all history is inexplicable, a fable, and the universe itself meaningless and without a purpose. The salvation of souls itself is in order to her, and God will have no children who are not also hers. As there is but one Father, so can there be but one Mother, and none are of the Father who are not of the Mother. Clear and explicit are all the Fathers and Saints as to this, and they plainly teach that it would dishonor her, and make God an adulterer, to suppose the salvation of a single soul of which she is not the spiritual Mother.

"God, in establishing his Church from the foundation of the world, in giving his life on the Cross for her, and abiding always with her in her tabernacles unto the consummation of the world, in adorning her as a Bride with all the graces of the Holy Ghost, in denominating her his Beloved, his Spouse, has taught us how he regards her, how deep and tender, how infinite and inexhaustible his love for her, and with what love and honor we should regard her. He loves us with an infinite love, and has died to redeem us; but he loves us and wills our salvation only in and through his Church. He would bring us to himself, and he never ceases as a lover to woo our love; but he wills us to love, and reverence, and adore him only as children of his Beloved. Our reverence and love must redound to his glory as her Spouse, and gladden her maternal heart, and swell her maternal joy, or he wills them not, knows them not.

"Oh, it is frightful to forget the place the Church holds in the love and Providence of God, and to regard the relation in which we stand to her as a matter of no moment! She is the one grand object on which are fixed all heaven, all earth, ay, and all hell. Behold her impersonation in the Blessed Virgin, the Holy Mother of God, the glorious Queen of heaven. Humble and obscure she lived, poor and silent, yet all heaven turned their eyes toward her; all hell trembled before her; all earth needed her. Dear was she to all the hosts of heaven; for in her they beheld their Queen, the Mother of grace, the Mother of mercies, the channel through which all love, and mercies, and graces, and good things were to flow to men, and return to the glory and honor of their Father. Humblest of mortal maidens, lowliest on earth, under God she was highest in heaven. So is the Church, our sweet Mother. O, she is no creation of the imagination! O, she is no mere accident in human history, in divine Providence, divine grace, in the conversion of souls! She is a glorious, a living reality, living the divine, the eternal life of God. Her maker is her Husband, and he places her, after him, over all in heaven, on the earth, and under the earth. All that he can do to adorn and exalt her he has done. All he can give he gives; for he gives himself, and unites her in indissoluble union with himself.

"Did we always reflect earnestly on what the Church is, did we consider her rank in the universe, her relation to God, the place she holds, so to speak, in his affections: the bare thought of the salvation of a single soul not spiritually begotten of her would make us thrill with horror.

"Here are the great mass out of the Church, unbelieving and heretical, careless and indifferent, and it is idle to expect to make any general impression upon them, unless we present the question of the Church as a question of life and death, unless we can succeed in convincing them that, if they live and die where they are, they can never see God. This is the doctrine, and the precise doctrine, needed. Is it true? Yes, or no? Is it denied? By those out of the Church, certainly, and hence the great reason why they are content to live and die out of the Church. Is it denied by those in the Church? What Catholic dare deny it? To what individual or class of individuals are we authorized by our holy faith to promise even the bare possibility of salvation, without being joined to the visible communion of the Church of God? No doubt, the truth is always to be adhered to, let the consequences be what they may.

"These poor souls, for whom our Lord shed his precious blood, for whom bleed afresh the dear wounds in his hands, his feet, his side, bound in the chains of error and sin, suspended over the precipice, ready to drop into the abyss below, admonish all who have hearts of flesh, or any bowels of compassion, to speak out, to cry aloud in awful and piercing tones to warn them of their danger, rather than by ingenious distinctions or qualifications to flatter them, or to have the appearance of flattering them, with the hope that, after all, their condition is not perilous."

Alas! a man must be really indifferent to God and religion, he must be without heart and without reason to tolerate quietly such religious errors. It is in the very nature of every honest man when he has the truth, to guard it with jealous watchfulness, and to repel with indignation every admixture of falsehood.

Look at the teacher of mathematics, when he discovers an error in the calculation of his pupils, does he not condemn it—is he not intolerant?

Look at the musician, the leader of a choir—is he not indignant when some one sings flat or out of time?

Look at the lawyer who has carefully studied the laws and is eloquently pleading his case. He quotes a certain law. He has read it even that very morning. Suppose you tell him that no such law ever existed. Is he not indignant at your denial? Is he not jealous of what he knows to be the truth?

Look at that experienced physician. Try if you can to make him believe that unnatural sins will not hurt the nervous system. You may as well try to convince him that poison will not kill.

Every honest man guards the truth with the most jealous care, and will you blame the good Catholic for jealously guarding the highest truth—that truth which God himself has revealed—that truth upon which depends our whole happiness, here and hereafter?

"Our intellect," says St. Thomas, "is formed for truth

and cannot help thinking according to truth. The intellect is not a faculty or power which is, in itself, free, as the will is. Wheresoever it sees the truth it cannot help embracing it. It is not free to accept or reject it, except when ignorance puts the mind in such a state as to render it unable to see the truth. Whenever the mind sees the truth, it is forced to accept it. When the mind does not see the truth it is inactive—it does nothing. If, in this case, it asserts one proposition rather than another, such assertion is merely an act of the will, and not an act of the intellect. For instance, if I am asked whether the moon is inhabited, I can assert that it is, merely because I choose to do so. But I am not compelled to make this assertion by any evidence, for I do not *know*. But if I am asked, to how much two and two amount, I cannot choose my answer; I am forced to say 'four.' The intellect, then, is bound to acknowledge the truth when it sees the truth. But the will may deny it. The intellect of any man cannot help acknowledging the existence of God, and of the first principles of right and wrong. But a perverse will may deny these truths."

Of all things that are good for men, truth is, without doubt, the greatest good.

Truth is the good thing for the intellect. As the eye was made to receive light, and the ear to receive sounds, and the hand to do all kinds of work, so the intellect was made to see and embrace the truth, to unite itself with the truth, and to find its repose in truth alone.

Truth is the good thing for the heart. The heart is bound to love something. Now, when the intellect does not show it a true, honest object of love, the heart is sure to soil itself in a sordid love.

Truth is the good thing for society. If truth does not guide its steps, society must fall into misery, and setting itself against the divine laws of the universe, will speedily be brought to utter ruin.

Truth is the good thing for men. They cannot attain their ultimate end—they cannot reach eternal goodness, except by means of the truth. So necessary is truth for men that the Son of God came down from heaven to teach them the truth.

Truth, then, is above all good things; it is a greater good than wealth and honors; it is above life and death, above men and angels. God is the only fountain of truth; truth alone leads to him, as it comes from him who is Truth itself. If this be so, what right can there be for any one to obscure the truth? What right can there be for a liberal-minded priest to profess Liberalism, a mixture of true and false principles? "A thing," says St. Thomas Aquinas, "becomes impure by mixing it with a worse substance, as, for instance, gold mixed with brass, or silver with lead; in like manner, truth becomes worse and loses the splendor of its purity by mixing it with error." Has not Protestantism risen in this way? What right then has a liberal-minded priest to assert or to endorse cheerfully so many falsehoods in the article "Queer Explanation?" what right has the liberal-minded Father Cronin to say "*what is needed in this country—if the country is to be ever converted to the Catholic faith—is more of such letters as the one in question (written by a liberal-minded priest and published by the liberal-minded Father Cronin) and less of such books that, through their inexact phrasing, furnish arguments to the enemies of the Church to represent her as teaching what she does not teach;*" in other words, we must have more liberal-minded priests that preach Liberalism all over the country, and less orthodox priests, that defend the doctrines of the Church, and then, of course, all Catholics will soon be liberal Catholics, and Protestants will easily become liberal Catholics, because they do no longer see much difference between Liberalism and Protestantism! Aye, what right has he to proclaim his erroneous teaching, which cramps the soul, sours the temper, dwarfs the conscience, and inflicts untold misery on the country and on the unhappy people who are brought within the reach of his fallacious assertions? No, there is no such right. Reason, and conscience, and the Catholic Church condemn such license, that is *such free discussion*, as he calls it.

Out of the Catholic Church there is No Salvation.

In an Allocution held by Pius IX. on Dec. 9, 1854, His Holiness says: "It is not without sorrow that we have learned another, not less pernicious error, which has been spread in several parts of Catholic countries, and has been imbibed by many Catholics, *who are of opinion that those who are not at all members of the true Church of Christ can be saved*. Hence they often discuss the question concerning the future fate and condition of those who die without having professed the Catholic faith, and give the most frivolous reasons in support of their wicked opinion. . . . .

"It is indeed of faith that no one can be saved outside the Apostolic Roman Church; that this Church is the one ark of salvation; that he who has not entered it, will perish in the deluge."

In his Encyclical Letter, dated Aug. 10, 1863, Pope Pius IX. says: "I must mention and condemn again that most pernicious error, in which certain Catholics are living, who are of opinion that those people who live in error and have not the true faith, and are separated from Catholic unity, may obtain life everlasting. Now this opinion is most contrary to Catholic faith, as is evident from the plain words of Christ: "If he will not hear the Church, let him be to thee as the heathen and the publican." Matt. xiii. 17; "He that believeth not, shall be condemned." Mark, xvi. 16; " He that despiseth you, despiseth me; and he that despiseth me, despiseth him that sent me." Luke, x. 16; "He that doth not believe, is already judged." John, iii. 18; "It is of faith that, as there is but one God, so also there is but *one faith*, and one baptism. To go beyond this in our inquiries is to be impious." (Allocution, Dec. 9, 1854.)

On the 18th of June, 1871, Pope Pius IX., in replying to a French deputation headed by the Bishop of Nevers, spoke as follows: "My children, my words must express to you what I have in my heart. That which afflicts your country, and prevents it from meriting the blessings of God, is *the mixture of principles* I will speak out, and not hold my peace. That which I fear is not the Commune of Paris, those miserable men, those real demons of hell, roaming upon the face of the earth—no, not the Commune of Paris; that which I fear is liberal Catholicism. . . .I have said so more than *forty* times, and I repeat it to you now, through the love that I bear you. The real scourge of France is Liberal Catholicism, which endeavors to unite two principles, as repugnant to each other as fire and water. My children, I conjure you to abstain from those doctrines which are destroying you. . . .if this error be not stopped, it will lead to the ruin of religion and of France." In a brief, dated July the 9th, 1871, to Mgr. Ségur, the Holy Father says: "It is not only the infidel sects who are conspiring against the Church and Society that the Holy See has often reproved, but also *those men who*, granting that they act in good faith and with upright intentions, yet *err in caressing liberal doctrines.*" On July 28, 1873, his Holiness thus expressed himself: "The members of the Catholic Society of Quimper certainly run no risk of being turned away from their obedience to the Apostolic See by the writings and efforts of the declared enemies of the Church; but they may glide down the incline of *those so-called liberal opinions which have been adopted by many Catholics*, otherwise honest and pious, who, by the influence of their religious character, may easily exercise a powerful ascendancy over men, and lead them to very pernicious opinions. Tell, therefore, the members of the Catholic Society that, on the *numerous* occasions on which we *have censured those who hold liberal opinions*, we did not mean those who hate the Church, whom it would have been useless to reprove, but those whom we have just described. *Those men preserve and foster the hidden poison of liberal principles, which they sucked as the milk of their education, pretending that those principles are not infected with malice, and cannot interfere with religion*; so they instil this poison into men's minds, and propagate the germs of those perturbations by which the world has for a long time been vexed."

Our faith, to be pleasing to God, must be sound; and according to the declaration of the Vatican Council, our faith is sound when we avoid not only open heresy, but also diligently shun, and in our hearts dissent from, those errors which approach it more or less closely, and religiously observe those constitutions and decrees whereby such evil opinions, either directly or indirectly, have been proscribed and prohibited by the Holy See. (Vatican Council, Canon iv.), as, for instance, "Opinions leaning to *naturalism*, or *rationalism*, whose sum and purpose is to uproot Christian institutions, and establish in society the rule of man, placing God out of consideration. An entire profession of Catholicity is by no means consistent with these opinions. Likewise, it is not lawful to follow one rule in private life, another in public life, namely, so that the authority of the Church may be observed in private life, and disregarded in public life. That would be to unite virtue and vice, and make man conflict with himself, when, on the contrary, he ought to be consistent with himself, and in nothing, no sort of life, depart from Christianity." (Leo XIII., Encycl. 1, Nov. 1885.) In other words, it is not lawful to be a liberal Catholic, and it is far worse to be a liberal-minded priest. It is the duty of all philosophers (far more so of all priests) *who desire to remain sons of the Church*, and of all philosophy, to assert nothing contrary to the teachings of the Church, and to retract all such things when the Church shall so admonish. The opinion which teaches the contrary, we pronounce and declare altogether erroneous and in the highest degree injurious to the faith of the Church, and her authority." (Litteræ Pii IX. "Gravissimas inter," ad Archiep. Monac. et Freising. Dec. 1862.)

A priest, therefore, who defends Liberalism, is in opposition to the teachings of the Church, and cannot remain a son of the Church.

A Liberal Catholic, then, is no true Catholic. The word Catholic is no vain and empty word. To be a true Catholic means to hold most firmly all those truths which Christ and his Apostles have taught, which the Catholic Church has always proclaimed, which the Saints have professed, which the Popes and Councils have defined, and which the Fathers and Doctors of the Church have defended. He who denies but one of those truths, or hesitates to receive one of them, is not a Catholic. He claims to exercise the right of private judgement in regard to the doctrine of Christ, and therefore he is a heretic. The true Catholic knows and believes that there can be no compromise between God and the devil, between truth and error, between orthodox faith and heresy, between divine and human faith, between true and false Christianity, between Catholics and Protestants. St. Paul, the Apostle, spoke freely and told the truth plainly from out of his prison-walls; it was because he was no compromiser. St. Peter spoke freely, plainly, and forcibly before the ancients, saying that it is better to obey God than men; it was because he was no compromiser. The Apostle St. Andrew proclaimed the plain truth from the wood of the cross; it was because he was no compromiser. St. Stephen, the first martyr, was no compromiser. When accused of being a follower of Jesus of Nazareth, he, in his turn, accused his enemies of being the murderers of Christ. All the holy martyrs of the Church were no compromisers. Being charged by the heathens with the folly of worshipping and following a crucified God, they, in their turn, charged the heathens with the impiety of worshipping creatures and following the devil. Why was our Holy Father, Pope Pius IX., and why is still our Holy father, Leo XIII., a prisoner? It is because neither the one nor the other could be a compromiser. Why were in Germany so many bishops and priests exiled or in prison? It is because they were no compromisers. Why was the Catholic Church persecuted in Germany and other parts of the world? It is because God, by means of persecution, purifies his Church from liberal or compromising Catholics. And as there are so many liberal Catholics in this country, persecution must come to separate them from the Church. Those compromising Catholics, said a well-known convert in Detroit, Mich., have kept me out of the Church for twenty years, until at last I met a good, conscientious, and learned priest, who taught me plainly that, if I wished to save my soul, I must become a member of Christ's Body—the Catholic Church—in order to become united to her head—Jesus Christ—from whom sanctifying grace will then flow upon your soul and prepare it for life everlasting.

"Undoubtedly," says Bishop Hay, "it is praiseworthy to show all indulgence and condescension to those who are without, and to behave towards them with all lenity and mildness.

"But to betray the truth with any such view must be a grievous crime, and highly prejudicial to both parties. Experience, in fact, shows that the loose way of thinking and speaking, which some members of the true Church have of *late* adopted, is productive of the worst consequences, both to themselves and to those whom they desire to favor.

"(1.) Those who are separated from the Church of Christ well know that she constantly professes, as an article of her creed, that without the true faith, and out of her communion, there is no salvation. When, therefore, they see the members of that Church talking doubtfully on this point, seeming to question the truth of the doctrine, and even alleging pretexts and and excuses to explain it away, what can they think ? What effect must this have upon their minds ? Must it not tend to extinguish any desire of enquiring after the truth which God may have given them, and to shut their hearts against any such good thought ? Self-love never fails eagerly to lay hold of everything that favors its wishes ; and if once they find this truth called in question, even by those who profess to believe it, they will consider it as a mere school dispute, and think no more about the matter.

" (2.) This way of thinking and speaking naturally tends to extinguish all zeal for the salvation of souls in the hearts of those who adopt it ; for whilst they persuade themselves that there is a possibility of salvation for those who die in a false faith, and out of the Church of Christ, self love will easily incline them not to give themselves any trouble about their conversion; nay, it has sometimes even gone so far as to make some think it more advisable not to endeavor to undeceive them, lest it should change their present *excusable ignorance*, as they call it, into a *culpable obstinacy;* not reflecting that, by their pious and zealous endeavors, they may be brought to the knowledge of the truth, and save their souls, whereas, through their uncharitable neglect, they may be deprived of so great a happiness. Woe to the world, indeed, if the first preachers of Christianity had been of such unchristian sentiments!

(3.) It is no less prejudicial to the members of the Church themselves to embrace such ways of thinking: for it cannot fail to cool their zeal and esteem for religion, to make them more careless of preserving their faith, ready for worldly motives to expose it to danger, and in time of temptation to forsake it entirely. In fact, if a man be thoroughly persuaded of the truth of his holy religion, and of the necessity of being a member of the Church of Christ, how is it possible he should ever expose himself to any occasion of losing so great a treasure, or for any worldly fear or favor to abandon it? Since experience shows, then, that many, for some trifling worldly advantage, do expose themselves to such danger, by going to places where they cannot practise their religion, but find every inducement to leave it, or, by engaging in employments inconsistent with their duty, expose their children to the same dangerous occasions, this can arise only from a want of a just idea of the importance of their religion; and, upon a strict examination, it is always found that some degree or other of the above latitudinarian sentiments is the radical cause.

"(4.) Besides, if a person once begin to hesitate about the importance of his religion, what esteem or regard can he have for the laws, rules, or practices of it? Self-love, always attentive to its own satisfaction, will soon tell him that, if it be not absolutely necessary to be of that religion, much less necessary must it be to submit to all its regulations; hence liberties are taken in practice, the commands of the Church are despised, the exercises of devotion are neglected, and a shadow of religion introduced under the show of liberal sentiments, to the destruction of all solid virtue and piety."

If you travel at night through a wild, desolate moorland, you will notice in some lonely spot a flame of fire that flickers and shoots, and recedes farther and farther as you follow it. It is called the will-o'-the-wisp, or the wandering light. This light is not from heaven, but from the deep, miry marsh. Woe to the foolish traveller who blindly follows it! It leads him on into a deep morass, into some black pool, where he perishes alone in the darkness! His last agonizing shriek, his trembling groan, is echoed by the hooting nightbird.

There are wandering lights, too, in the human mind, that lead many astray. Men may think that these lights come from above, from the Holy Spirit, but they proceed only from self-conceit, from passion, from pride, and often from the demon of hell.

No doubt, it was not a little poppy of a devil that was sitting on the shoulder of S. O. to dictate to him his "Queer Explanation;" only a fallen angel of the higher ranks could conceive and suggest that malicious article.

Coxe, and Fulton, and other narrow-minded bigots have now something better than *Familiar Explanation* to take hold of. They will henceforth take hold of the "Queer Explanation," written by S. O.; they will not twist it into another sense than it really has; they will prove from it that their faith in Christ and in all the facts of his divine life is precisely the same as that of Catholics; and, as all Protestants believe that all Catholics who live up to their faith are saved, so, in like manner, all Protestants who live up to their faith in Christ will now believe that they will be saved, precisely because their faith in Christ is the same as that of Catholics.

Coxe and Fulton will now assure all their Protestant brethren not to be afraid of the final sentence of the Eternal Judge; for his words, "I know you not whence you are, depart from me all ye workers of iniquity," (Luke xiii. 26–

27.) will be addressed, not to Protestants, but only to bad Catholics. What a consoling hope for Protestants at the Particular and General Judgment!

Coxe, and Fulton, and their Protestant brethren do not know Christ and his doctrine as taught by the Catholic Church; and therefore as "No man will be condemned on account of his ignorance, neither Protestant nor heathen," all of them will be saved who die in their ignorance. This is quite certain according to the logic of S. O. And not to entertain even the least doubt of his salvation, "Every sincere, God-fearing Protestant, and even every God-fearing heathen, has but to lift up, in the hour of death, his heart to God his Creator, and to acknowledge his sins and offenses against God with true contrition, and to ask forgiveness, and to add always, trusting in the merits of Jesus Christ my Saviour,' or, ' for the love of my Redeemer, who died on the cross for me,' and this *surely* obtains God's forgiveness."

What a wonderful power is not attached to these words by S. O.! and why should not Coxe and Fulton let their people know it? You see, according to the infallible oracle of S. O., those words are *sacramental words*, producing their effects *ex opere operato*, as soon as they are pronounced; that is, they produce at once divine faith, true Christian hope, perfect sorrow, which proceeds from perfect charity; they force God the Father, and God the Son, and God the Holy Ghost, to enter the soul and unite themselves with it in the most intimate manner, and remain thus united with it for all eternity in heaven! And if at the same time many a bitter cry for forgiveness goes up to God, such a wonderful effect will also be brought about by the above words, even in the soul of the Protestant, "who, knowing so much of the truth of the Catholic religion as he does, failed to have the courage of his convictions and to embrace it! It is a grievous sin to reject the known truth, but grievous as it is, even that and any other sin will be forgiven to him, no matter what his religion may be, who makes an act of perfect contrition and has the will to comply with every other condition which a merciful God imposes as a condition of forgiveness, though he may not know explicitly what those conditions are. And *to such*, this *Explanation of Christian Doctrine* notwithstanding, *there is no condemnation!*"

What an easy and wide road to heaven! S. O. tells every man, no matter what his religion may be, to raise himself into heaven like the man who tried to lift himself up into the air by taking hold of his own boot straps!

Alas! Which of the two, Coxe or S. O., is most oblique-minded, and suffers most from mental strabismus? Which of the two—

Fulton or the most prominent priest of the U. S., is the most infatuated, lunatic-like man. Which of the three, S. O., or Coxe, or Fulton—suffers most from softening of the brain? Which of the three permitted himself to be drawn most into the cyclone of so many heretical errors? Which of the three has been lifted most off his feet, and "*is the cap of all fools alive.*" (Shak.)

Alas! the article "Queer Explanation," written by S. O. in favor of Protestants, will do more harm, not only to liberal Catholics, but even to sincere Protestants who honestly seek the truth, than all the rantings of such men as Coxe and Fulton, because it is calculated to confirm them in their errors and make them believe that they can be saved out of the Catholic Church; and yet the Rev. Father Cronin solemnly declares that it was *sorely needed!* and the Rev. A. Young is of the same opinion!

We read in Holy Scripture that the Bishop of Pergamus, though quite orthodox himself, did not use energetically enough the sword of the Word of God, with which he was armed to oppose certain false, pernicious principles of his time and country, and warn the Christians against following them. Hence it happened that those erroneous principles spread more rapidly and infected even many of the Christians. For this neglect, and the evil consequences thereof, the Bishop is severely reprimanded by our Lord, who threatens him and his flock with everlasting punishment, if they do not repent. (Apoc. ii. 12–16.)

Dark clouds of error and weakness in faith have settled thickly around us since the time of the so-called Reformation. It is the special duty of priests to scatter these clouds by speaking freely and plainly on the great truths of our religion, especially on the great fundamental truth, that our religion is revealed by God, and that his revelation is invested in an infallible divine teaching authority, and that no one will be saved without being willing to accept this teaching authority—the Catholic Church—for his guide on the road to heaven. On these great truths, priests must speak with a lively faith, in language glowing with love for those truths, in words that work miracles, that is, in words that create in the mind of the hearers so profound a conviction of the truths of our religion, and which, at the same time, enkindle in their hearts so great a love for them, as are apt to make them believe and live up to these truths with a holy joy and spiritual delight.

This is, indeed, what Jesus Christ expects every priest to do, especially in our time, when faith in the great truths of our holy religion grows weaker every day, not only among the higher classes of society, but even among the lower classes, especially among young men and young women. But, alas! the divine Master is sadly disappointed in all those priests who speak so coldly of him and his doctrine as to make believe that their own faith is rather weak.

Such coldness is generally found in those who, considering themselves learned and wise, rely too much on their own opinion and judgment in religious matters. They guide themselves only by their lights, and for want of humility care not to rise higher than human reason. Thus they are grovelling all their life-time in the littleness of their own ideas and sentiments—a littleness increditable in all that regards the great truths of our religion.

Such men are in the habit of always thinking first how a tenet, or a practice, or a fact is most presentable to the Public. This habit soon and almost imperceptibly leads them to profaneness, and easily produces the spirit of liberalism and rationalism in matters of faith.

Their too delicate and fastidious taste has too much regard for the feelings of a certain class of people. We are aware that Christian charity demands of us to have due regard for the feelings of our neighbor, and we are thoroughly convinced that no one was ever yet benefited by harsh means. Charity, however, is not only not incompatible with truth, but it ever demands that the whole truth should be told well, especially when its concealment is a cause of error, or of perseverance in error and sin, in matters, too, of the greatest importance.

Hence, to judge from the works of our greatest Catholic theologians, it appears that the deeper theologian a man is, the less does he give way to the studious desire of making difficulties easy at any cost short of denying what is positively *de fide*.

They handle the truth religiously and conscientiously just in the way that God is pleased to give it to us, rather than to see what they can make of it themselves by shaping it for controversy, and so, by dint of skilful manipulation, squeeze it through a difficulty. No doubt, all such priests are out of harmony with the spirit of the Church and the Saints. They do much harm, not only to themselves, but also to those who come into contact with them. By their example and principles they lead into error those persons who easily suffer themselves to be guided by them, forgetting the advice of St. John the Apostle: "Believe not every spirit, but try the spirits, if they be of God." (I. John, iv. 1.)

I have now only to add that I submit this, and whatever else I have written, to the better judgment of our Bishops, but especially to the Holy See, anxiously desirous to think nothing, to say nothing, to teach nothing but what is approved of by those to whom the sacred deposit of Faith has been committed—those who watch over us and are *to render an account to God for our souls*—those who are the Pastors of that glorious Church, out of which there never was, since her establishment, nor is, nor ever will, be any salvation!

All hail to thee, dear and ever-blessed Mother, thou chosen one, thou well-beloved, thou Bride adorned, thou chaste, Immaculate Spouse, thou Universal Queen! all hail to thee! We honor thee, for God honors thee; we love thee, for God loves thee; we obey thee, for thou ever commandest the will of thy Lord. The passers-by may jeer thee; the servants of the prince of this world may call thee black; the daughters of the uncircumcised may beat thee; earth and hell may rise up in wrath against thee, and seek to despoil thee of thy rich ornaments and to sully thy fair name; but all the more dear art thou to our hearts; all the more deep and sincere the homage we pay thee; and all the more earnestly do we pray thee to receive our humble offerings, and to own us for thy children and watch over us, that we may never forfeit the right to call thee our Mother.

www.ingramcontent.com/pod-product-compliance
Lightning Source LLC
Chambersburg PA
CBHW022105150426
43195CB00008B/277